Endorsements

T0307852

In recent years, educators' understanding of how people learn has shifted in some big ways, but we haven't had a go-to manual for applying that research in the classroom. *Powerful Teaching* is that manual and so much more. With specific examples, actionable strategies, and tips for realistic implementation, Agarwal and Bain bridge the gap between cognitive science and education, showing us exactly how to put four key strategies into practice in any subject area and any grade level. Teachers who want to see dramatic improvement in student learning must read this book!

—Jennifer Gonzalez, educator and director of Cult of Pedagogy

Teachers need this book. Students need this book. It's as simple as that. This book will create a more efficient and effective classroom and improve learning. *Powerful Teaching* should be required reading for all teachers. If this book isn't in your school's professional development library, you're missing out. Our classrooms are in dire need of this information and I cannot wait to lead a book study on *Powerful Teaching*.

—Blake Harvard, blogger and AP Psychology teacher,
James Clemens High School

Powerful Teaching is an incredible book with a very powerful message for teachers as to how *we* can transform education. A practical read, explained clearly and explicitly, this book will impact and improve teaching and learning. I love the fusion of educational research with real-life practical classroom examples.

—Kate Jones, author of Love to Teach
and History Teacher, Abu Dhabi

In *Powerful Teaching*, educators at every level will find a treasure trove of new techniques they can put to use in their classrooms, all of which are grounded in the latest research on how students learn. Accessible prose, practical strategies, and solid scientific support—these elements combine to make this a book that will benefit all teachers and, more importantly, their students.

—*James M. Lang, author of* Small Teaching: Everyday Lessons from the Science of Learning

We've arguably learned more about the brain—how it works and more pressingly how it learns—in the last 20 years than we did in all of human history up to that point. Yet many educators have done precious little to adjust their teaching to what we now know. Fortunately this book provides a golden opportunity to do that. "Golden" because the authors have taken the science and distilled it into its most powerful form: a limited number of simple but powerful ideas with guidance on how to use them with insight and fidelity. They've made it easy to be smarter about how you—and your students—learn. Who doesn't want that?

—*Doug Lemov, author of* Teach Like a Champion 2.0, Practice Perfect, *and* Reading Reconsidered

Powerful Teaching shines a spotlight on the partnership between teachers and students in learning, by emphasizing student responsibility in the classroom. Using a set of clearly defined Power Tools, this book equips educators to empower students to take charge of their own learning.

—*Mandy Manning, 2018 National Teacher of the Year*

Powerful Teaching brings cognitive science and education together in one book! It's a digestible, evidence-based resource for educators (of all subject matter and age groups), parents, and students alike to easily implement for tremendous impact. I've already shared multiple ideas and activities with co-workers and I'll be asking all our staff to read it!

—*Megan Nellis, program director of Imagine Scholar,*
South Africa

Other books about learning draw on academic research or on experience in the classroom. In *Powerful Teaching*, Pooja Agarwal and Patrice Bain combine the best of both to offer teachers, parents, and others concerned with education the most accurate and most useful information on how students learn.

—*Annie Murphy Paul, author of* Origins
and The Cult of Personality

I have been anxiously awaiting *Powerful Teaching* and I am especially excited to put Chapter 4: Energize Learning with Spacing and Interleaving to work in my school. The data behind the science are visually presented so that teachers can instantly see why they should be using these strategies. The authors provide multiple practical applications that can be adapted to any educational setting—a book that will truly create powerful teachers and learners!

—*Lisa A. Pulley, District Instructional &*
Technology Coach and Social Studies teacher

Anxiety and fear of making mistakes was sometimes the culprit for failing to remember what I *really* knew at the right moment. Learning about retrieval strategies with *Powerful Teaching* not only clarified for me why I would get anxious in school about making mistakes, but also provided a toolbox of strategies to truly make learning low-stakes and even fun for our students. From the creation of a welcoming community on day one to the day of the test, the ideas and resources offered in this book ensure that students succeed, take advantage of mistakes, and feel enthusiastic about learning.

—Oscar Ramírez, adult education principal,
The Next Step Public Charter School

This easy-to-read book makes the phrase "science of learning" real for anyone responsible for teaching students. It's chock full of practical tips (not fads) and, mercifully, devoid of academic mumbo jumbo. If you want to unlock the full power of students' minds, please read this!

—Benjamin Riley, founder of Deans for Impact

The authors have combined years of scientific expertise and practical experience to create a marvelous book about understanding and applying the science of learning in the classroom. This book is highly readable and a boon to all teachers who want to improve their students' learning.

—Henry L. Roediger, III, co-author of Make it Stick:
The Science of Successful Learning

Powerful Teaching

Powerful Teaching

Unleash the Science of Learning

Pooja K. Agarwal, Ph.D. and
Patrice M. Bain, Ed.S.

JB JOSSEY-BASS™
A Wiley Brand

Jossey-Bass
A Wiley brand
111 River St, Hoboken, NJ 07030
www.josseybass.com

ISBNs: 9781119521846 (Hardback), 9781394324903 (Paperback), 9781119521853 (ePDF), 9781119521839 (ePub)

Jossey-Bass books and products are available through most bookstores. To contact Jossey-Bass directly, call our Customer Care Department within the U.S. at 800-956-7739, outside the U.S. at +1 317 572 3986, or fax +1 317 572 4002.

Wiley also publishes its books in a variety of electronic formats and by print-on-demand. Some material included with standard print versions of this book may not be included in e-books or in print-on-demand. If this book refers to media such as a CD or DVD that is not included in the version you purchased, you may download this material at http://booksupport.wiley.com. For more information about Wiley products, visit www.wiley.com.

Library of Congress Control Number is Available

Cover Design: Wiley
Cover Image: © ARTQU/Getty Images
Author Photos: (Agarwal) photo by Michelle Schapiro,
(Bain) courtesy of the Author

SKY10086354_093024

To the teacher who first asked me, "If you could build a school, what would it look like?" That single, simple question led to this book.
— Pooja Agarwal

To educators who create classrooms where students internalize success.
— Patrice Bain

Contents

Introduction

Do you remember your first day teaching, with students eagerly (or not eagerly) awaiting your instruction? Perhaps you felt terrified. Elated. Cautious. Ready. Not ready. Almost ready?

In the days leading up to that first day, you may wonder, "What am I going to say? What am I going to teach? What are they going to think of me? What should I do when my lesson plans tank?"

But how often do you ask, "*How* am I going to teach?"

Let's travel back in time to 2006. Patrice was starting her twelfth year teaching and Pooja had just graduated from college with a degree in elementary education. A veteran teacher and a newly minted teacher. Strikingly, the critical question on their minds was identical: What works best in education?

By this point, Patrice had noticed that her students were remembering what they learned years *after* her class – much more than what they remembered from other classes. Patrice also noticed that most teaching strategies were based on anecdotes, passed down from teacher to teacher. Year after year, teachers would come and go, but ineffective teaching methods would stay. *How* could there be such a disconnect between what was working in Patrice's classroom and ineffective fads permeating many other classrooms?

A few years earlier, Pooja had taken a course in cognitive science, without really knowing what that meant. She was astounded to realize that there is rigorous research on how humans learn and remember. *How* could there be such a disconnect between Pooja's education classes on one side of campus and her cognitive science classes on the other side of campus – both all about learning, but one based on anecdotes and the other based on science?

Suddenly, just like pieces in a puzzle, *it all came together*. Researchers at Washington University in St. Louis received grant funding to conduct cognitive science research in classrooms. Up until this point, most research within this specific field took place in laboratory settings with college students, using fairly simple materials to examine how students learn and remember information. Now, with this new grant, the long-overdue opportunity to bridge the gap between learning in the classroom and learning in the lab had arrived.

On a sunny Wednesday in August, Patrice and Pooja met for the first time – just inside the school's entrance, near the cafeteria, next to the principal's office. Shaking hands and walking up the stairs to Patrice's classroom, the energy was unmistakable; Patrice would be one of the first K–12 teachers to partner with cognitive scientists in her classroom, and Pooja would be one of the first cognitive scientists to conduct full-time research in an authentic school setting. This initial meeting of the minds became a teacher-scientist bond that continues today.

This book is the culmination of our extensive collaboration to understand what works best in education. Enter *the science of learning*. What, exactly, is the "science of learning?" It's so simple, and yet counterintuitive. Why can we remember scenes from our favorite movies but struggle to remember our students' names? Why is it easy to learn some things and hard to learn other things? Why can we read a book and feel we learned a lot, only to find that we've forgotten most of it a year later? Why can we think back and remember our first day of teaching, but not our tenth day of teaching?

Cognitive scientists conduct research on all of these things – how we learn stories, names, facts, important events, unimportant events, and more. Research on the science of learning dates back more than 100 years. Fads feel like they've persisted for 100 years, too. Sometimes we run into fads during pre-service programs and professional development, and other times through word of mouth or online blogs. We've all had the experience of being excited about a "new" teaching idea, only to file the materials away for a rainy day. Rarely are these new strategies utilized. Professional development programs often feel like a waste of time.

So why do we keep reinventing the wheel with teaching strategies based on the "fad of the semester," when scientifically based strategies are waiting to be unleashed? We feel there are two main reasons:

1. The science of learning sits dormant in academic journals, rather than easily accessible in pre-service textbooks and professional development materials.

2. The science of learning has recently been featured in newspapers, blogs, and social media, but it's hard to know if these are trusted sources or simply people concocting more fads.

For these reasons (and more), teachers are given the impossible challenge of finding time to seek out good research, make sense of it, and apply it in classrooms. We frequently get asked, "Why haven't I heard about this research before? Why didn't I learn about this in my pre-service program or professional development?" It's because this research isn't accessible – literally and figuratively. There is valuable research on the science of learning out there, but it's sitting behind lock and key.

Until now. For more than a decade, we have developed a rare partnership of scientist-and-teacher, research-into-practice – one that is true to the rigors of cognitive science and also practical with today's teachers in mind. In *Powerful Teaching: Unleash the Science of Learning*, we decipher cognitive science research, illustrate how we have applied the science of learning in our own teaching, and provide evidence-based recommendations to empower educators to unleash the science of learning in their classrooms.

> There is valuable research on the science of learning out there, sitting behind lock and key. Until now.

By drawing on empirical research by fellow cognitive scientists and practical strategies from educators around the world, *we focus on four powerful teaching strategies based on the science of learning*: retrieval practice, spaced practice, interleaving, and feedback-driven metacognition.

1. *Retrieval practice* boosts learning by pulling information *out* of students' heads (e.g., quizzes and flashcards), rather than cramming information into students heads (e.g., lectures). Retrieval practice is a no-stakes learning opportunity that increases student performance, beyond formative and summative assessments.

2. *Spaced practice* boosts learning by spreading lessons and retrieval opportunities out over time so learning is not

crammed all at once. By returning to content every so often, students' knowledge has had time to rest and be refreshed.

3. *Interleaving* boosts learning by mixing up closely related topics and encouraging discrimination. For example, learning increases when students practice addition, subtraction, multiplication, and division problems all mixed up, rather than one type of problem at a time.

4. *Feedback* boosts learning by providing the student the opportunity to know what they know, and know what they don't know. This increases students' *metacognition* or understanding about their own learning progress.

Critically, research demonstrates that these four powerful strategies:

- Raise student achievement by a letter grade, or even two – *from a C to an A*. Research we conducted in Patrice's classroom and additional classrooms demonstrated a consistent and reliable increase in students' grades, confidence, and engagement.

- Boost learning for diverse students and subject areas. Our book applies to all grade levels and disciplines (e.g., STEM, social studies, language arts, fine arts, special education, and foreign languages).

- Enhance higher-order learning and students' transfer of knowledge. We provide research and examples demonstrating that these strategies apply for basic fact knowledge, skill learning, and critical thinking.

When it comes to retrieval practice, spaced practice, interleaving, and feedback-driven metacognition, *the combination of being research-based and classroom-proven is paramount.* The rigor of science gives us confidence that these strategies aren't fads, and successful classroom implementation gives us confidence that these strategies work in the real world, not just in the laboratory. In addition, the better you understand the research behind the strategies, the more effectively you can adapt them in *your* classroom – and you know your classroom best.

By this point, you may be thinking, "These strategies sound great, but they probably take a lot of time and effort to use them." Actually, they don't! The research-based strategies we describe in this book can be implemented *in less than a minute without additional prep or grading time*. In addition, as teachers, we already use many of these strategies: retrieving what we know, spacing it out over time, mixing it up, and giving our students feedback. The difference is that we share how to use these evidence-based strategies *purposefully, intentionally, and frequently*.

We start this book by sharing the research behind retrieval practice and why it's foundational for learning. Next, we share specific, actionable strategies to implement retrieval practice in the classroom. We continue with research and classroom strategies for spacing, interleaving, and metacognition, followed by recommendations on how to overcome potential challenges, engage in conversations with students and parents, and lead evidence-driven professional development at the school, district and university level.

We have even more activities, templates, and downloads available on our website, www.powerfulteaching.org. Lastly, we have intentionally embedded retrieval, spacing, interleaving, and feedback throughout this book. In other words, we practice what we preach, we model these strategies in each chapter, and we boost *your* learning from this book!

With *Powerful Teaching: Unleash the Science of Learning*, you will:

- Develop a deep understanding of powerful teaching strategies based on the science of learning, whether you are a past, present, or future educator.

- Go behind the scenes and explore key findings from cognitive science research.

- Gain insight into how scientifically-based strategies are effectively implemented in a variety of academic settings without additional preparation, classroom, or grading time.

- Think critically about your current teaching practices and classroom environment from a research-based perspective.

- Develop tools to share the science of learning with students and parents, ensuring success inside and outside the classroom.

- Identify next steps to transform teaching and unleash the science of learning in your classroom.

As educators, we must look forward – using evidence-based strategies – to propel and guide student learning. We must stop driving instruction with anecdotes and fads, we must stop reinventing the wheel, and we must stop riding in circles when it comes to classroom instruction.

Instead, it's our responsibility to *ask for evidence*. Evidence for which strategies are effective, not just which strategies are popular. Evidence for why we teach the way we teach, not just because we've always taught that way.

Most importantly, after reading this book, we hope that on the first day of the school year, you won't be asking, "What should I teach?" Instead, you'll be asking, "*How* should I teach? *How* can I turn my teaching into *powerful teaching*?"

The science of learning exists. *Now, it's time to unleash it.*

Chapter **1**

Discover the Power Behind Power Tools

Before we dive into all the powerful research and strategies in this book, I (Pooja) would like to tell you a story.

I was visiting family in Oakland, California, on Christmas Eve, 2017. I needed to write and so I asked my brother if he had a favorite coffee shop nearby. "Yes!" he said. "It's only a few blocks away from the house, and it's an easy walk." Perfect, I thought – I can get some peace and quiet and write (while avoiding chaotic family time back at the house). He told me which streets to walk on and where to turn. It sounded pretty simple.

Except the next morning, when I wanted to walk to the coffee shop, I couldn't remember where it was or how to get there. Thanks to my smartphone, I got directions and I took one last look at the map. After my five-minute walk, I arrived! It's a good thing I found my way, too – it had great coffee, a cozy atmosphere, and very kind owners.

You may be thinking "Gee, I thought this was a book about learning." It is! Learning is as complex as remembering and using directions to a coffee shop, even if we don't think about it that way. To explore something so complex, cognitive scientists often refer to the three stages of learning: *encoding, storage,* and *retrieval.*[1]

Figure 1.1 illustrates the three stages of learning:

- *Encoding* is when we get information in and absorb knowledge, almost like a sponge.
- *Storage* is where we hope that once we encode information, our knowledge sticks around.
- *Retrieval* is when we reach back and bring something we previously learned into mind.

Now, what do these three stages of learning have to do with my trip to a coffee shop? Let's relive my journey, but this time through the lens of learning.

First, I asked my brother about a nearby coffee shop and he gave me the name of one down the street. At this point, I *encoded* or "inputted" the coffee shop details, but I was distracted by Christmas celebrations in the background. I expected that the coffee shop's name would be *stored* in my memory until the next

Figure 1.1 A simplified three-stage model of learning: encoding (getting information *in*), storage (when information *sticks*), and retrieval (getting information *out*).

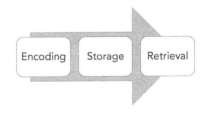

morning. When I woke up, however, I tried to *retrieve* the directions to the coffee shop, but I couldn't. *How could I forget something so simple?*

A few days later, I wanted to return to the same coffee shop. And yet again, I couldn't remember how to get there! It was literally four blocks away from my brother's house, but the directions had vanished from my head. This is a perfect example of a quirk when it comes to learning: *Just because you know something once doesn't mean you'll always remember it.*

One of the best ways to make sure something sticks and gets stored is to focus on the *retrieval* stage, not the encoding stage. In my situation, for example, if I had practiced *retrieving* the coffee shop directions before going to bed, I would have remembered them the next morning.

This brings us to the first *Power Tool* that will serve as the foundation for our book: *retrieval practice*. Retrieval practice is the same thing as the retrieval stage of the learning process: It's when we practice bringing information to mind. We tend to think that most learning occurs during the encoding stage, but a wealth of research demonstrates that learning is strengthened during retrieval.[2]

When I couldn't remember the directions, what did I do? I looked up the coffee shop on my phone, of course! Without even thinking about it, I gave myself *feedback*. It's second nature for us to seek more information, fill in the gaps, and check whether we're on the right track. First, I had to recognize I needed help, and then I gave myself feedback using my phone. This mental process is what's called *metacognition,* or, literally, "thinking about thinking." *Feedback-driven metacognition* is another Power Tool that significantly boosts learning. It isn't new and you probably give students feedback all the time; the difference is that *how* you give feedback has a large impact on encoding, storage, and retrieval.

Now, I can't help but re-retrieve the directions to the coffee shop. I'm 99% sure I'll remember them the next time I visit my brother in Oakland! This act of retrieving something over time is another Power Tool called *spacing*, which strengthens long-term learning and decreases forgetting. Lastly, *interleaving* is a Power Tool where learning increases when we mix up what we need to learn – like learning the directions to multiple coffee shops and trying to keep them all straight. It might sound challenging, but as we'll discuss in greater depth, challenges are a *good* thing for learning.

In this brief, everyday situation, I engaged in the three stages of learning. Even when we try to remember names, birthdates, or our favorite recipe, we engage in encoding, storage, and retrieval. But what does this mean when it comes to your classroom? Students encode, store, and retrieve, too! In this book, you'll learn quick, simple, everyday tools that transform learning. Each Power Tool we share has been supported by decades of scientific research *and* decades of classroom implementation. You probably use many of these strategies already; the difference is that when you understand how learning works, you can harness these evidence-based strategies and increase student achievement even more.

Get ready to move beyond the coffee shop and on to unleashing the science of learning. *Let Powerful Teaching begin!*

HOW DID PATRICE'S TEACHING EVOLVE INTO *POWERFUL* TEACHING?

I (Patrice) made a discovery at the end of my first year working with Pooja.

In my sixth-grade history class, Pooja and I gave a "pop" final exam. The students were not told in advance, so there was no opportunity to study or "cram." Students' exam scores were not recorded in the grade book, so test anxiety was minimal.

My discovery occurred when, after the pop final exam, I looked at the score of my top GPA (grade point average) student. She had done well on all homework, quizzes, and tests throughout the year. However, she was not number one on this pop final exam. In fact, although she did well, she was only in the top *half* of the class. Why?

Indeed, I had several questions to ponder. Why didn't my highest-GPA student score higher at the end of the year? Knowing exactly what I had taught, why would I get confused looks upon bringing up something from earlier in the year? How could students get a 100% on homework and not be able to discuss it in class a day or two later? Why do I prioritize grading homework and having it returned 24 hours later, when none of this seems to increase learning?

A summer of pondering allowed me to realize the solution to all of my questions was *retrieval practice*. Digging into research and applying my own years of teaching experience helped me make changes the following year. It took me, however, a few more years to perfect my tools.

My own essential question turned into, "How can I support my students to become more accountable for learning?" I realized that many of my students, including my top GPA student, had mastered the system of doing homework. Look for the correct answer, copy it down, next question. Their homework grades were 100%. But learning was negligible. And, to be honest, some papers looked surprisingly similar – copying from friends? Copying from the book? A little too much parental involvement? I was also extremely frustrated at the hours I had spent grading those "A" papers when my students lacked the breadth and depth to answer essential questions. What could I do differently? How could I evolve my teaching into *powerful teaching*?

THE FOUR POWER TOOLS: RESEARCH-BASED AND CLASSROOM-PROVEN

As we all know, we could fill warehouses with all the books, blogs, and worksheets out there promising to transform classrooms.

Powerful Teaching is more than just another promise. *Powerful Teaching* is different. How?

- It's based on rigorous research by cognitive scientists.

- It's based on decades of experience by classroom teachers.

In *Powerful Teaching*, we show you how to harness four evidence-based strategies, which we call *Power Tools*:

Retrieval Practice

Retrieval practice boosts learning by pulling information out of students' heads, rather than cramming information into students heads.

Spacing

Spaced practice boosts learning by spreading lessons and retrieval opportunities out over time so learning is not crammed all at once.

Interleaving

Interleaving boosts learning by mixing up closely related topics, encouraging discrimination between similarities and differences.

Feedback-Driven Metacognition

Feedback-driven metacognition boosts learning by providing the opportunity for students to know what they know and know what they don't know.

When it comes to Power Tools, we're all about being practical. No need to revamp what you're already doing! Here's why:

- *You already use Power Tools.* Retrieving what we know, spacing it out over time, mixing it up, and giving our students feedback are no-brainers! They're intuitive strategies, and that's what makes them so simple and flexible. And they're not new – *100 years of research* demonstrate they significantly improve learning. You can harness these evidence-based strategies that have stood the test of time and make them a regular part of your classroom practice.

- *You don't have to spend more time grading.* Will Power Tools increase grading time? No! In fact, keeping these strategies as grade-free as possible lowers the stakes and increases learning. In fact, we'll talk about how to remove grades all together. There's no need to collect papers, assign points, or enter anything into the gradebook.

- *You'll save time, not spend it.* Engaging students in Power Tools might take a tiny amount of class time (one minute or less, we promise). But in the long term, students will remember *more* and you can re-teach *less*. In fact, just a few quick quizzes in K–12 classrooms have raised students' grades from a C to an A. You'll learn more about small strategies that make a big difference for students.

- *You can use Power Tools your way, in your classroom.* From preschool through medical school, and biology to sign language, these strategies increase learning for diverse students, grade levels, and subject areas. There are multiple ways to use these strategies to boost students' learning, making them flexible in *your* classroom, not just any classroom.

- *You can use Power Tools for free.* Yes, free. There are many great technology websites, tools, and apps available that take advantage of these strategies, but old-fashioned paper and pencil are perfect, too.

Evidence-based strategies that are simple, quick, flexible, and free – too good to be true? Definitely not! By the end of this book, we hope to convince you that these strategies answer a number of today's challenges when it comes to teaching and learning – precisely because they're research-based *and* classroom-proven.

Even if you're already using Power Tools, how learning works isn't always intuitive. Consider these myths about learning, which you'll read more about throughout the book:

Myth: When students learn something easily, they will remember it well.

Myth: Forgetting should be prevented as much as possible.

Myth: It's better for learning if we give feedback *before* students make errors.

In this book, we focus on *how* students learn, not *what* students learn. While we give examples from teachers in a variety of content areas, we don't focus on content-specific knowledge because research demonstrates that Power Tools are effective for *all content areas*.

Unleash these four Power Tools your way, with your content, in your classroom.

Because you know your classroom best, we will help you take these flexible research-based strategies and unleash them your way, with your content, in your classroom.

When it comes to *Powerful Teaching* and Power Tools, one teacher put it best:

I do this all the time, but it's nice to have a name *and* know why it works.

POWER TOOLS IMPROVE MORE THAN MEMORIZATION

In the following chapters, we dive into each Power Tool, the research behind it, and how to unleash it in your classroom. Before we do, we want to address the single most frequent question we are asked: "Do these strategies improve *more* than just memorization?" Here's our answer, based on years of cognitive science research and classroom practice:

Yes!

These four Power Tools improve students' higher-order learning, ranging from a deep understanding of mitosis to effectively resuscitating someone using CPR.[3] As educators, we know that boosting learning beyond the memorization of facts is critical. And that's why we advocate for the use of these strategies – because decades of research demonstrates that they improve much more than just memorization. We share specific research studies and teaching tips to emphasize that retrieval practice, spacing, interleaving, and feedback-driven metacognition boost students' basic understanding of information, and students' higher-order learning and transfer of knowledge, too.

> ## Power Up
>
> Earlier, we talked about three stages of learning in the context of going to a coffee shop.
>
> Challenge yourself: Describe the three stages of learning in a situation from your everyday life!

POWER TOOLS ARE *DESIRABLE DIFFICULTIES* THAT ARE *GOOD* FOR LEARNING

When it comes to teaching, we might lecture, show videos, and encourage note-taking during class. When it comes to studying, students might re-read their textbooks, highlight information, and review their notes before an exam. We've all had the experience of feeling like these teaching and studying methods work. So what's the problem?

The problem is that these methods only lead to *short-term* learning. Have you ever asked students about material you covered months earlier, only to find that they've forgotten everything? This common situation arises because of an assumption we make about learning. We assume that when information comes to mind easily and it feels *fluent*, we'll remember it.

In contrast, researchers have demonstrated that the *opposite* is true: When information feels fluent, we forget it. In other words, *just because we learn something easily does not guarantee we'll remember it*. As Anne Agostinelli, a math teacher from Illinois, put

When it comes to learning, easier isn't better.

it, "I thought my students learned it, but then they forgot it. Which makes me wonder: Did they ever really know it in the first place?"

Why do retrieval practice, spacing, interleaving, and feedback-driven metacognition boost learning? It's because they *challenge* learning. This is what's called *a desirable difficulty*, a term coined by cognitive scientist Robert Bjork in 1994.[4] Power Tools are challeng-

Power Tools are desirable difficulties. They challenge learning, and that's a good thing!

ing, and that's a good thing! Decades of research have shown that fast, easy strategies lead to short-term learning, whereas slower effortful strategies lead to long-term learning.

> **Power Up**
>
> When it comes to your teaching, ask yourself: Are you supporting *short-term* learning or *long-term* learning?

There's a second component to unleashing powerful, challenging strategies: Students can be resistant because of the added struggle. Remember Patrice's top GPA student from earlier? Sometimes students who have done really well up to this point are the most resistant to desirable difficulties. In addition, students who struggle most can be even more reluctant to engage in challenging strategies like retrieval practice and spacing.

In other words, desirable difficulties are good for learning, but they can be tough for us and also for our students. In the first half of this book, we highlight how retrieval practice, spacing, interleaving, and feedback-driven metacognition challenge learning, which is why they improve learning. In the second half of this book, we discuss how to make desirable difficulties a regular part of your classroom, how to foster buy-in with students, and how to engage in conversations with parents about this shift from short-term learning to long-term learning.

From here on out, if a student says, "My brain hurts," you'll say, "That's a good thing!"

WHAT EXACTLY IS THE SCIENCE OF LEARN-ING AND COGNITIVE SCIENCE?

In the next chapters, we dive into the four Power Tools and specific research-based teaching strategies. Before we do, we want to answer this common question: What exactly is "the science of learning" and "cognitive science?"

Fundamentally, because learning is an incredibly complex behavior, *the science of learning* is actually an umbrella term that spans many research fields including psychology, computer science, and neuroscience.

Our research sits in the field of cognitive science or, more specifically, *cognitive psychology*. In cognitive psychology, we typically examine mental operations, or "behind the scenes" behaviors occurring *inside* our heads, like perceiving, attending, remembering, thinking, and decision making. One way to think about it is that the word *cognition* comes from the Latin word for "to know," similar to the word *cognizant*, which means "to be aware."

Cognitive psychologists examine "invisible" everyday behaviors we rarely stop to reflect on. For example, have you ever talked on a cellphone while driving a car? There's a lot that goes into being able to multi-task and do both things at once: We have to pay attention to a lot of information, we need to react quickly, and we're talking while moving our hands and arms – all pretty seamlessly. (Or so we think! Based on cognitive science research, talking on a cellphone while driving is much more dangerous than we realize.[5])

Here's another example: You meet someone at a party and later you remember details about your new friend – where she lives, where she works, and so on – but you struggle to remember her name. Strategies from cognitive psychology can help you remember names, concepts, and much more – just like learning in the classroom!

In contrast to cognitive psychology, research on social-emotional learning (e.g., growth mindsets and character development) investigates how we interact with the world around us; in other words, what happens *outside* our heads. This field is typically referred to as social and personality psychology, and social psychologists examine behaviors such as how we develop relationships, how we're affected by culture, and why we form stereotypes. Of course, how we learn and how we interact with our environment are intertwined, and learning doesn't happen in a vacuum (especially not in education!). Even so, think of cognitive psychology and social psychology as looking at the same human behavior – learning – but using different approaches.

While research on learning – arguably the most complex cognitive process – can be based on observations, surveys, or correlations, most of our research in cognitive psychology is experimental. We use experiments to examine how students learn everything from basic facts and vocabulary words to how students apply their knowledge using complex higher-order materials. Or we might compare popular study methods, such as re-reading or highlighting, to see which ones lead to longer-lasting learning. In this book, we focus on cognitive psychology or the "inside" behaviors of how learning works, in order to emphasize specific, practical teaching strategies for the classroom.

While cognitive psychology is probably the most appropriate term for the field of research we describe in this book, we rarely use the term *psychology* to avoid confusion due to many misconceptions and myths about the field of psychology.[6] For example, clinical psychologists examine behaviors related to clinical populations and provide therapy for mental health conditions. Cognitive psychologists, by contrast, conduct experiments in laboratories (and classrooms more recently!) on everyday learning and memory in typical human populations.

To describe our research, we've chosen to use the phrases *cognitive science* and *the science of learning* interchangeably. These fields are more comprehensive when it comes to learning, and they help emphasize the *science* of learning, not the fads or anecdotes of learning. We are thrilled to share the science behind how learning works *and* share how to put it into action in your classroom.

WE PRACTICE WHAT WE PREACH AND MODEL BEST PRACTICES

Finally, we wanted to mention that in *Powerful Teaching*, we practice what we preach: We engage you in frequent retrieval practice! If you are going to make teaching powerful by getting information out, then you should get information out while reading this book, too.

Boxes, like the one earlier in this chapter, are called Power Ups! When you see a Power Up, you should literally pause and complete our retrieval, spacing, interleaving, and metacognition exercises. In the first Power Up, for example, we asked you to *retrieve* a situation from your life and apply it to a *spaced* concept, which were the three stages of learning we described earlier.

With these exercises, we:

- Improve your long-term learning and remembering from this book.

- Provide you with the experience of desirable difficulties.

- Model what Power Tools look like – quick, simple, and no-stakes whatsoever.

- Give you the opportunity to put on your "teacher hat" *and* your "learner hat!"

For example, we'll keep you on your toes with spaced exercises (e.g., we may ask you to retrieve information from three chapters prior!), metacognition prompts (e.g., questions to help you reflect on your own learning), and key information about scientific research. We use a mix of question types, too: basic, complex, short-answer, multiple-choice – all research-based best practices, of course.

We also have a wealth of downloads, resources, templates, retrieval exercises, and more at our website, www.powerfulteaching.org. Visit our website and explore more strategies, spark ideas, and connect with powerful teachers all over the world.

Finally, we provide additional retrieval exercises in your own *Do It Yourself Retrieval Guide* in Chapter 12, to solidify what you've learned and also to use as a reference in the future. We don't provide chapter summaries; we all have a tendency to flip straight to them rather than challenging our own learning! Instead, experience powerful teaching as you read and challenge yourself to pull information *out* of your head, rather than cramming information *into* your head.

Evidence-based strategies that are simple, quick, flexible, and free – too good to be true? Definitely not!

NOTES

1. Melton, A. W. (1963). Implications of short-term memory for a general theory of memory. *Journal of Verbal Learning and Verbal Behavior* 2: 1–21.

2. Brown, P. C., Roediger, H. L., and McDaniel, M. A. (2014). *Make It Stick: The Science of Successful Learning.* Cambridge, MA: Harvard University Press.

3. Dunlosky, J., Rawson, K. A., Marsh, E. J., et al. (2013). Improving students' learning with effective learning techniques: Promising directions from cognitive and educational psychology. *Psychological Science in the Public Interest* 14: 4–58.

4. Bjork, R. A. (1994). Memory and metamemory considerations in the training of human beings. In: *Metacognition: Knowing about Knowing* (ed. J. Metcalfe and A. Shimamura), 185–205. Cambridge, MA: MIT Press.

5. For research on attention, multi-tasking, and more, we recommend the book *The Invisible Gorilla: And Other Ways Our Intuitions Deceive Us* by Christopher Chabris and Daniel Simons (Crown Publishing, 2009).

6. For more about myths and misconceptions in psychology, we recommend the book *50 Great Myths of Popular Psychology: Shattering Widespread Misconceptions about Human Behavior* by Scott O. Lilienfeld, Steven Jay Lynn, John Ruscio, and Barry L. Beyerstein (Wiley-Blackwell, 2010).

Chapter 2

Build a Foundation with Retrieval Practice

We'd like to start this chapter with a few questions. Think about them carefully and write down your answers:

Power Up

What did you have for breakfast yesterday?[1]

At what age did King Tut become a pharaoh?[2]

What was your favorite vacation?[3]

What's one thing you've learned from this book so far?[4]

In 2017, Pooja asked some of these questions during an interview with Jennifer Gonzalez for the podcast Cult of Pedagogy. Here's what Jenn came up with:

Pooja: What did you have for breakfast yesterday?

Jenn: I have the exact same thing every day: spinach, mushrooms, eggs, and oatmeal.

Pooja: Wow. That's much nicer than my coffee! Okay, here's another question: In what year did King Tut become a pharaoh?

Jenn: Oh my gosh. Do you know, I used to know all about King Tut. When I was in fifth-grade my teacher was obsessed. I have no idea. It was a BC, right?

Pooja: Yep, yep.

Jenn: 500 BC? Am I anywhere near?

Pooja: Do you remember how old he was?

Jenn: Oh, he was a kid, wasn't he? Wasn't he like 10 or something?

Pooja: Yes, he was 9 or 10 years old!

Jenn: Right!

What's with these harebrained questions? Well, they help us talk about something that's tough to pinpoint – learning. In this example, you may have learned something at some point, but forgot it (e.g., King Tut's age), or you can simply think back and bring something to mind even if you didn't intentionally learn it (e.g., your breakfast yesterday). You may have a fond memory for something you haven't thought about in a while (e.g., your favorite vacation) or you can probably remember something you recently learned with a little bit of effort (e.g., one thing from this book).

Sound confusing? It's because it is. *Learning is complex and messy.* It's not something we can touch, and it's really hard to define. You might even say that the learning process looks more like a blob than a flowchart. Reading Pooja and Jenn's conversation gives us initial insight into what learning and remembering "look" like. Now, get ready to dive in and explore the blob of learning!

THE THREE STAGES OF LEARNING AND THE CRITICAL IMPORTANCE OF RETRIEVAL

In Chapter 1, we talked about three stages of learning: encoding, storage, and retrieval.

- Encoding is when we initially learn something.
- Storage is how long something is retained in mind.
- Retrieval is when we access information and bring it to mind.

Using the three stages of learning and thinking about your responses to the four questions we just asked, complete the following table.

	Did you intentionally try to encode this information?	How long have you had this information stored?	How many times have you retrieved this information?
What you ate for breakfast			
King Tut's age			
Your favorite vacation			
One thing about this book			

When it comes to the classroom, where do we focus our activities and teaching practices – encoding, storage, or retrieval? Do you think of these stages as linear – like the arrow figure in Chapter 1 – or do you envision a meandering path across a map?

As teachers, we typically think of learning as getting something in through encoding; we hope what we teach gets stored in our students' heads; and we determine whether our students learned something by having them retrieve during an assessment.

Power Up

Where do you focus your teaching: encoding, storage, or retrieval?
Do you focus on one stage more than another stage?

In other words, we typically focus on getting information *into* students' heads. On the contrary, one of the most robust findings from cognitive science research is the importance of getting information *out* of students' heads. Based on a century of research, in order to transform learning, we must focus on getting information *out* – a strategy called *retrieval practice*. In fact, research demonstrates that retrieval practice is more potent than other techniques commonly used by teachers and students, such as lecturing, re-reading, or taking notes.

Retrieval and the process of getting information *out* is so simple, intuitive, and flexible. For instance, even though the four questions we just asked are very different, they are all examples of retrieval – we're reaching back and pulling information out about breakfast, kings, vacations, and books. Formative assessments and exit tickets are another intuitive form of retrieval. But why do we still default to traditional encoding-assessment methods, like "I lecture, you write a paper" and "I teach a lesson, you take a test?"

When we think about learning, we typically focus on getting information into students' heads. What if, instead, we focus on getting information out of students' heads?

In this chapter, we highlight the critical importance of retrieval for learning, not just encoding. More specifically, we focus on our first Power Tool, *retrieval practice*, and we present conclusive scientific evidence that it significantly benefits learning.

THE POWER OF RETRIEVAL PRACTICE IN PATRICE'S CLASSROOM

After a long day of teaching, I (Patrice) stopped at a Thai restaurant for take-out dinner. While I was waiting, two former students I hadn't seen in six years came in. The second they saw me, they came over and exclaimed: "Mrs. Bain!" They started a rapid-fire litany of knowledge learned in my class. Each time one student retrieved a fact, it would trigger more retrieval from the other student. They continued to rattle off information; I felt like I was watching a ping-pong volley of knowledge. And their facts were correct! What was exciting to me was that we hadn't expected to see each other; there was no preparation on their part. Yet, how was it possible, after a delay of six years, for them to pull out so much information?

Was this an isolated incident? Absolutely not! As another example, I received a lovely note from a parent this year. Her daughters were in my class a few years previously. The family had taken a trip to Europe over the summer and the mother was astonished by the facts and stories the girls told her at each historical site. Each time the girls were asked how they knew this information, their replies were always: "Oh, we learned that in Mrs. Bain's class." In fact, rarely does a school year go by when I have *not* been contacted by surprised parents – and students – with similar stories of delight in remembering details from years past.

Students often ask, "Why do I remember so much from your class, but I don't remember that much from my other classes?"

Why do teachers get the deer-in-the-headlights look from students when they don't remember information from year to year? Or semester to semester? Or even week to week? At the same time, why do my students retain so much information? It's because of the strategies I use. In this case, *retrieval practice*. Not only does research overwhelmingly support retrieval practice, I have used it for over 10 years in my classroom. The success rate of my students is consistent. Retrieval practice works.

THE SCIENCE BEHIND POWER TOOL #1: RETRIEVAL PRACTICE IN THE LABORATORY

First, how do we know that the process of retrieval improves learning? Consider a landmark study conducted in 2006 by our colleagues Henry L. Roediger, III ("Roddy") and Jeffrey Karpicke.[5] In this simple laboratory study, college students at Washington University in St. Louis read brief passages about topics like sea otters and the sun. After reading the passages once, some students were instructed to

Figure 2.1 College students remember information after re-reading in the *short term*, but retain significantly more after retrieval practice over the *long term*.

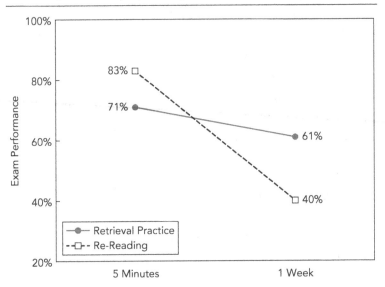

re-read them over and over again, whereas other students retrieved information by writing down everything they could remember.

Importantly, Roddy and Jeff measured students' performance on an exam five minutes later and also one week later using the same "write down everything you can remember" method. What they found was pretty stunning (Figure 2.1):

- After five minutes, student performance in the re-reading condition was much higher (83%) compared to the retrieval condition (71%).

- After one week, this pattern completely switched – student performance in the retrieval condition (61%) was now much higher than performance in the re-reading condition (40%).

Consider it this way: In the span of one week, when students re-read passages, they forgot more than *half* of what they once knew! On the other hand, when students engaged in a simple, quick retrieval method, they forgot a little bit (which is expected), but they forgot much *less* over the one-week delay.

In addition to examining short-term and long-term learning, Roddy and Jeff also asked college students, "How much will you remember in one week?" They asked this question for passages that were re-read and also for passages that were followed by retrieval practice.

Power Up

Do you think college students predicted they will remember more after re-reading or after retrieval practice? Why?

On a 0–7 point scale, students said they'd remember more after re-reading (a rating of 4.8) than after retrieval (a rating of 4.0) – the opposite from the actual results. Time and time again, cognitive scientists find this same pattern or *illusion of fluency*, where students think they'll remember something well after re-reading, but that's actually when they forget the most.[6]

This study by Roddy and Jeff is one simple example that when we deliberately recall information, it forces us to pull our knowledge out and examine what we know. We won't go into all the research here, but thousands of laboratory and neuroscience studies demonstrate that retrieval practice significantly increases learning.[7]

In typical laboratory experiments, college students do the following:

1. They study a set of material (e.g., foreign language vocabulary words, reading passages).

2. They engage in retrieval practice (e.g., via free-recall or multiple-choice quizzes).

3. They complete a final exam immediately or after a delay (e.g., ranging from minutes, to hours, to days).

Consistently, when students engage in retrieval activities that bring knowledge to mind, researchers see a dramatic increase in both short-term and long-term learning.[8]

Quick question: Who was the fourth president of the United States? Instantly, a plausible answer may have jumped to mind, only to realize you had to mentally struggle to think of the actual answer. As we discussed in Chapter 1, it's precisely this struggle or *desirable difficulty* during retrieval that improves learning. Now that you have struggled with this question, check the answer at the end of this chapter.[9] Thanks to our first Power Tool, you'll probably remember the name of the fourth president much better after retrieval practice than if we simply told you the name!

THE SCIENCE BEHIND POWER TOOL #1: RETRIEVAL PRACTICE IN AUTHENTIC CLASSROOMS

We know that learning about sea otters and basic trivia facts can be fun, and these simplistic materials work well in controlled laboratory environments. But what about a chapter in a real Advanced Placement (AP) Biology book or formulas from a college engineering course? Does retrieval practice improve long-term learning in authentic classroom settings for real classroom materials?

Yes!

Research in classrooms has demonstrated that retrieval practice improves learning for:

- Diverse student populations (e.g., K–12 students to medical school students)

- Subject areas (e.g., introductory history to CPR skills)

- Time delays (e.g., ranging from weeks to months)

- Developmental stages (e.g., preschool, young adults, and older adults)[10]

Even with fire alarms, snow days, assemblies, absences, and the day-to-day chaos in classrooms, *scientists have raised grades from a C to an A* for thousands of students, simply with retrieval practice. How? Let's dive into our bread and butter: research with real students, real materials, in real classrooms.

In one of the first studies to explore retrieval-based learning in an authentic classroom setting, students in Patrice's sixth-grade social studies class received three brief low-stakes quizzes via clicker remotes. For a chapter on Ancient Egypt, for example, all information was covered during Patrice's lesson, but half of the chapter material was presented on

Research has shown that retrieval practice can increase students' grades from a C to an A.

the clicker quizzes and half the chapter material wasn't quizzed. In other words, students engaged in retrieval practice for only part of the chapter material, but all of the material was covered during Patrice's lessons.

The team of researchers from Washington University in St. Louis (Pooja, Roddy, Mark McDaniel, and Kathleen McDermott) found that student performance was significantly greater for quizzed material than for nonquizzed material (94% vs. 81%) on a chapter test. Even at the end of the semester (approximately one to two months after Patrice's lessons), student performance was still significantly greater for quizzed material than nonquizzed material *by an entire letter grade* (79% vs. 67%; see Figure 2.2).[11]

Figure 2.2 Patrice's sixth-grade students had significantly higher exam performance when her lessons included retrieval practice (three brief quizzes) compared to lessons without retrieval practice.

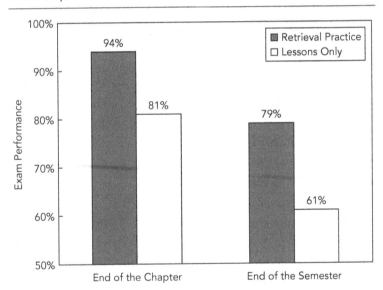

By this point, we hope you're thinking, "Of course, students do better when they're quizzed versus not quizzed. They're seeing the material more often." Now you're thinking like a scientist! In a follow-up experiment, researchers added a condition where students could read material via the clicker software, but they couldn't click in. In other words, if simply seeing the information is as effective as retrieval practice, then scores should be the same in both conditions. Sure enough, on the end-of-chapter exam, quizzes again raised students' grades by an entire letter grade (91% vs. 81%). Even something as simple as three quizzes made a huge impact on student learning.

Consider one study by Keith Lyle and Nicole Crawford in college statistics classes at the University of Louisville.[12] The classes were split into two conditions:

- One class engaged in retrieval practice via short-answer questions at the end of each lecture.

- Another class continued with "business as usual" lectures. They didn't receive any short-answer questions and the lectures continued a little longer to fill the same amount of time as the retrieval practice condition.

When Keith and Nicole looked at four exams throughout the semester, performance for students in the retrieval practice condition was nearly a letter grade higher (86%) compared to students in the lecture-only condition (78%).

Scientists have shown that even medical students benefit from retrieval practice.[13] In one study by Doug Larsen and colleagues, medical students taking a course on neurology participated in three initial learning conditions:

- Students listened to a lecture and then practiced identifying neurology conditions with a standardized patient (an actor who is trained to engage in conversation as a patient).

- Students listened to a lecture and then took a written quiz on key topics.
- Students listened to a lecture and studied a review sheet of key topics.

After six months, performance on a written test was significantly greater when students had initially engaged in the two retrieval conditions (61%) than when they only studied a review sheet (48%). When the final test assessed students' performance on a new standardized patient, initial retrieval practice with a standardized patient (the first condition) led to the greatest performance after six months (59% vs. 49% vs. 43%, respectively).

While this is just the tip of the scientific iceberg so far, in each chapter we'll continue to present research that demonstrates that such a small adjustment during teaching – like a quick quiz – can make a *big* difference for student learning.

HOW TO DEFINE RETRIEVAL PRACTICE IN YOUR CLASSROOM

Throughout this book, when we talk about retrieval practice, it is described as bringing information to mind or pulling information out. We retrieve every day, all the time – from our favorite movie scenes to whether we turned off the kitchen stove (we hope you did!).

And even though we retrieve information nearly every second of every day, it's an abstract concept that can be difficult for us to describe when we talk with students, parents, and other teachers. From our experience, everyone defines retrieval practice in different ways. And that's not a bad thing! But how can we be equipped to describe it to others so we're all on the same page?

Doug Lemov, author of *Teach Like a Champion 2.0*, defines retrieval practice as follows:

Retrieval practice occurs when learners recall and apply multiple examples of previously learned knowledge or skills after a period of forgetting.[14]

Doug breaks down his definition as follows:

- Retrieval practice is relevant to skills (hitting a baseball, solving for the perimeter of an octagon) and to knowledge (historical dates, formulas, vocabulary).

- In the classroom, retrieval practice is intentional, beyond simply asking questions.

- Retrieval practice requires at least a short delay after something has been learned because once you've started to forget you have to work harder to remember.

In a survey we conducted with teachers around the world in 2018, we asked how they define retrieval practice. Here are a few of our favorites:

- Having to strain your memory in order to do something previously learned

- Reaching into the recesses of your brain to grab knowledge that's stored there

- Recalling what you've been learning, without the pressure of having your results evaluated

- Digging for information and bringing it up to the learning surface

- Actively generating knowledge from memory as opposed to simply reading

Whether you define retrieval practice as recalling examples, digging into your brain, or pulling information out, we encourage you to think about (and retrieve!) how you define retrieval practice for yourself, for students, and also for other teachers. It's complex, it's powerful, and it's also just a fun part of everyday life.

> **Power Up**
>
> How do you define retrieval practice?

TEN BENEFITS OF RETRIEVAL PRACTICE

In Chapter 3, we dig into specific ways to incorporate retrieval practice in your teaching. Before we talk about the *how* of retrieval practice, we'd like to first present the *why*. In other words, *why* should you consider using this Power Tool at all?

Here are 10 (of the many) important benefits of retrieval practice, adapted from a list by Roddy, Adam Putnam, and Megan (Smith) Sumeracki.[15] Retrieval practice:

1. Improves students' learning and retention of information over the long term

2. Increases students' higher-order thinking and transfer of knowledge

3. Identifies students' gaps in knowledge, which provides formative assessment for teachers and students

4. Increases students' metacognition and awareness of their own learning

5. Increases students' engagement and attention in class

6. Increases students' use of effective study strategies outside of class

7. Increases students' advance preparation for class

8. Improves students' mental organization of knowledge

9. Increases students' learning of related information that isn't initially retrieved

10. Increases students' learning in the future by blocking interfering information

More than 100 years of research demonstrates that learning can be enhanced, boosted, and transformed with something as simple as getting information out.[16] In fact, retrieval practice yields even *more* benefits for learning when it's used as the basis on which we add more Power Tools we'll be talking about in this book: spacing, interleaving, and feedback-driven metacognition. Without retrieval practice, additional Power Tools improve learning on their own; but *with* retrieval practice, these strategies make a huge impact on student learning.

RETRIEVAL PRACTICE BOOSTS HIGHER-ORDER THINKING AND TRANSFER OF KNOWLEDGE

By now, you may be wondering, "Retrieval practice sounds great, but it still sounds pretty basic." Over the years, we've had the same concerns, too! Fortunately, in the lab and in the classroom, research demonstrates that retrieval practice boosts students' higher-order thinking, application of knowledge, and skills like writing and math. We'll provide research on how retrieval practice boosts more than just memorization, but before we do, let's take a look at complex learning in Patrice's classroom.

Higher-Order Thinking in Patrice's Classroom

Learning facts is crucial and it is the first step. But learning is much more than the simple regurgitation of facts. Learning is also higher-order thinking; it's the synthesis and evaluation of information. For example, if you ask a student, "What color is the sky?" you can anticipate that from pre-K on, the answer will be blue. That is a terrific answer for early elementary grades.

However, we can't stop there. From upper elementary grades on, we should ask, "*Why* is the sky blue?" Immediately, students are forced to pull out or retrieve information and synthesize it into an answer. The higher the grade level, the more information can be retrieved and synthesized.

One of the ways I (Patrice) encourage higher-order thinking in my classroom is by using the acronym *HOT*. In fact, when students write an essay or answer an essential question, I emphasize: *Let's make this so HOT it sizzles!*

It is vital to take learning beyond lower-level thinking. Knowing facts readily assists students in the ability to form opinions and answer essential questions. But I strive for higher-order thinking, where students ponder, synthesize facts, and analyze how the puzzle fits together.

It's important to know that students earn high grades in my class. Students who earn Cs and lower in other classes usually earn As and Bs in mine. Is it because my class is easier than others? *Quite the contrary.* Because of the Power Tools I use, students not only learn facts – they are able to engage in higher-order thinking, too.

Research Demonstrates Retrieval Practice Boosts Students' Knowledge *and* Higher-Order Thinking

Retrieval practice boosts students' higher-order thinking, application of knowledge, and skills like writing and math.

Of course, the development of students' higher-order thinking is a critical component of education. From both an educational perspective and a scientific perspective, it is of practical interest to develop robust strategies that improve higher-order thinking and learning. What, exactly, is higher-order thinking and learning? While there are few agreed-on definitions, higher-order thinking is frequently classified using *Bloom's Taxonomy*, first published in 1956, followed by a revision to the taxonomy in

2001.[17] Based on Bloom's Taxonomy (frequently depicted as a pyramid), higher-order thinking is considered to comprise the apply, analyze, evaluate, and create categories closer to the top of the pyramid. On the other hand, recognition, memory, and comprehension fall under the remember and understand categories near the bottom of the pyramid.

Does retrieval practice improve more than skills at the bottom of the pyramid? Yes! In one study in an eighth-grade science classroom, the same team from Washington University in St. Louis mentioned earlier found that when retrieval practice included both fact questions and application questions, students' performance on the final exam was higher than if they didn't receive retrieval practice at all.[18] Importantly, the application questions had the biggest boost on performance on the final exam with complex questions. Similarly, in an experiment conducted in Patrice's classroom as part of Pooja's dissertation, a mix of basic concept questions and higher-order questions during retrieval practice produced the highest exam performance – more than basic questions alone.[19]

Research also demonstrates that retrieval practice improves students' learning of skills, like math and language arts. In one study led by Charles Kromann, researchers looked at how well medical students could perform CPR. After students received training, some students practiced CPR on a dummy for 10 minutes while other students didn't. When assessed on the key steps of CPR after two weeks, students who initially engaged in retrieval practice significantly outperformed students who didn't engage in any practice (83% vs. 73%).[20]

When it comes to retrieval practice, *how far up the pyramid can we move student learning*? If we want students to think on a higher-order level, then we should make sure our retrieval questions are basic *and* higher-order. It's shortsighted to think, "Gee, well, if I have students retrieve a vocabulary word, they should be able to apply this in a higher-order example or a higher-order type of material." Based on research, *provide a mix of fact-based retrieval and higher-order retrieval* if that's the type of learning you want to see in your students.[21] In other words, move from *pyramid learning* to *powerful learning* in which all levels of thinking and learning are engaged during retrieval practice (Figure 2.3).

Figure 2.3 Move from *pyramid learning* to *powerful learning* by providing *a mix* of fact and higher-order retrieval practice.

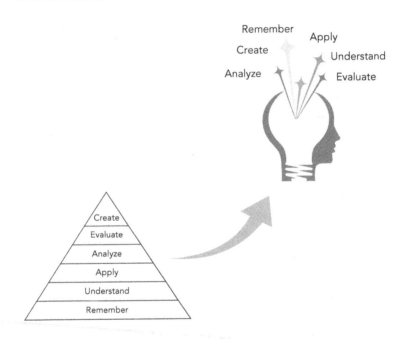

Keep in mind that learning basic knowledge is a good thing! Can a surgeon perform surgeries well without an understanding of basic anatomy? Knowledge plays a critical role in providing a foundation for learning, problem solving, and building connections.[22] Emerging research suggests that learning is not unidirectional or a hierarchy; we don't need to necessarily learn facts before we can think critically, analyze, or engage in higher order thinking. Instead, particularly in the context of retrieval practice, a bi-directional route and a mix of basic and complex knowledge can be more beneficial for students' higher-order thinking.

One additional note about knowledge: Recently, Pooja had the opportunity to video chat with high school students in Indiana. A few hours later, Pooja led a video chat with teachers at a high school in South Carolina. Within the same day, *both* high school students and high school faculty asked this: What does Google mean for learning, memory, and knowledge? Do we have to learn or teach basic facts?

Fascinating question! Of course, we've all had the experience of Googling something, perhaps without even attempting to retrieve it (e.g., how well can you remember how ice cream is made? Can't remember? Google it!). Because students have Google at their fingertips, they may not need to learn specific dates, locations, and facts to the same extent as decades ago. At the same time, students can't rely on Google for everything. Sticking with our surgeon analogy, you wouldn't want a surgeon Googling instructions in the middle of a challenging operation! As another example, how can a student understand the nuances of a complex political event without understanding the basics of the political parties involved?[23]

Scientist and professor Jason Finley, who specializes in interactions between memory and technology, put it this way:

> We don't really know all the implications of Google yet. We know that people are memorizing facts less and it's becoming more important to know how to *find* information than to have it all in your head.

Back to the bigger picture: Knowledge enhances higher-order thinking (and vice versa). With retrieval practice, include complex questions, not just fact questions. Anecdotally, we've heard from teachers who use retrieval practice to help students learn

Buddhism, sign language, and dressage (a performance discipline for riding horses). Talk about knowledge *and* higher-order thinking!

Research Demonstrates That Retrieval Practice Boosts Students' Transfer of Knowledge

Let's say a teacher teaches a lesson on the water cycle. A few days later, a student is walking outside. She notices that a puddle from the morning has vanished by the afternoon. How can the teacher enhance the student's understanding that evaporation has occurred? How can students successfully apply what they have learned from one lesson to another, from one class to another, or from school to the real world?

Transfer happens when students take something familiar and apply it to something unfamiliar.

Transfer of learning, or simply called transfer, is the application of concepts or information in new situations.[24] In other words, transfer happens when students take something *familiar* and apply it to something *unfamiliar*. In the same way, a fundamental goal is that student learning *inside* the classroom is applied *outside* the classroom – the hallmark of deep understanding and flexible knowledge.

Retrieval practice enhances students' transfer of learning, which can take many forms. For example, a type of *near transfer* could involve students learning how to calculate the Pythagorean theorem, followed by calculating the theorem with a new set of numbers. In contrast, *far transfer* would be when a medical student learns something from a textbook and then applies it when diagnosing patients (see Figure 2.4 for more examples).[25]

In a meta-analysis from 2018, scientists Steven Pan and Tim Rickard at the University of California, San Diego, found that retrieval practice produces more robust transfer than any other

Figure 2.4 Retrieval practice improves students' transfer of knowledge, ranging from near to far transfer and also transfer in a variety of settings.

	NEAR TRANSFER			FAR TRANSFER
Knowledge	Ancient Egypt in 1330 BC vs. 1325 BC	Ancient Egypt vs. Ancient China	Ancient Egypt vs. Modern United States	Ancient Egypt vs. Romantic Literature
Physical	Same classroom	Different classroom at the same school	Different schools	School vs. home
Time	During the same lesson	During the same day	Weeks or months later	Years later
Task	Algebraic calculation with new numbers	Algebraic calculation with novel diagrams	Algebraic calculation with word problems	Algebraic calculation with real world examples
Format	Same format as before	Multiple-choice vs. short answer	Multiple-choice vs. essay	Multiple-choice vs. projects

research-based strategy to date.[26] Why does retrieval practice boost transfer? Because it's a desirable difficulty. Students learn information in a deeper manner than when they simply review information. With this increased effort and broader engagement, students don't simply recall information; they have to use existing knowledge in new and different ways.

Here's the catch: While we might *know it when we see it*, transfer of learning can be *easier said than done*, too. For example, when students are asked, "On what day did the Allies invade Normandy?" (D-Day) and then later asked, "Where did the Allies invade on D-Day?" (Normandy), it's surprising that students struggle to transfer their knowledge; transfer from one specific part of a fact to another can be tough.

> While we might know it when we see it, transfer of learning can be easier said than done.

Here's another situation where college students surprisingly struggle to transfer their knowledge. In the 1980s, researchers created a "fortress problem" and a "tumor problem." In the fortress problem, a military general wanted to capture a fortress in the center of a country. The problem was that large groups of soldiers could not travel on the same road to the fortress. The simple solution was that *soldiers had to travel in small groups, taking different roads to reach the fortress.*

In the tumor problem, a physician was trying to irradiate a tumor. The problem was that a single dose of radiation strong enough to destroy the tumor would also severely damage nearby tissue. Can you guess the solution? It might be obvious to you, but it wasn't to the college students! The vast majority of the college students (80%) failed to transfer and apply the fortress solution to the new tumor problem (note that this sample was small; only 15 students).[27]

Thankfully, not all is lost! Even though retrieval practice improves students' transfer, scientists have demonstrated there are two additional strategies to ensure success: *hints* and *feedback*. For the fortress and tumor problems, when students were given a helpful hint, nearly all of them (92%) generated the correct solution.

Why is transfer more challenging than we expect?

- Students may not *recognize* that their knowledge should be applied in a novel situation.

- Students may recognize that they need to apply their knowledge, but they can't *remember* the knowledge to be applied. If they can't remember it, they can't transfer it.

- Students may not correctly *apply* knowledge to the novel situation.

How can we reduce these challenges and ensure successful transfer?

- Hints help students recognize when and what to transfer.
- Retrieval practice helps students remember what to transfer.
- Feedback helps students apply their knowledge correctly.

When it comes to higher-order thinking, skill learning, and transfer of knowledge, retrieval practice is a key Power Tool. Combined with helpful hints and meaningful feedback (which we discuss in greater detail in Chapter 5), retrieval practice is for more than just memorization or basic fact learning – *much* more. Daniel Willingham, professor and author of *Why Don't Students Like School*, put it this way:

> A great deal has been written about the impact of retrieval practice on memory. That's because the effect is sizable, it has been replicated many times and it seems to lead not just to better memory, but deeper memory that supports transfer.

RETRIEVAL PRACTICE IS NOT THE SAME AS FORMATIVE OR SUMMATIVE ASSESSMENTS

You're probably familiar with these two forms of assessment:

Formative assessment is when we check on and monitor students' progress. Kind of like inserting a toothpick into a cake to see how it's doing while baking, formative assessment is a strategy to see if things are on track.

Summative assessment is when we discover what students have learned through various forms of measurement. This is when we get to celebrate accomplishments, perhaps like enjoying a cake after baking, while also noticing what could be done differently next time.

But where does retrieval practice fit in?

In keeping with our cake analogy, *retrieval practice* is the process of learning how to crack an egg, measure ingredients, and mix it all together (perhaps using a Power Blender!). This is when we embrace mistakes rather than emphasize perfection because challenges are a *good thing* for learning.

Consider an additional comparison to a file drawer:

- Retrieval practice: Organize the files so it's easier to access next time.

- Formative assessment: Peek into a file drawer and see what's inside.

- Summative assessment: Inventory all the files before moving to the next cabinet.

There are, of course, similarities and differences between retrieval practice, formative assessment, and summative assessment:

- *Similarity.* All three require retrieval! From the outside, it can look like one seamless process, and that's a good thing.

- *Difference.* Retrieval practice doesn't require any data collection, grading, or points. *Nothing* needs to be recorded in the gradebook. Retrieval practice is a *no-stakes opportunity* when students can experiment, be challenged, and improve over time.

Retrieval practice is a learning strategy, not an assessment strategy.

This is why retrieval practice does *not* equal assessment. While formative and summative assessment are valuable for *checking* learning, retrieval practice activities, like brief quizzes we'll discuss in Chapter 3, are valuable for *increasing* learning. Similarly, retrieval practice is *a learning strategy*, not an assessment strategy.

It's also crucial that we think of retrieval as a *good* thing for learning, not a bad thing that's only associated with assessment. We must foster a classroom culture of retrieval that's *positive, not negative*. By keeping retrieval practice no-stakes, we (and our students!) get away from thinking of retrieval as more tests and move toward retrieval as being *more learning*.

> *Get away from thinking of retrieval as more tests and move toward retrieval as being more learning.*

Cognitive scientists used to refer to retrieval practice as the *testing effect* (and occasionally still do in the research literature). But you won't find the word *test* in this book very often. It's because retrieval and pulling information out is what dramatically improves learning. Retrieval practice can take many forms – including *Think-Pair-Share* and flashcards – not just tests.

Lastly, retrieval practice is *not* a call for more testing; *it's the opposite*. Retrieval practice is successful when we foster learning in a supportive, no-stakes environment that values oddly shaped cupcakes over a perfect wedding cake.

Power Up

We described three reasons why students struggle to transfer their knowledge. What is one of those reasons?

TAKE RETRIEVAL PRACTICE FROM YOUR CLASSROOM TO YOUR EVERYDAY LIFE

Now that you have a firm understanding of retrieval practice and the science behind it, pay attention to it; not only inside your classroom, but also in your daily life. When you start paying attention to your own retrieval habits, you'll be surprised at how often you bring information to mind *outside* the classroom.

Then, take it to the next level and start practicing retrieval for all sorts of things: where you parked your car, the name of a book you want to recommend to a colleague (hint!), and even details from your day you want to share with a loved one. Start incorporating retrieval practice into your everyday life and experience firsthand how desirable difficulties are a good thing for your *own* learning.

It's time to move from what we ate *yesterday* to transforming learning *tomorrow*. Get ready, get set – let's go!

NOTES

1. Yesterday, Pooja probably had coffee for breakfast, and Patrice likely had Greek yogurt and half a banana.

2. Don't cheat! Take a guess and write it down before checking the answer.

3. Pooja's favorite vacation was a two-week road trip through Uruguay. Patrice's favorite vacation was snorkeling around the US Virgin Islands.

4. We mean it! We know you're near the beginning of the book, but we hope you've learned at least one thing already. Pause and write down one thing you've learned so far!

5. Roediger, H. L., and Karpicke, J. D. (2006). Test-enhanced learning: Taking memory tests improve long-term retention. *Psychological Science* 17: 249–255.

6. Agarwal, P. K., Karpicke, J. D., Kang, S.H.K., et al. (2008). Examining the testing effect with open- and closed-book tests. *Applied Cognitive Psychology* 22: 861–876.

7. Nadel, L., Hupbach, A., Gomez, R., and Newman-Smith, K. (2012). Memory formation, consolidation and transformation. *Neuroscience & Behavioral Reviews* 36: 1640–1645.

8. Pashler, H., Bain, P., Bottge, B., et al. (2007). *Organizing Instruction and Study to Improve Student Learning.* Washington, DC: National Center for Education Research, Institute of Education Sciences, U.S. Department of Education.

9. The fourth president of the United States was James Madison.

10. Fazio, L. K., and Agarwal, P. K. (2019). *How to implement retrieval-based learning in preschool and elementary school.* Vanderbilt University. Available at www.powerfulteaching.org.

11. Roediger, H. L., Agarwal, P. K., McDaniel, M. A., et al. (2011). Test-enhanced learning in the classroom: Long-term improvements from quizzing. *Journal of Experimental Psychology: Applied* 17: 382–395.

12. Lyle, K. B., and Crawford, N. A. (2011). Retrieving essential material at the end of lectures improves performance on statistics exams. *Teaching of Psychology* 38: 94–99.

13. Larsen, D. P., Butler, A. C., Lawson, A. L., et al. (2013). The importance of seeing the patient: Test-enhanced learning with standardized patients and written tests improves clinical application of knowledge. *Advances in Health Sciences Education* 18: 409–425.

14. Lemov, D. (2017, October 3). Retrieval practice: A teacher's definition and video examples [Blog post]. Retrieved from www .teachlikeachampion.com.

15. Our list of ten benefits of retrieval practice is adapted from Roediger, H. L., Putnam, A. L., and Smith, M. A. (2011). Ten benefits of testing and their applications to educational practice. In: *Psychology of learning and motivation: Cognition in education* (ed. J. Mestre and B. Ross), 1–36. Oxford: Elsevier.

16. Adesope, O. O., Trevisan, D. A., and Sundararajan, N. (2017). Rethinking the use of tests: A meta-analysis of practice testing. *Review of Educational Research* 87: 659–701.

17. Anderson, L. W., Krathwohl, D. R., Airasian, P. W., et al. (2001). *A taxonomy for learning, teaching, and assessing: A revision of Bloom's taxonomy of educational objectives* (abridged ed.). New York, NY: Addison Wesley Longman, Inc.

18. McDaniel, M. A., Thomas, R. C., Agarwal, P. K., et al. (2013). Quizzing in middle-school science: Successful transfer performance on classroom exams. *Applied Cognitive Psychology* 27: 360–372.

19. Agarwal, P. K. (2019). Retrieval practice and Bloom's taxonomy: Do students need fact knowledge before higher order learning? *Journal of Educational Psychology* 11: 189–209.

20. Kromann, C. B., Jenson, M. L., and Ringstead, C. (2009). The effect of testing on skills learning. *Medical Education* 43: 21–27.

21. In the cognitive science literature, a match between the format of initial learning to the format of final learning is referred to as *transfer appropriate processing*. Morris, C. D., Bransford, J. D., and Franks, J. J. (1977). Levels of processing versus transfer-appropriate processing. *Journal of Verbal Learning and Verbal Behavior* 16: 519–533.

22. Willingham, D. T. (2006, Spring). How knowledge helps: It speeds and strengthens reading comprehension, learning, and thinking. *American Educator.*

23. For more examples of the interplay between knowledge and complex learning, we recommend the book *Learn Better* by Ulrich Boser (Rodale, 2017).

24. Pan, S. C., and Agarwal, P. K. (2018). *Retrieval practice and transfer of learning: Fostering students' application of knowledge.* University of California, San Diego. Available at www .powerfulteaching.org.

25. Barnett, S. M., and Ceci, S. J. (2002). When and where do we apply what we learn? A taxonomy for far transfer. *Psychological Bulletin* 128: 612–637.

26. Pan, S. C., and Rickard, T. C. (2018). Transfer of test-enhanced learning: Meta-analytic review and synthesis. *Psychological Bulletin* 144: 710–756.

27. Gick, M. L., and Holyoak, K. J. (1980). Analogical problem solving. *Cognitive Psychology* 12: 306–355.

Chapter 3

Empower Teaching with Retrieval Practice Strategies

In the previous chapter, we went behind the scenes of our first Power Tool, retrieval practice, and why it transforms learning. Decades of research findings on retrieval practice are rock solid: Retrieval practice and bringing information to mind dramatically improves learning over the long-term for diverse students, content areas, and education levels.[1]

In this chapter, let's move research into the classroom with specific strategies that are quick, flexible, and practical. With an understanding of the basic principle of desirable difficulties from Chapter 2, we are confident that you can effectively adapt each strategy in your classroom, for your content area, regardless of grade level. Keep in mind that we focus on retrieval practice as a *learning* strategy, not an assessment strategy, like a test or exam.

Retrieval practice is intuitive and simple. That's why we love it! But you can't stop there. James Lang, professor and author of *Small Teaching: Everyday Lessons From the Science of Learning*, said it well:

> You don't have to think too hard about how to give your students effective retrieval practice; *you just have to do it.*[2]

Let's jump in, get our hands dirty, and focus on getting information *out.*

BRAIN DUMPS: WRITE DOWN EVERYTHING YOU CAN REMEMBER

For our first retrieval practice strategy, here's a small technique that makes a big impact on student learning: *Brain Dumps.*

1. Pause your lesson, lecture, or activity.

2. Ask students to write down everything they can remember.

3. Continue your lesson, lecture, or activity.

Yes, it's that simple! Simply ask students to Brain Dump and write down what they remember individually, then move on. How do we know that Brain Dumps improve learning? Research, of course! In scientific lingo, writing down what you remember is called *free-recall,* and it's a common retrieval strategy in laboratory studies because of its simplicity and opportunity for open-ended responses.

In fact, scientists have demonstrated that Brain Dumps:

- Boost students' learning of past and future content[3]

- Boost students' organization of knowledge[4]

- Boost students' inferential reasoning[5]

Across the board, evidence-based Brain Dumps boost learning for all students. As Jillian, a fourth-grade teacher, shared with us, "My fourth-graders tried Brain Dumping today. It was a huge success!"

Brain Dumps are pretty straightforward, which is one reason why we love them. Here are three additional recommendations to keep in mind:

1. *Provide as much – or as little – time as you'd like on a Brain Dump in class.* You can even play it by ear, depending on how students are progressing. Depending on your students, it could take them 30 minutes or more to write down everything they know! While that's fabulous, we also know there are classroom constraints when it comes to time. Even if students retrieve only a subset of what they know, learning will be boosted for related information that's not retrieved.[6]

2. Scientists are currently exploring whether Brain Dumps are more effective if written by hand versus typed; include structure (organize as you go along) vs. no structure; or include prompts ("describe how clouds are made") versus no prompts. So far, there are no hard-hitting winners when it comes to optimal structures compared to a simple "write down what you can remember" approach.[7] We encourage you to *do what's practical for you and your classroom* and focus on retrieval, not format.

3. Avoid using Brain Dumps as a substantial part of a grade (e.g., as an exam or paper assignment). By keeping Brain Dumps low-stakes, students will feel less pressured and more comfortable writing down everything they can retrieve, even if they make mistakes (which are good for learning!). They can be used as a learning tool for you via formative assessment, but steer clear of using them as high-stakes summative assessments.

What should students do after a Brain Dump? *Simply move on with your lesson!* No collection of papers, no grading, no class discussion, other than acknowledging students' engagement in retrieval practice, of course. Often, Brain Dumps provide a simple *confidence boost* for students, especially when they can compare an earlier Brain Dump to their most recent one. Students are able to write down what they know, without being limited to the questions asked of them, and there is a large amount of satisfaction when students simply see what they know written down in front of them.

Provide the opportunity for *peer feedback*. Ask students to swap their Brain Dump with a neighbor for 1–2 minutes, *have them add something new* that wasn't already written down, and pass back the Brain Dump. This is quick and instant feedback, but it could also be followed with extended discussion.

Use Think-Pair-Share following a Brain Dump. Students have already completed the *think* stage individually. During the *pair* stage, here are some questions you can ask to prompt discussion:

- Is there anything in common that *both of us* wrote down?
- Is there anything new that *neither of us* wrote down?
- Did either of us write down any *misinformation*?
- *Why* do you think you remembered what you did?

Give students ownership. Once students have Brain Dumped once or twice, have the class come up with a name for this strategy. Patrice's middle school students call this activity a *Brain Drain* and Pooja's college students call this activity *free-recall.* As we discuss in Chapter 9 on sparking conversations with students, shared language makes a huge difference in emphasizing that Power Tools are a *good* thing for learning.

With such a powerful, simple strategy like Brain Dumps, you can unleash the science of learning and your students can unleash it, too.

We asked teachers around the world for alternative names for Brain Dumps and here were their top suggestions:

Free Recall	Stop and Jot
Brain Drain	Free Flow
Brain Pop	Total Recall
Brain Drop	Learning Deposit
Brain Inventory	Tell Me Everything
Data Dump	Information Extraction
Knowledge Bombs	Information Unpacking
Knowledge Download	Learning Sync
Show What You Know	Learning Unplugged

As you can see, there are many ways to describe retrieval practice! The words *exam* and *test* are nowhere to be found. Keep Brain Dumps no-stakes or low-stakes, include feedback when you can, and engage students in the process.

Power Up

Now that you've learned more about retrieval practice, how would you describe it to students?

Brain Dumps in Patrice's Classroom Boost Student Confidence

During the first quarter of the school year, one of my students' favorite activities is a Brain Drain focused on Ancient Egypt. I pass out lined paper that states on the top: "What I Know about Ancient Egypt." After a few quizzical looks, they begin to write. And write and write (take a look for yourself in Figure 3.1). My only rule for students: Your writing must be in complete sentences and reflect

Figure 3.1 Thirty-five minutes into Patrice's Brain Drain, sixth-graders continue to write.

what you learned in our unit. It's rare for a student to finish before the end of class, and more often than not, I find a note at the bottom, "I could have written so much more!" I have also seen and been told:

- "I learned so much more than I thought I knew!"
- "I could have written for hours!"
- "I would write one thing and then my brain would flood with information about it – and that would lead to more!"

Every student retrieves on average four to five *pages* of correct facts. I often share my students' Brain Drains during parent-teacher conferences (see examples in Figure 3.2). I see parents' mouths drop open, with incredulous looks on their faces. Some of my favorite conferences have been with parents of my special education students; this is where I see the tears. Often, parents have never seen

Figure 3.2 Examples of students' Brain Drains in Patrice's classroom.

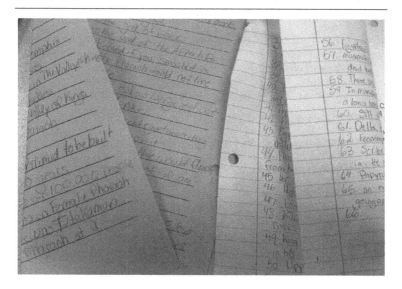

such an example of their child's work. And the students themselves? Students confirm that they are learning how to learn. I love witnessing their pride and accomplishment, especially when they compare how much they've learned between the beginning and end of a unit. Their confidence truly soars.

Power Up

In a landmark study of retrieval practice by scientists Roddy Roediger and Jeff Karpicke mentioned in the Chapter 2, how did college students engage in retrieval practice?[8]

TWO THINGS: A QUICK STRATEGY FOR THE BEGINNING, MIDDLE, AND END OF CLASS

How can we use retrieval practice to break up our lessons, quickly and easily, without pausing to hand out quizzes, facilitate class discussion, or collect papers? Let's explore a no-quiz strategy we simply call *Two Things*:

At any point during a lesson, stop and have students write down Two Things about a specific prompt. For example:

- What are Two Things you learned so far today?

- What are Two Things you learned yesterday (or last week)?

- What are your two takeaways from this unit?

- What are Two Things you'd like to learn more about?

- What are two examples from your own life that relate to today's lesson?

Now what? Just like the other strategies we've discussed so far, simply move on with your lesson. In this way, retrieval practice can take one minute or less. Recently, Pooja instructed her students, "Write down Two Things you remember about neuroscience we discussed a few weeks ago." Students wrote down their thoughts and she promptly moved on. That's it!

Note: Your students might give you odd looks after this exercise. They may automatically hand you their paper. They may not understand why you're moving on. Actually, this is a perfect time to *flip retrieval from a negative to a positive*! Yet again, emphasize that Two Things is a learning strategy, not an assessment strategy. Also, remind students that the challenge from retrieval is a desirable difficulty – it's good for learning!

Retrieval practice can take one minute or less.

There are two additional benefits from Two Things:

- By retrieving Two Things, students have notes they can keep and use in the future – without taking notes during class.

- During a small group or class discussion, have students share *one* of their Two Things. They already have something written down, so they won't need to think of something on the fly, saving classroom time and also decreasing anxiety. By sharing, students confirm their Two Things are on point and they learn more things they didn't write down from each other.

> **Power Up**
>
> The next time you read a book, ask yourself, "What are Two Things I learned?" In fact, take a moment and write down Two Things you've learned from this book so far!

RETRIEVE-TAKING: A POWERFUL SPIN ON TRADITIONAL NOTE-TAKING

What do your students do during lessons? Are they listening? Discussing? Retrieving? Taking notes?

If you teach in upper-grade levels (high school, college, and above), chances are, your students take notes. Why? Note-taking can help students organize information, and it provides a record of topics students can use to study at home. At the same time, not all students are good note-takers. They may have a tendency to transcribe literally what you are saying or struggle to identify which concepts are most important to write down.

How can we turn note-taking into retrieval practice? We call it *Retrieve-Taking*! Here are the steps:

1. Teach your lesson as usual. Students listen and participate, but they *can't* take notes (yet!)

2. Pause your lesson. Students write down important topics they want to study.

3. Give students quick feedback about important topics or facilitate a discussion where students share what they wrote down.

4. Continue with your lesson.

Did you notice the tiny change? Instead of taking notes *during* a lesson, students simply retrieve notes when you *pause* your lesson. This tiny change swaps students' half-attentive, somewhat disorganized note-taking with Retrieve-Taking, which becomes notes for students after class!

With Retrieve-Taking, students take closed-book notes, not open-book notes. They retrieve what they know, rather than write down what you know.

Here's another way to think about it: In many surveys, most students report taking notes while reading (or re-reading!) a textbook. With note-taking, students focus on getting information in, not out. Luckily, students can swap note-taking with Retrieve-Taking *outside* of class, too!

1. Students read their book.
2. Every so often, students *close* their book.
3. Students engage in Retrieve-Taking.
4. Students open the book. Voila!

A few "notes" to keep in mind (get it?):

- Model Retrieve-Taking during class in a no-stakes environment, so students become comfortable using Retrieve-Taking outside of class.

- Retrieve-Taking with index cards or on a computer helps students organize their thoughts afterward, as opposed to the more traditional process of organizing notes during note-taking.

- What students write down during Retrieve-Taking becomes a study tool, just like note-taking. Students can stay within their comfort zone without copying information out of a book.

- With Retrieve-Taking, students will save themselves study time in the long run. They won't have to re-read if they retrieve and retain more in the first place.

Encourage students to dip their toes into this desirable difficulty by guiding them from traditional note-taking on the fly to Retrieve-Taking – *just close the book!*

RETRIEVAL PRACTICE STRATEGIES IN PATRICE'S CLASSROOM: RETRIEVAL GUIDES AND MINI-QUIZZES

Ever since I (Patrice) started teaching, I've been using "guides" that students fill in during a lesson. Initially, I referred to these as study guides; I later changed the name to *Retrieval Guides*. Prior to my work with Pooja, I thought of them as a means to take important information from a text, put it in outline form, and become a paper from which to study. However, by simply changing *how* the guides were completed, I transformed these outlines into a powerful tool for retrieval. I now combine Retrieval Guides with daily Mini-Quizzes to help students retrieve information.

Retrieval Guides: A Powerful Spin on Traditional Study Guides

To get started, I outlined every lesson in my text and created *clozes,* or phrases with intentional words or ideas left blank. (And, yes, it took a summer to outline the text.) For each lesson, I created Retrieval Guides with about 15 fill-in-the-blank or short-answer questions for students to complete (you can download sample Retrieval Guides at www.powerfulteaching.org).

Here's what it looks like in my classroom:

1. All text reading is done aloud, usually by the students. I am intentional in this process as the students are unfamiliar with much of the vocabulary. I want them to listen to the

terms out loud so they can decipher correct pronunciation and I can continue to relate previously learned information. Shi Huangdi, Lady Murasaki Shikibu, and Queen Amanishakheto are a few examples of difficult pronunciation. Usually, when a name or term is particularly difficult to pronounce, I have the student pause, I say the word correctly, students repeat it, and the student continues reading.

2. During this read-aloud, *all pencils are down*. After several paragraphs, I pause the reading and encourage students to retrieve and write down the required information in the Retrieval Guide without using their books. Students have the option of going back and finding answers in the text, but by the second quarter, it is rare for students to look up answers. Students enjoy the challenge of not having to look back at the text. This is how *study guides* become *Retrieval Guides*. Students are *retrieving* important information, not just looking it up.

3. After students have written down answers, I conduct a group discussion to ensure correct answers. Also, while reading is paused, I tie in questions from earlier learning. I often have students Think-Pair-Share to help reinforce the information. By switching the timing from filling in the guide *during* the read aloud to retrieving *after* the read aloud, a mechanism for powerful learning had been created.

The benefits of Retrieval Guides have been numerous for both students and me. For example:

- I became familiar with my curriculum; I had my whole year outlined.

- I was able to see trends and establish ideas for essential questions.

- While in class, I was able to monitor student engagement, receive formative feedback, and ensure all students were receiving the same information.

Most 11-year-olds do not yet know how to pull out important information from reading a text, book, journal, or online source. Through the Retrieval Guides, I am able to teach and model this process. In addition, students become familiar with and comfortable seeing information in outline form. At the bottom of each guide is an *outcome statement*. I ask students, without looking at notes or text, to write down the most interesting thing they learned. The outcome statements are my version of an exit ticket and are yet another great tool for retrieval. Additionally, the finished outline is a great resource for at-home study. A major plus: Students aren't doing hours of history homework each night!

Mini-Quizzes: A No-Grade, Low-Stakes Basket of Clues

I came up with this idea several years ago and continue to use it. Here is what works for me. Students do the same amount of classwork, *but I no longer spend hours at night grading it*. Rather, I came up with the idea of daily Mini-Quizzes:

1. Take anything discussed in the previous class or questions from Retrieval Guides, write clues on small slips of paper, cut up each clue, and put them into a basket.

2. Students number 1–5 on paper. (Cut-up recycled paper works well).

3. Randomly choose five slips of paper from the basket of clues.

4. Read each clue twice. (For example, what is the term for the person at the top of Russia's social pyramid from the 1800s to the early 1900s?[9])

5. At the end of the Mini-Quiz, read all five clues one last time.

6. Students turn in Mini-Quizzes.

7. As soon as students' Mini-Quizzes have been collected, provide immediate feedback by going over the answers. (These are low-stakes or no-stakes quizzes – at most, they are worth five points; sometimes I don't grade them at all.)

8. At the end of the Mini-Quiz, all clues go back into the basket, and again, they're chosen randomly for the next class.

9. I conduct an analysis of the Mini-Quizzes after school; students know I conduct this analysis, which encourages accountability for their answers.

10. Handing the Mini-Quizzes back the following day allows for double retrieval: the day of the Mini-Quiz and the following day as we go over answers again.

The following example illustrates the decreased stress and anxiety of the students as they retrieve a previous day's lesson. If a student misses an answer (or more), rather than internalizing failure, they often think, "Hmm . . . I don't know that one *yet*. Now I know what to work on." I would say about 50% of the Mini-Quizzes have comments or doodles. I credit these "positives" to the fact that the students feel proud of their accomplishments. When students feel successful at the middle school level, they are unsure as to what to do with that feeling. Often, they gift it to the teacher (see Figure 3.3). Rather than internalizing that I am "best teacher ever," my heart swells because I know students are experiencing success.

Students are also held accountable. They know each class will begin with a Mini-Quiz. In fact, all I have to do to begin class is to ask, "What time is it?" They joyfully begin singing, in a song I teach at the beginning of the year, "It's time for a Mini-Quiz . . ." (Please keep in mind I teach sixth-grade!) Because Mini-Quizzes are an everyday occurrence, there is little anxiety and students see that what is discussed or written from notes is not busy work. I am

Figure 3.3 Example of a student's Mini-Quiz in Patrice's classroom.

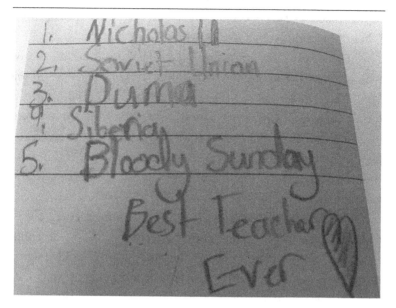

able to build on what was learned to create deeper thinking. By using Mini-Quizzes, I have removed the detours that can lead to a negative impact on learning, i.e., copying or getting answers from another, poor organization, and/or incomplete homework . . . to name a few. My own time spent grading went from several hours at night for my 150+ students to a 15–20 minute analysis after school. Through my analysis, I have a clear idea of what may or may not require more coverage the following day. Most importantly, students are retrieving. They are learning. That's powerful.

With a year's worth of learning, how do I select the items I include in the Mini-Quizzes? I know my curriculum. I know my essential questions. I base my questions on what I want the students to retain. I connect previous knowledge with new knowledge, reinforcing retrieval.

If students are absent, they are required to read the text and fill in the Retrieval Guide over what they missed. I go over these one on one with the students upon their return to check for accuracy and answer questions. However, because Mini-Quizzes are low- or no-stakes, and each week is filled with retrieval opportunities, I do not have students make up Mini-Quizzes.

Keep in mind that my Mini-Quiz questions are often recall-type questions. For example, *Who was the King of France in the late 1700s?* Or, *What was the name of the law-making body formed by the Third Estate in 1789?*[10] Questions for the Mini-Quizzes are usually taken from the previous day's learning. My purpose for giving these questions is to assist students in determining how well they can retrieve the answers. The questions assist with the students' retention of basic knowledge.

Of course, I have my naysayers. When presenting at conferences, or simply talking with other teachers, I have heard, "But learning is so much more than the regurgitation of facts." I couldn't agree more! However, how can we expect our students to answer essential questions, to go to deeper levels of understanding, without first knowing the facts? Through daily retrieval, students learn what they know and what they still need to learn. We compare, contrast, differentiate . . . and this continues with each new chapter and unit. *We retrieve every step of the way.*

Meanwhile, my essential questions require higher-order thinking. At the beginning of each chapter, I have the essential question written on the board. As new facts are learned, I ask the students to relate this new information to the essential question. I may encourage *Turn and Talks* followed by class discussions. These are questions that one could not simply "Google" an answer. The questions are often more like an essay and are given as part of the test at the end of a chapter. An example might be: *After being a republic, why did French citizens give up their power to an absolute ruler? How do the two types of government differ?* Or, often I will combine different chapters with questions such as: *Compare and contrast the French Revolution with the Russian Revolution. State five reasons how they were alike and five reasons how they were different. Could either of them have been avoided? Defend your answer.* Another essential question: *Did the Treaty of Versailles play a role in World War II?* (The steps and strategies I use in building essential questions can be found at www.powerfulteaching.org.)

These types of questions encourage retrieval of higher-order concepts. However, what never ceases to put a smile on my face is how incredulous the students are as we begin a new chapter. They see the essential question and shake their heads in disbelief that they would ever know the answer. Yet, within a few weeks, they answer the essential questions like pros! As the year progresses, their confidence grows as they *know* they will be able to answer these questions.

Power Up

As we discussed in Chapter 2, what does it mean to move from pyramid learning to powerful learning? Write a description or draw your own diagram.

RETRIEVAL PRACTICE STRATEGIES IN POOJA'S CLASSROOM: WEEKLY QUIZZES AND STRUCTURED CLASS DISCUSSION

Based on this wealth of research on retrieval practice, I practice what I preach. I incorporate retrieval practice in all my psychology classes as frequently as possible.

I engage college students in retrieval from day 1; I ask students to respond to the question, "What is psychology?" On day 2, I ask students, "Write down Two Things you remember about the syllabus from yesterday." After this prompt, I have students go around the room individually and quickly share just one of the Two Things they wrote down. In this way, students are retrieving and reviewing the syllabus, rather than me reiterating it for absent (or inattentive) students.

One of my central methods for incorporating retrieval practice in my classroom is in the form of brief low-stakes quizzes at the beginning of each week (see Figure 3.4). Note that I'm referring to them as "quizzes" here for simplicity, but I only call them "retrieval practices" in my classroom:

Figure 3.4 Example of a low-stakes weekly retrieval practice in Pooja's classroom. Students complete short-answer questions for 20–30 minutes, followed by discussion activities and feedback.

Retrieval Practice: Week 3

1) Last week, we watched 7 Science Brief videos from previous semesters. List **three specific things** you learned (from any of the videos). (3 points)

1. Coursing is healthy. One scenario could be to liberate some "steam" when you're mad or hurt

2. Naps between 12-4 pm are good to "recharge" yourself for the othe half of the day

3. People can be addicted to their phones, there's a similar reaction in the brain than with actual drugs.

2) What was your initial reaction to your book reading? Was it interesting? Boring? Confusing? Why? Be specific. (1 point)

I'm very happy with my book. It's insanely interesting and easy to read, but most of all USEFUL

3) Should research be conducted on animals? Why or why not? **Write a persuasive argument.** (3 points)

Doing harmfull research with humans is not allowed, it should be the same for animals. Why? It's not common to test humans to cure animals, what right do we have to make animals do that for us?

Unharmfull research are acceptable in humans and animals.

1. Students walk into the classroom and immediately pick up a double-sided retrieval practice.

2. Students have a seat and write silently for approximately 20 minutes, responding to four or five short-answer questions.

3. Students engage in small-group and whole-class discussion for approximately 20–30 minutes.

In the first step, by starting class with retrieval practices immediately, students have an incentive to attend class on time. I collect the retrieval practices once all the on-time students complete it, so any students who are tardy miss out on additional time. This writing time at the beginning of class also gives me the opportunity to get settled – I have a few minutes to get my laptop set up, get my lesson plans in order, and take attendance. An added bonus: The room is quiet during students' writing, which is a nice break from the hustle and bustle during everyone's day.

In the second step, I find silent writing time invaluable. Building on the strategy *Everybody Writes* by Doug Lemov, all students have time to think and reflect at their own pace.[11] Once they have time to think, they're more comfortable and confident participating in class discussions.

Also, my short-answer questions are written in a way that intentionally provides a springboard for class discussion. My short-answer questions include a mix about the reading for the week, concepts learned recently or from weeks ago, and concepts we'll discuss that day.

Here are some examples of my short-answer questions:

- Describe one of the 10 psychology myths we learned about last week.

- Are all humans scientists? Why or why not?

- What are Two Things you learned from your book reading this week? Be specific.

- How would a scientist conduct an experiment to see which type of shoe makes people jump higher, Nike or Adidas?

As you may have noticed, my questions aren't Google-able; they don't always have a right or wrong answer. Each retrieval practice includes an optional Retrieval Warm-Up on the back, such as, "Have you ever gone skydiving? Why or why not?" (See Chapter 8 on fostering a supportive environment for more information.) Students know that any content throughout the semester is "fair game," boosting learning with spacing (stay tuned for this Power Tool in Chapter 4).

What do students do if they finish before others?

- I always put up a slide of reminders, so that students can read through them in the meantime.

- I encourage them to take advantage of the time and read ahead (or catch up on their reading!).

- I use the time as "office hours," where students can chat with me outside the classroom about projects, class, or anything else on their mind.

- I also point students toward something productive to occupy their time – reading, checking their grades, working on their group projects, etc.

In the third step, once students have retrieved individually, I use a combination of Think-Pair-Share, small-group, and whole-class discussions for feedback. In line with our fourth Power Tool, feedback-driven metacognition (see Chapter 5), my structured discussions are opportunities to check student understanding, clarify misunderstandings, and provide feedback. For example:

- In a small-group discussion, students are assigned into groups based on their major, or they can choose discussion stations based on the reading.

- For a whole-class discussion, students might line up single file based on their short-answer responses (e.g., ranging from definitely yes, all humans are scientists – to no, they're absolutely not scientists!). Students pair off from opposite ends of the line for discussion, and then they move back into a single-file line to see if their position has shifted. (Learn more about Metacognition Line-Up in Chapter 5.)

I've thought about offering my retrieval practices online in order to free up 20 minutes of class time. At the same time, scientists have found that when students expect open-book quizzes, they study less; this is one hesitation on my part to switch to online retrieval practice.[12] I also dislike grading online writing, since I find it much easier to read (or skim) students' responses on paper. If I were to offer weekly quizzes for blended learning or fully online courses, I'd include a word limit for responses, which would encourage students to be persuasive and decrease the amount of time it would take me to grade. But for now, my quizzes will remain paper-and-pencil at the start of class.

You may be wondering, "Won't students be frustrated by these weekly retrieval practices?" At the beginning of the semester, my students are hesitant. They're concerned about retrieval as an *assessment* rather than retrieval as a *learning* exercise. They ask a number of questions: How much are they worth? (2% each) What types of questions should I expect? (short-answer) How many questions are there? (3–5 questions) Are there makeups? (Nope!)

By the end of the semester, however, students have realized the benefits from weekly retrieval practices. Here are a few quotes from my students:

- "Retrieval practices are the bomb. Keep that up."
- "Love that we have nothing for a final! Best thing ever!"

- "If I had to remember one thing about this course, it would probably be the use and advantages of retrieval practices. I want to remember it because of how applicable it is to the field of education with how I plan to teach my students." (pre-service teacher)

Here's the takeaway: My weekly retrieval practices are not simply for boosting learning; *they're a core part of my class.* I find such value in dedicating nearly half my class to retrieval *and* discussion.

What does this mean for you? First, low-stakes assignments and quizzes can take some trial and error. Our methods have been refined over the years, which is okay! One thing we've both done is to take something familiar to students (e.g., study guides and quizzes) and turn them into something that emphasizes learning (e.g., Retrieval Guides and weekly retrieval practices).

Brain Dumps
Write down everything you can remember!

Two Things
What are Two Things you learned?

Retrieve-Taking
Retrieve and take closed-book notes after a lesson!

Retrieval Guides
Retrieve during lessons without looking up the answers.

Mini-Quizzes
Successful retrieval with a daily basket of clues.

These are strategies that work best for us and we hope you can start small – even just from a quick Brain Dump – and move toward making retrieval practice *a core part of your instruction.*

THREE SYSTEMS TO BUILD RETRIEVAL ROUTINES INTO YOUR CLASSROOM

The previous strategies work great on the fly. But are you worried you'll have students digging through their backpacks each time you want them to engage in a Brain Dump or Two Things? Put these systems in place to build *Retrieval Routines* into your classroom and save time:

- *Bell work or exit tickets.* Give small slips of paper at the very beginning of class as students are entering the classroom (*bell work*) or before students leave the classroom (*exit tickets*) that include questions about content learned in class or in previous classes (more information on spaced practice in Chapter 4). The question could even be a simple prompt written on the board at the front of the classroom – yet another strategy that requires no prep and can be created on the fly. This engages students in retrieval practice and uses time effectively right at the start or end of class. You'll find that many students will show up on time and stay in their seats until the bell rings – just for retrieval practice!

- Colored index cards. All students can have their own set of colored index cards, with the letters A, B, C, and D on them (or true/false, or 1, 2, 3, etc.). Ask a question on the fly, and then have students close their eyes while raising the appropriate colored index card to identify their response. It's an easy, cheap alternative to using clickers or tech tools, and you can give immediate feedback after students respond. This method is low-cost, requires no prep, and it provides you with formative assessment at any point during a lesson.

Figure 3.5 Example of a student's answer on a homemade whiteboard in response to the question, "Who ruled Ancient Sumer for 56 years?"

- *Homemade whiteboard.* Insert a piece of paper or cardboard into a page protector (see an example in Figure 3.5). This becomes a cheap, do-it-yourself dry erase board or *homemade whiteboard* for each student. You can call out a question and students can write down an answer with a dry erase marker – even a short-answer response – and hold up their homemade whiteboard. Again, you can quickly scan the room and provide appropriate feedback.

> **Power Up**
>
> *Why* should retrieval practice be used as a learning strategy and *not* an assessment strategy?

RESEARCH-BASED TIPS FOR POWERFUL RETRIEVAL PRACTICE STRATEGIES

So far, we've highlighted some quick, no-stakes strategies and a few practical low-stakes strategies for retrieval practice. Still, there are so many ways to use retrieval in our classrooms! It's flexible, but that also means there can be a number of lingering questions and approaches. Next, we provide some detailed tips on using retrieval practice effectively, based on research in the laboratory and in the classroom.

Retrieval Practice Boosts Learning for More than Vocabulary and Facts

As we discussed in Chapter 2, retrieval practice improves learning of both basic concepts *and* complex concepts. The key is that, if you want students to learn facts, concepts, and higher-order topics, implement retrieval practice using fact-based, concept-based, and complex questions. Don't just stick to one type or another. Put differently, think of this phrase often attributed to music and sports: "practice how you're going to play." Think about your lesson, curriculum, or course objectives, and be sure to *incorporate a range of question complexity* if you want students to think and understand across a range of concepts, situations, and content.

Retrieval Practice Boosts Learning with Multiple-Choice, Short-Answer, and Free-Recall Questions

Consider this simple but important question: What should retrieval practice "look like?"

Research from K–12 to higher education demonstrates that multiple-choice, short-answer, and free-recall retrieval practice (i.e., Brain Dumps) enhance learning.[13] In other words, when it comes to the format of retrieval practice, questions can be all of the above! As long as students are retrieving, use the format that's most practical for you. Technology tools are typically used for multiple-choice questions, whereas for bell work, exit tickets, or brief quizzes, short-answer questions might be more practical.

But what about multiple-choice questions specifically? While weighing the pros and cons of multiple-choice questions for student learning, an economics professor, Kevin Block-Schwenk, put it well: "Compared to a short-answer quiz, is a multiple-choice quiz equal to, slightly-less-good, substantially less good, or all-but-worthless?"

When we think about multiple-choice questions, here are a few potential concerns:

- Multiple-choice questions don't require as much thinking as short-answer questions or Brain Dumps.
- Because multiple-choice questions aren't as challenging, they may not benefit learning as much as short-answer questions or Brain Dumps.
- Students may learn incorrect information from the alternative answer options.

At the same time, multiple-choice questions can be easier to administer and quicker to grade – especially via clickers, tech tools, and online platforms. So what's the verdict? Confirmed by a review of the literature by scientist Andrew Butler in 2018, multiple-choice questions are *a good thing* for learning![14] Research demonstrates:

- Multiple-choice questions can be just as effective – or sometimes more effective – than short-answer questions.[15]
- Providing students with feedback decreases or eliminates students' learning of misinformation from multiple-choice questions.[16]
- Multiple-choice questions enhance learning for related information that wasn't even on the quiz![17]

While they are quick to administer and grade, scientists Jeri Little and Elizabeth Bjork recommend creating multiple-choice questions and alternatives very carefully for a larger retrieval benefit.[18] What makes for good multiple-choice questions and competitive alternatives?[19]

Try these multiple-choice questions for yourself:

What are two characteristics of angiosperms?
A. They produce pollen and cones.
B. They sing and dance.
C. They produce flowers and fruits.
D. They have arms, legs, fingers, and toes.

What is 49 + 79?
A. 108
B. 118
C. 128
D. 138

Which of these multiple-choice questions has alternatives that were easy to narrow down? Which questions had alternatives that were harder to narrow down?[20]

We hope you noticed that the first question about angiosperms had alternatives that are easy to eliminate (angiosperms can't sing and dance!). You might have initially thought that the question about angiosperms was harder than the addition problem. We intentionally created multiple-choice alternatives that were *easier* to eliminate for the first question and harder for the second seemingly-simple math question. This demonstrates the importance of making multiple-choice retrieval practice beneficial for learning by creating *competitive* alternative answer options, rather than easy options where students don't have to engage in retrieval at all.[21]

Even if a topic is complex, like biology, multiple-choice questions can be easy. It's also possible to write multiple-choice questions for complex or higher-order material, like predicting how an author or character will react in a completely new situation. Here's an example of a complex multiple-choice question from Pooja's research conducted with college students:

> The political scientist you read about would agree with which statement?
> A. Welfare programs could work, but they rarely meet the needs of the people.
> B. Welfare programs waste taxpayer money on people who don't really need help.
> C. Welfare programs can never work, because they are always too expensive.
> D. Welfare programs are harmful, because they make bad situations even worse.

This multiple-choice question was pretty complex and nuanced, even for college students. Of course, it can be challenging and time consuming to create good multiple-choice questions – whether for K–12, college, or medical school courses. There are many tech tools and teacher resources online with already-developed multiple-choice questions for a range of content areas. Another option is to have students develop multiple-choice alternatives as part of a low-stakes retrieval activity, which you can then use for an upcoming exam or subsequent activity; win-win!

Retrieval Practice Before and After Lessons Boosts Learning

Benefits from Pre-Tests depend on your learning objectives and goals. Based on both research and classroom experience, Pre-Tests improve *understanding* in the short term (e.g., for the lesson immediately after). At the same time, benefits from Pre-Tests on long-term *retention* (e.g., after weeks and months) are less clear.

We both use Pre-Tests right before our lessons for a few reasons:

- They engage students and prepare them to think about upcoming material.

- They provide an opportunity for formative assessment, to get a sense of where our students are already.

- We can tailor our lessons and facilitate learning immediately after Pre-Tests.

- The process informs elaborative feedback days and weeks later using spaced practice to highlight the progress students have made from the Pre-Tests to where they are now.

In addition, in laboratory studies by Phil Grimaldi and Jeff Karpicke, Pre-Tests improved student performance on tests after a few minutes.[22] For these reasons, we feel that Pre-Tests benefit student understanding and engagement for upcoming lessons.

Meanwhile, in an eighth-grade classroom[23] and a college classroom,[24] Pre-Tests improved student performance on tests in the short term, but they didn't increase test performance after a few weeks or months. In comparison, retrieval practice *after* lessons provided a bigger boost to long-term retention than retrieval practice *before* lessons.

What does this mean in your classroom? It depends:

- Retrieval practice *before* a lesson is beneficial for understanding in the short term, *but*

- Retrieval practice *after* a lesson is beneficial for retention in the long term.

We feel it's ideal to use retrieval practice before *and* after a lesson, as we do in our classrooms – the more the better!

Open-Book Quizzes Increase Learning But May Decrease Studying

In research with college students, Pooja and her colleagues found that retrieval practice via open-book quizzes and closed-book quizzes produce similar results in terms of improving students' performance on a final exam.[25] However, *if* students know in advance that they will be taking an open-book quiz, *they spend less time studying and have poorer performance on a final exam*, compared to if they know they are taking a closed-book quiz.[26]

Be mindful about whether students are retrieving and writing something *down* without access to notes, or whether students are looking something *up* with access to notes. The more students retrieve and get information "down and out," the longer learning may last. Note that research using open-book quizzes and assessments with college-level materials (e.g., engineering) is limited, so it's unclear whether having access to math formulas during retrieval might be more beneficial for learning than having to retrieve all mathematical information from mind.[27] In the meantime, we recommend using closed-book retrieval activities and quizzes to ensure that students are studying at home accordingly and also retrieving fully in-class.

Retrieval Practice Boosts Learning When Students Generate Their Own Questions

A question we get asked by both teachers and students is whether students can engage in retrieval practice by generating their own questions. Sometimes, students generate their own questions as preparation for an exam, in hopes they're creating an "exam" that mimics what they'll actually receive as an assessment. But does self-generation improve learning?

Yes! There is research demonstrating that when students self-generate their own questions, it's beneficial for learning. In one laboratory study led by Yana Weinstein, retrieval practice with teacher-generated questions and student-generated questions boosted learning more than re-reading.[28] There were, however, two caveats: First, the student-generated condition required additional time. Second, students predicted that they'd remember more after self-generation than teacher-provided questions, but later test performance was equivalent.

If students are going to self-generate questions, we suggest they create a variety of questions in terms of format (short-answer and multiple-choice), complexity (detailed and broad), and content (overall themes and specific concepts), in line with our recommendations for teachers. We also suggest students work with a peer, where they both come up with questions independently and then administer their "exams" to each other. In this way, students can not only answer their peer's questions, but also discuss how the two sets of questions are similar or different.

On a related note, there is research demonstrating that teaching someone improves learning.[29] In other words, if one student teaches another student without access to notes, they are engaging in retrieval practice! As we all know, this benefit for learning from teaching applies to us as educators. Having taught our material to students frequently, we know it like the back of our hand!

Retrieval Practice Boosts Learning More than Concept Mapping

Sometimes, retrieval practice can look like nothing's happening at all or it can look like students are intensely taking an exam (see Figure 3.1). We might feel that our students need to do something "active," otherwise it looks like we're not teaching and students aren't learning.

Actually, we know from research that just because something is active doesn't always mean that students are learning or remembering information. In a laboratory study with college students at Purdue University, researchers Janell Blunt and Jeff Karpicke compared concept mapping to retrieval practice.[30]

In *concept mapping*, students are typically asked to create nodes around a central concept. For example, if students are learning about blood cells, they draw nodes off of that central concept like white blood cells, plasma, oxygen, and so on (almost like a spider web). In this study, concept mapping was compared to a retrieval practice condition, where college students were asked to write down everything they could remember after reading a passage (exactly the same as a Brain Dump mentioned earlier). After one week, students remembered far more information in the retrieval practice condition (67%) compared to the concept mapping condition (45%).

Just because something seems "active" doesn't mean that learning sticks. The key question to ask is this: Are students engaging in retrieval practice during "active" instruction? We hope you will be mindful with your instructional strategies and include as much retrieval practice as possible, not just activity for engagement's sake.

Engage *All* Students in Retrieval Practice, Not Just One or Two

Many of us already use retrieval practice in the classroom by calling on individual students to answer questions throughout a lesson (also known as cold calling). But cold calling doesn't guarantee that *all* students are engaged in retrieval practice. The students who aren't called on are "off the hook" and no longer responsible for thinking about a response. In fact, research led by Sarah Tauber has demonstrated that when students engage in retrieval practice *covertly* (in their head, as opposed to an overt written or verbal response), *their learning doesn't increase.*[31] In other words, we may expect that all of our students are retrieving when we ask questions during lessons, but it's likely that they aren't receiving any benefit *unless they're the one being called on.*

It's important to have all students write down or verbally share their responses *individually*. Compared to calling on one student at a time, individual writing ensures that *all* students are retrieving, engaged in pulling information out, and bringing it to mind. By engaging every student in retrieval practice, every student has the opportunity to boost long-term learning.

When It Comes to Learning, Encoding and Retrieval Go Hand in Hand

Yes, encoding is an important part of learning, but we have a tendency to focus all of our effort on it. Even when it comes to complex material like anatomy and chemistry, we should spend less time than we typically do on encoding and more time on retrieval. If we keep trying to cram information in before any retrieval takes place, students have a hard time mentally keeping track of everything.

So yes, start with encoding – presenting material, discussion, videos, etc. But try to intersperse retrieval *during* encoding, not just after everything has been crammed in. Here's another way to think about it: Retrieving helps students encode. In other words, when students are retrieving, they're also encoding.

When students are retrieving, they're also encoding.

USE RETRIEVAL PRACTICE TO CHALLENGE LEARNING *AND* SIMPLIFY TEACHING

In Chapter 4, we describe two more Power Tools: spacing and interleaving. But before we get there, pause and reflect. What does it look like to challenge learning *and* simplify teaching?

As a first step toward simplifying your teaching, start *small*. With Power Tools, there's no need to make it more complicated. With the simple strategies we present, what are small tweaks you can make in your classroom? Here's one idea: Lecture less – this shares what you know. Retrieve more – ask students what *they* know.

Second, keep retrieval practice *short*. The shorter it is, the easier it'll seem for students (even though it's a desirable difficulty!). By keeping it short, emphasize that we don't just retrieve during a big test or exam – it can be as simple as writing down one takeaway and moving on.

Third, we challenge *you* to retrieve. If you haven't already, simply flip to the back of this book for our Retrieval Guide. Try to complete as much of it as possible (without looking up the answers!) and continue retrieving as you read. We practice what we preach – and hope you will, too. Challenge your own learning with Power Tools!

> ### Power Up
>
> Retrieval practice can take one minute or less! How can you incorporate just one of these strategies and start small *tomorrow*?

NOTES

1. Agarwal, P. K., Roediger, H. L., McDaniel, M. A., et al. (2018). *How to Use Retrieval Practice to Improve Learning*. Washington University in St. Louis. Available at www.powerfulteaching.org.

2. Lang, J. M. (2016). *Small Teaching: Everyday Lessons From the Science of Learning*. San Francisco, CA: Jossey-Bass.

3. Arnold, K. M., and McDermott, K. B. (2013). Free recall enhances subsequent learning. *Psychonomic Bulletin & Review* 20: 507–513.

4. Zaromb, F. M., and Roediger, H. L. (2010). The testing effect in free recall is associated with enhanced organizational processes. *Memory & Cognition* 38: 995–1008.

5. Karpicke, J. D., and Blunt, J. R. (2011). Retrieval practice produces more learning than elaborative studying with concept mapping. *Science* 331: 772–775.

6. Rowland, C. A., and DeLosh, E. L. (2014). Benefits of testing for nontested information: Retrieval-induced facilitation of episodically bound material. *Psychonomic Bulletin & Review* 21: 1516–1523.

7. Smith, M. A., Blunt, J. R., Whiffen, J. W., et al. (2016). Does providing prompts during retrieval practice improve learning? *Applied Cognitive Psychology* 30: 544–553.

8. College students in the Roediger & Karpicke (2006) study engaged in free-recall (i.e., Brain Dumps)! Free-recall continues to be a common strategy for retrieval practice in laboratory studies.

9. The person who was at the top of Russia's social pyramid from the 1800s to the early 1900s was called a tsar.

10. The king of France in the late 1700s was Louis XVI. The name of the law-making body formed by the Third Estate in 1789 was the National Assembly.

11. Lemov, D. (2010). *Teach Like a Champion: 49 Techniques that Put Students on the Path to College.* San Francisco, CA: Jossey-Bass.

12. Agarwal, P. K., and Roediger, H. L. (2011). Expectancy of an open-book test decreases performance on a delayed closed-book test. *Memory* 19: 836–852.

13. McDermott, K. B., Agarwal, P. K., D'Antonio, L., et al. (2014). Both multiple-choice and short-answer quizzes enhance later exam performance in middle and high school classes. *Journal of Experimental Psychology: Applied* 20: 3–21.

14. Butler, A. C. (2018). Multiple-choice testing in education: Are the best practices for assessment also good for learning? *Journal of Applied Research in Memory and Cognition* 7: 323–331.

15. Smith, M. A., and Karpicke, J. D. (2014). Retrieval practice with short-answer, multiple-choice, and hybrid tests. *Memory* 22: 784–802.

16. Butler, A. C., and Roediger, H. L. (2008). Feedback enhances the positive effects and reduces the negative effects of multiple-choice testing. *Memory & Cognition* 36: 604–616.

17. Bjork, E. L., Little, J. L., and Storm, B. C. (2014). Multiple-choice testing as a desirable difficulty in the classroom. *Journal of Applied Research in Memory and Cognition* 3: 165–170.

18. Little, J. L., Bjork, E. L., Bjork, R. A., et al. (2012). Multiple-choice tests exonerated, at least of some charges: Fostering test-induced learning and avoiding test-induced forgetting. *Psychological Science* 23: 1337–1344.

19. Little, J. L., and Bjork, E. L. (2015). Optimizing multiple-choice tests as tools for learning. *Memory & Cognition* 43: 14–26.

20. Angiosperms produce flowers and fruits (alternative C) and 49 plus 79 equals 128 (alternative C).

21. Marsh, E. J., and Cantor, A. (2014). Learning from the test: Dos and don'ts for using multiple-choice tests. In: *Integrating Cognitive Science with Innovative Teaching in STEM Disciplines* (ed. M. A. McDaniel, R. F. Frey, S. M. Fitzpatrick and H. L. Roediger). St. Louis, Missouri: Washington University in St. Louis.

22. Grimaldi, P. J., and Karpicke, J. D. (2012). When and why do retrieval attempts enhance subsequent encoding? *Memory & Cognition* 40: 505–513.

23. McDaniel, M. A., Agarwal, P. K., Huelser, B. J., et al. (2011). Test-enhanced learning in a middle school science classroom: The effects of quiz frequency and placement. *Journal of Educational Psychology* 103: 399–414.

24. Carpenter, S. K., Rahman, S., and Perkins, K. (2018). The effects of prequestions on classroom learning. *Journal of Experimental Psychology: Applied* 24: 34–42.

25. Agarwal, P. K., Karpicke, J. D., Kang, S. H. K., et al. (2008). Examining the testing effect with open- and closed-book tests. *Applied Cognitive Psychology* 22: 861–876.

26. Agarwal, P. K., and Roediger, H. L. (2011). Expectancy of an open-book test decreases performance on a delayed closed-book test. *Memory* 19: 836–852.

27. Durning, S. J., Dong, T., Ratcliffe, T., et al. (2016). Comparing open-book and closed-book examinations: A systematic review. *Academic Medicine* 91: 583–599.

28. Weinstein, Y., McDermott, K. B., and Roediger, H. L. (2010). A comparison of study strategies for passages: Rereading, answering questions, and generating questions. *Journal of Experimental Psychology: Applied* 16: 308–316.

29. Koh, A. W. L., Lee, S. C., and Lim, S. W. H. (2018). The learning benefits of teaching: A retrieval practice hypothesis. *Applied Cognitive Psychology* 32: 401–410.

30. Karpicke, J. D., and Blunt, J. R. (2011). Retrieval practice produces more learning than elaborative studying with concept mapping. *Science* 331: 772–775.

31. Tauber, S. K., Witherby, A. E., Dunlosky, J., et al. (2018). Does covert retrieval benefit learning of key term definitions? *Journal of Applied Research in Memory and Cognition* 7: 106–115.

Chapter 4

Energize Learning with Spacing and Interleaving

So far, we've focused on retrieval practice – improving learning by bringing information to mind. There are many ways to define it and many ways to foster retrieval in our classrooms. But *when* and *how often*? Is more retrieval practice better than less?

Here's the key to unleashing retrieval practice: Don't have students simply engage in retrieval once or even repeatedly. In this chapter, we feature research and strategies for two more powerful teaching approaches: *spacing* and *interleaving*.

Our second Power Tool is what cognitive scientists call spaced practice, or simply *spacing*. In a nutshell, spacing is a combination of engaging in retrieval practice *multiple* times, while also engaging in those retrievals *over time*. In contrast, when students engage in retrieval practice but it's crammed all at once, learning isn't nearly as robust.

As we talked about in Chapter 2 on retrieval practice research, retrieval is much more powerful for learning than reviewing material, re-reading, or re-studying notes. But does it matter whether retrieval happens within a short period of time (e.g., five Mini-Quizzes on Ancient Egypt in one week) or spaced over time (e.g., five Mini-Quizzes on Ancient Egypt, spread over three weeks)? Can such a small adjustment make an impact on student learning? Surprisingly, yes!

Power Up

Why do you think your students cram the night before an exam?

THE SCIENCE BEHIND POWER TOOL #2: SPACING

Consider research conducted by cognitive scientists, Doug Rohrer and Kelli Taylor, at the University of South Florida. In this experiment, college students completed mathematical permutation problems, where they calculated all possible letter sequences from strings of letters like AABBCC. For these math problems, students either completed 10 problems crammed into one week, or they completed 10 problems that were spaced over two weeks. That's it! This was a very simple change in how retrieval practice was spread out over time. Importantly, students spent the exact same amount of time solving problems in both conditions – they simply crammed all the problems into one week or spread out the problems over two weeks.[1]

As shown in Figure 4.1, after one week, the cramming condition led to slightly higher exam performance compared to the spacing condition. After four weeks, however, performance in the cramming condition dropped by *more than half*, while exam

Figure 4.1 When college students completed practice problems using a crammed approach (10 problems in one week) or a spaced approach (5 problems across two weeks), short-term exam performance was higher after cramming, but long-term exam performance was higher after spacing.

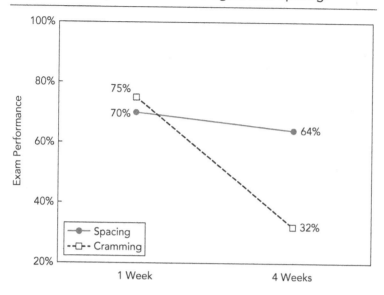

performance for the spacing condition decreased only a little bit, from 70% to 64%. In other words, simply completing 10 math problems spaced out over two weeks instead of one week dramatically reduced forgetting.

Remember the study we discussed in Chapter 2 by Roddy Roediger and Jeff Karpicke on retrieval practice? The graph in Figure 4.1 shows the exact same pattern: What's good for learning in the short term, like re-reading and cramming, leads

Just because something boosts learning in the short term doesn't mean learning will stick around over the long term.

to a huge drop-off in learning over the long term when compared to challenging strategies like retrieval practice and spacing.[2]

From our Power Up box earlier, did you figure out why students cram the night before an exam? It's because it works! In line with many scientific studies, tell your students that there is scientific evidence that cramming works! *But only in the short term.* When students cram, they forget more over the long term and they'll have to spend *more* time studying to catch up. But with spacing,

Cramming works, but only in the short term.

students learn *more* in the long term and can study *less*.[3]

THE POWER OF SPACING IN PATRICE'S CLASSROOM

Most of my students are blank slates when it comes to world history. It is the first time in my district's curriculum map that this course is taught. One of my first tasks is to create a *hook*. I use this hook analogy with my students. If, for example, we are studying the ancient Nile River civilization, I urge them to create this hook or place to store the knowledge in their mind. The more we learn about a particular topic, the more the hook is strengthened.

Pre-Tests: A Strategy to Hook Students' Thirst for Knowledge

I generally start this process with a *Pre-Test*. It helps me set the stage for what is to be learned, provide an introduction to new material, and form a platform for retrieval and spacing. Although various tools and methods could be used, I prefer to use teacher-led, interactive, multiple-choice questions via clickers. Using these devices, students are able to interact with the material, see immediate feedback, hear my explanations, and understand how it ties in with previous learning. Because this is an introduction, individual Pre-Test scores never go into the gradebook. I do, however, keep track of *class* averages – and these usually range between 30% and 40% correct. Not only am I frontloading information to students via Pre-Tests, I also receive a benefit: It establishes an important baseline for me in determining the areas requiring the most focus.

As I am explaining the correct answers on the Pre-Test, I frequently use retrieval practice to tie in this new information with previously learned facts. For example, I might ask: "We are now studying the Nile River; how is it similar and different to the Tigris and Euphrates?" or "What factors of the Treaty of Versailles possibly led to the outbreak of WWII?"

Students are engaged. I discuss each question. I explain why a particular answer is correct. I use choral work. As we continue throughout the unit, I consistently refer back to the Pre-Test and encourage students to retrieve the information from day one. My dialogue goes like this: "Who remembers the meaning of x from the Pre-Test? First, ponder for 10 seconds. Next, discuss with your neighbor. Now, let's hear a few of your responses." This Think-Pair-Share is powerful and often takes less than 90 seconds. Each student has had a chance to retrieve individually and with a partner, and hearing other students' replies reinforces information learned. Each and every time I refer back to the Pre-Test, I'm using spacing. I have intentionally left an interval of time for the students to retrieve this information.

> *Each and every time I refer back to the Pre-Test, I'm using spacing.*

Moving from a Pre-Test to a *Blast from the Past*

Here is the easiest method of all I use for spacing: I simply do *Blasts from the Past,* such as "Remember when we learned about X, think about it, and Turn and Talk to your partner." I call on several students and as a class, retrieval occurs. I will usually follow up with the prompt, "Now let's ponder how this relates to our current topic." This is spacing! I honestly don't think a day goes by when I'm not bringing something from the past forward. Spacing in my classroom is not a chance occurrence; it is purposeful.

For example, I teach students about the French Revolution, which occurred in the late 1700s. Later, I teach students about the Russian Revolution, which occurred in the early 1900s. When I begin teaching the Russian Revolution, I encourage students to find that place in their mind, the *hook*, where we learned about the French Revolution and then we discuss how the French Revolution relates to the Russian Revolution. This less-than-two-minute exercise has brought forth previous learning, spacing across several weeks of content. I see the light bulbs turn on in my students' eyes as they retrieve what they know about the French Revolution and connect it to what they're learning about the Russian Revolution.

> *I see the light bulbs turn on in my students' eyes as they retrieve what they know about the French Revolution and connect it to what they're learning about the Russian Revolution.*

Big Basket Quizzes: Space Out Retrieval with a "BBQ"!

In order to space important information even more over the long haul, I came up with the following strategy: the *Big Basket Quiz*, or BBQ. (You can also substitute the word *Bin* for *Basket*.) Every Friday, we have an end-of-the-week BBQ. It contains not only the questions from the daily quizzes throughout the week but also questions from *previous* weeks. This is spacing: The students retrieve material from the current week *plus* they have to find that hook to retrieve previously learned material. I randomly choose 10 questions and the students write down their responses. Similar to my Mini-Quizzes, the BBQs get turned in and we discuss answers. The 10 questions go back into the big basket and the following class will be given random questions from the basket. (This random choosing of questions is also a great way to circumvent the hallway question, "What was on the quiz?")

How do I keep my big basket from overflowing by the end of the semester? Oh, we teachers are a creative lot. At the end of each chapter or unit test, I leave in only those questions that I know will be revisited throughout the semester or year via essential questions, themes, big topics, final exams, and so on. The powerful duo of retrieval and spacing has strengthened students' knowledge, and it is time well-spent.

> ### Power Up
>
> What is one example in your everyday life where you purposely *retrieve* information in order to remember it, rather than focusing on *encoding* to remember it?

THE KEY TO SPACING IS FORGETTING (BUT NOT TOO MUCH)

Let's take a moment to talk about spiraling. Spiraling is a term frequently used when deciding when information is taught, whether it be in textbooks or curriculum design. It involves deciding where a "big topic" is taught at each grade level and how this idea comes back each year and is consequently taught at a deeper level. Spiraling is used in every discipline. However, spiraling is *not* spacing. Too often, these big topics are discussed, reviewed, tested, and then not covered again until the following year. This is one of the main reasons for the "deer-in-the-headlights" look each year when previously learned information is lost. We teach content over and over again, only for students to forget year after year.

We teach content over and over again, only for students to forget year after year.

As we know from spiraling, sometimes spacing can be spread out over too much time. For example, you might have a recipe for cookies that you really like to bake. If you use the recipe every month, you will probably have the recipe memorized after a few months. On the other hand, if you use the recipe to make cookies for a birthday party only once a year, you may need to refer back to the recipe each time you make it. This happens because too much time has passed from batch to batch, party to party, or year to year.

Why do we remember the cookie recipe better when we bake it every few months? This is because some forgetting has occurred, but not too much. We're able to refresh our memories while we still have something lingering in the back of our heads. We don't use the cookie recipe once and then never again – just as we wouldn't engage in retrieval practice on one topic and then never again until the following year.

There are two key reasons why spacing is an effective teaching strategy:

- Spacing takes advantage of forgetting *during* learning.
- This forgetting is a desirable difficulty.

This is why spreading out practice problems in the study we described earlier (spacing our discussion about spacing research!) is so beneficial for learning: literally spacing things out and coming back to them increases learning by harnessing forgetting. It may sound counterintuitive, but *a little forgetting is the key to spacing*: When we let time pass and space things out, students' knowledge has time to solidify and "simmer."[4] We know from experience that by taking a step back and letting things settle, we have a better understanding of what we're trying to learn. This space gives us a mental break – literally time to forget – so that we can return to what we know and don't know with a fresh perspective (and a fresh batch of cookies, too).

Spacing and Goldilocks: Getting It Just Right

A common question we encounter is how much spacing is ideal. If spiraling content once a year is too much of a delay, and cramming is too close together, how much spacing boosts learning?

In a large internet-based study led by Nicholas Cepeda in 2008, researchers found that the optimal amount of spacing for long-term retention was approximately a 1:10 ratio.[5] For example, in order for research participants to remember information for 30 days, it was optimal to space retrieval every 3 days; in order for participants to remember information for 200 days, it was optimal to space retrieval every 20 days. That being said, we want students to remember information for longer than 200 days! So what does this mean for us and our teaching?

In a classroom study with eighth-grade anatomy students, Pooja and her colleagues combined both retrieval practice and spacing.[6] In this study, students received clicker quizzes (followed by immediate feedback) on part of an anatomy unit and no clicker quizzes on the rest of the unit. More specifically, students had a pre-quiz before the teacher taught her lesson, a post-quiz right after the lesson, and a review quiz a few days after the lesson. They were interested in precisely this question: How many quizzes are ideal for long-term retention, and when should happen throughout a unit of material?

Pooja and her colleagues tried eight possible combinations of quizzes: clicker quizzes before, after, and a few days after the lesson; just a pre- and a post-quiz; just a pre- and review quiz, and so on. What they found on the end-of-the-chapter test was that a combination of all three quizzes led to the highest level of student performance on the end-of-unit exam. By the end of the semester, almost six months later, they found a very similar pattern: Student performance on the end-of-semester exam was higher when students received all three quizzes, but also high when students received only one review quiz a few days after the teacher's lesson (see Figure 4.2). In other words, student performance increased the more the space between the lesson and the quiz increased, even with just one quiz. Note that this doesn't mean that pre- and post-quizzes are ineffective – they boosted learning more than zero quizzes. But when it comes to the "biggest bang for your

Figure 4.2 Students received the biggest benefit from retrieval practice on review quizzes (two days after a lesson) compared to other combinations of spaced quizzes. Even one review quiz significantly boosted learning at the end of the semester.

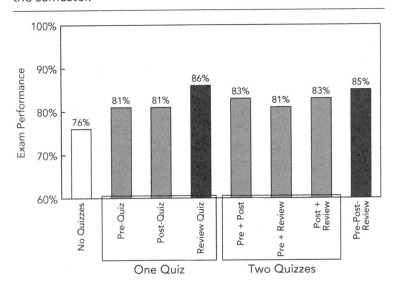

buck," quizzes that are spaced and delayed a few days after initial learning are the most powerful for long-term learning.

Based on Pooja's classroom research, we recommend spacing retrieval practice at least a few days after a lesson. Why? Again, the more challenging the retrieval, the better; so the more spacing, the better. Yet any schedule of retrieval practice is better than none at all. As a very simple example of spacing, don't give students homework on what they learned in class earlier that day; challenge them by providing homework on content learned *last week*. In other words, focus more on the *amount* of spacing, and less on *when* it should occur. Classrooms are messy, learning is complex, and luckily, Power Tools – like spacing – are flexible!

What about spaced retrieval practice *during* a lesson, lecture, or assigned reading? In a laboratory experiment led by Oyku

Uner, college students read 40-page biology textbook chapters. To examine the optimal placement of questions, students:

- Completed questions *within* a textbook chapter
- Completed questions *after* reading the chapter
- Completed questions twice, *both* within and after the chapter
- Read the chapter once without questions (no retrieval)
- Read the chapter once, followed by reading the answers (no retrieval)

After two days, the retrieval practice conditions led to greater final test performance than the two reading-only groups – regardless of whether questions were within or after the textbook chapter.[7] Importantly, answering questions both during and after the chapter produced the most learning. What's the takeaway? Regardless of the placement of questions, retrieval practice enhanced learning more than reading or re-reading long textbook chapters. In other words, encourage students to retrieve using practice questions, whether they do it *while* they read or *after* they read. The same could apply to lessons: For the greatest boost in learning, provide retrieval opportunities during or after lessons – and any is better than none!

When it comes to the "biggest bang for your buck," quizzes that are spaced a few days after initial learning are the most powerful for long-term learning.

Keep in mind that spacing – even throughout the semester – doesn't require a lot of prep time or coordination. Here's an example of semester-long spacing from Patrice's classroom on a unit about carbon-14 dating: Prior to studying the Iceman of the Alps, Patrice has students become archeologists as they go on a scavenger hunt finding clues the Iceman left behind. In groups of four, one is the recorder, one the reporter, and all are brainstormers as they speculate on possible conclusions. The class ends with each group's reporter stating findings to the class. The following day, students learn about the Iceman. Students are engaged as they compare their findings to the scientific findings. Students discover how carbon-14 dating allowed scientists to determine that the Iceman died approximately 5,000 years ago.

As students study different civilizations throughout the year, Patrice returns to this concept by asking, "What is one way we could figure out that Queen Amanishakheto ruled Kush around 27 BCE?" And students' immediate response? Carbon-14 dating! Even if students had not understood the concept from the earlier lesson, after a few spaced examples, all students strengthen their learning and understanding of carbon dating.

Power Up

How do you already use spacing in your classroom?

An Added Benefit of Spacing: Savings

Another thing that happens after time passes is what cognitive scientists call *savings*. Savings is when we return to something we learned before and we experience an "aha!" moment.

For example, for my birthday this year, I (Patrice) received a new bicycle. It is a beauty and it was love at first sight! I hadn't ridden a bike in over 20 years, and so many fun memories popped up from the past as I raced to my new gift. I immediately remembered how to swipe my foot in just the right way to raise the kickstand and get on the bike. I couldn't wait to re-live the familiarity of a breeze against my face and the feeling of soaring.

But I began to experience a bit of trepidation. The handlebars were different; in fact, the brakes, the seat, and the height were all different. I remembered how to set the pedals at the correct balance for me to engage and take off, but I wobbled. I nearly ran into a parked car across the street. It took me about a quarter of a block to get used to the handlebars and the brakes, and then I was on my way – combining my old knowledge from bicycle riding with my new knowledge from trial and error.

How is it that, even with minor adjustments, we can pick up knowledge from our past – sometimes from long ago like Patrice's example – and begin where we left off? This experience of savings is a direct result from spaced learning; we don't see savings – or the "banking" of knowledge – when we cram or re-read.[8] Students can bring that savings or refresh what they know much more quickly after spacing, compared to cramming.

With savings from spacing, knowledge returns more quickly and fluently. It may feel unsteady for our students (and us) at first, but quickly a feeling of "I *do* know this!" kicks in. Students are surprised by their own knowledge after a delay, which builds their confidence, their comfort with forgetting, and their long-term learning.

With spacing, students are surprised by their own knowledge. This surprise builds their confidence, their comfort with forgetting, and their long-term learning.

An example of savings arose recently when Patrice ran into a previous student who is now in high school. He enthusiastically announced that his scholar bowl team had won a match and he attributed it to something he had learned in sixth-grade. The answer was: Mansa Musa. Beaming, he said, "After the match, we all just looked at each and said at the same time: Mansa Musa was the Muslim Mali king who made a pilgrimage to Mecca!"

Key Recommendations for Spacing: More Is Better and Any Is Better than None

From both our research-based and classroom-based perspectives, we recommend two approaches to spacing:

- More is better.
- Any is better than none.

When students encounter a spaced retrieval opportunity, student performance may be lower than we'd like. But forgetting can be a *good* thing – a desirable difficulty that powerfully increases student learning, especially when combined with retrieval practice. In your classroom, try to normalize forgetting! Explain to your students that some forgetting happens naturally and that it's actually a *good* thing for learning.

So far, we've talked about spacing, or spreading out concepts over time, as a powerful teaching strategy. But in order to space, what should you teach in between? Great question! Get ready for Power Tool #3: interleaving.

THE SCIENCE BEHIND POWER TOOL #3: INTERLEAVING

A number of my (Pooja's) students at the Berklee College of Music complete a major in music therapy. As part of the program, students have to learn a variety of instruments, songs, and genres of music because of the different populations of clients and patients with whom they serve. One student in particular, Jaylyn, was struggling to learn a song for her upcoming practicum at a nursing home ("On the Sunny Side of the Street," a jazz standard written in 1930). She could sing the beginning of the song and she could sing the end, but she was struggling with the middle few verses.

Instantly, a research-based approach of mixing up the song came to my mind. Instead of practicing her song from start to finish, I asked Jaylyn to start by singing the third verse. After that, I asked her to sing the fifth verse, followed by the first verse, followed by the chorus, followed by the last verse, and so on. In other words, I asked Jaylyn to sing the song in a mixed up order – not beginning to end, or even backwards. Within 10 minutes, Jaylyn had the song memorized. She was amazed!

This strategy of mixing things up during spacing is called *interleaving*. Years of cognitive science research have established that interleaving – simply *re-arranging* the order of retrieval opportunities during spacing *without* changing the content to be learned – can increase (and even *double*) student learning.[9] Research by Doug Rohrer demonstrates that the simple approach of mixing up concepts to be learned can result in a large benefit for student learning – whether learning songs, math, science, vocabulary words, art history, and even baseball.[10] Most research on interleaving has been conducted using math content, so while we present examples from math, think about how interleaving can be adapted in your classroom (and we'll provide some strategies in a bit).

Consider this basic example of practice problems in any math course:

Problem Set 1: AAAA BBBB CCCC DDDD

Problem Set 2: ABCD ABCD ABCD ABCD

Both problem sets have the same practice problems; they've simply been rearranged. If the letters represented addition, subtraction, multiplication, and division, then Problem Set 1 requires students to perform a procedure, but it doesn't require students to know which procedure to use. Students can safely *plug and chug* without thinking about the strategy they need to use in the first problem set. This is what scientists call *blocked practice*. The second set with mixed-up problems is *interleaved practice*; students can no longer plug and chug because each problem may or may not require a different formula. In other words, students have to *choose* and retrieve the appropriate strategy for each interleaved practice problem.

Another example of interleaving we find helpful is from the book *Make It Stick: The Science of Successful Learning*, co-authored by our research collaborators Roddy Roediger and Mark McDaniel.[11] In this example, imagine a batter practicing with a pitcher. If the batter receives 10 fastballs, followed by 10 changeups (slower pitches), and then 10 curveballs, the batter will know he only has to change his batting strategy after

10 pitches. The batter literally knows what's coming. But, if the batter doesn't know which type of pitch is coming – if the pitches are mixed up – the batter will have to determine and retrieve which batting strategy works best. Now before you move on, complete these word problems:

> A bug flies 48 miles east and then 20 miles south. How far is the bug from where it started?
>
> A bug flies 48 miles east and then 14 miles north. How far is the bug from where it started?
>
> A bug flies 48 miles east and then 6 miles west. How far is the bug from where it started?

What did you come up with? These word problems appear to be similar and you may have applied the Pythagorean Theorem. But did you notice that the last problem requires a different strategy to solve it correctly?[12] Tricky! Because these problems were presented side-by-side, you yourself may have plugged and chugged, using the same strategy for each problem. If students realize that various problems may be mixed up and interleaved, they'll be more likely to *choose* a formula to apply, not just *use* a formula without thinking.

In terms of the science behind interleaving, consider one research study by the same colleagues mentioned earlier, Kelli Taylor and Doug Rohrer. In this study, fourth-grade students completed math problems on prisms and faces. They completed a blocked set of prism problems followed by faces problems, or the two types of problems were interleaved. As shown in Figure 4.3, student performance immediately after practice was higher for the blocked condition, but then students showed a giant drop-off in learning after 24 hours. When completing interleaved math problems, students had nearly *double* the exam performance after 24 hours (77%) compared to students who initially completed blocked problems (38%).[13]

In another study using graph and slope problems from a seventh-grade classroom, students who completed interleaved

Figure 4.3 When fourth-grade students completed math problems, immediate exam performance was perfect after blocked practice, but after only 24 hours, exam performance for the blocked condition dropped dramatically and interleaving was significantly better for learning.

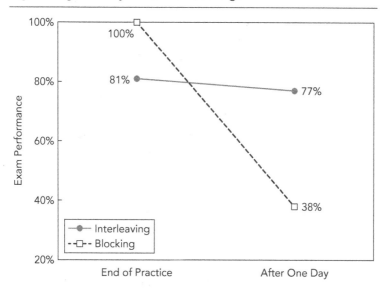

practice problems outperformed students who completed blocked practice problems by more than a letter grade (80% vs. 64%). Again, after a delay, performance for the interleaved group was almost *double* compared to performance for the blocked group one month later (74% vs. 42%).[14] In other words, simply mixing up problems using interleaving improved mathematics performance for real students, in a real classroom with real practice problems, even one month after reviewing course material.

As one more example, consider high school history. Justin Cerenzia is a high school history teacher and director of the Merck Center for Teaching at St. George's School in Rhode Island. Similar to Patrice's experience we describe next, once Justin learned about interleaving research and strategies, he noticed the following:

At first glance, interleaving felt like it could be problematic given the chronological study of history. An example of this might be studying different revolutions throughout history, and understanding how the three time-scales influenced the nature and outcome of a revolution.

Now, I'm interleaving more intentionally than ever before in my classes, because it gives students varying perspectives on how we experience history. In a way, I'm interleaving concepts of time throughout what is otherwise a traditional chronological history class. Interleaving definitely bolsters student understanding as they begin to weave in threads of knowledge that were otherwise disconnected before.

THE POWER OF INTERLEAVING IN PATRICE'S CLASSROOM

In most of the studies I (Patrice) have read, interleaving was linked with math and sports. I don't teach math, nor am I a coach. While we were writing this chapter, I pondered whether I use interleaving in my classroom. I started to write, and write, and write. . . until I realized, "Holy cow! I use interleaving all the time!" It is planned, purposeful, efficient, and effective. Each time I bring up specific examples and learning from the past, I am using spacing. Also, when I am asking students to differentiate different cultures, places, ideas, I am using interleaving. I urge you to ponder: In your own discipline, have you also been interleaving? Have you been encouraging students to discriminate, and detect similarities and differences between concepts?

One of the first units of the year is on ancient river civilizations. Throughout the six-week unit, I frequently ask students to retrieve information regarding all of the river civilizations. I don't just cover one ancient river civilization and then move on to the next; I conduct a well-organized, purposeful "dance of facts." I combine retrieval, spacing, and interleaving; students must compare, contrast, differentiate, and synthesize river civilizations through the lens of different parts of the world. I am continually fostering retrieval practice of all of the civilizations throughout the unit. I know that by simply asking my students questions, based on available research, I am increasing their knowledge. Interleaving takes no extra time, no extra materials, and it is free. An added benefit? Students can easily answer deep, essential questions throughout and after each unit.

Another example using spacing and interleaving was done by a science teacher in my school. Previously, when teaching mitosis, she taught the basics in a class period. Students read the material, had a discussion, and answered questions. However, by simply changing up *when and how* it was taught, she found different results. This time, she taught mitosis along with animal reproduction, and a few weeks later, taught it again using plant reproduction. Spacing *and* interleaving. After a three-week delay, she gave the same test she had given in the previous year – where mitosis had been taught in one class period. After using spacing and interleaving, the students had a dramatic increase in the following:

- Answering questions about particular terms
- Generating terms to fill-in-the-blank
- Writing essays describing mitosis
- Illustrating the process of mitosis

No extra supplies, gadgets, materials, etc. were needed. Changing the "hows and when" in classrooms and utilizing spacing and interleaving led to increased results.

Spacing and interleaving are important tools that lead to powerful learning (Figure 4.4; this figure is available online at www.powerfulteaching.org). They encourage retrieval practice. They reinforce the hook. They bring confidence to students. They encourage higher-order thinking and allow students to apply, compare and contrast, answer essential questions, and *learn*.

Figure 4.4 Combining the Power Tools of retrieval, spacing, and interleaving leads to powerful learning.

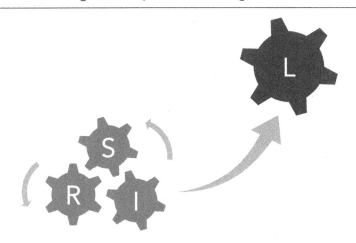

THE KEY TO INTERLEAVING IS DISCRIMINATION

Why does interleaving help our students remember songs and civilizations? There are two reasons why interleaving is powerful:

- Interleaving promotes students' *discrimination*.

- Interleaving increases students' learning of information in the *middle* of a unit.

First, in order to encourage *discrimination*, the key is mixing up *similar* ideas. Students have to *choose* a strategy, decide which song verse does and doesn't come next, and carefully apply a concept. For example, the benefits from discrimination apply if we present two paintings by similar artists side-by-side, two song verses, two world revolutions, and so on.[15]

As another example, how would you describe your ideal fruit salad? Perhaps a variety of citrus fruits, including oranges and grapefruits. Or maybe a fruit salad with berries: blueberries, strawberries, and raspberries. But would you put carrots or broccoli into your fruit salad? Probably not!

This fruit salad analogy from Betty Curry, an academic coach at Trinity University, helps drive home the point that effective interleaving is similar to a fruit salad where we need to mix *similar* things. By mixing similar things, interleaving becomes a true desirable difficulty. When students have to choose and look at all their options with interleaving, this added difficulty improves learning.

Second, interleaving helps students learn the *middle* of a unit. As we know from decades of cognitive science research – and from everyday life – we tend to remember things at the beginning and end of a movie, song, or textbook unit, but not the middle.

For example, retrieve and write down a list of all the US presidents. Which ones do you remember? Which ones have you forgotten? Most likely, you are experiencing what scientists call the *serial position effect*[16] – you remember the first few presidents and the most recent ones, but you've probably forgotten the presidents in the middle (aside from Abraham Lincoln!).[17]

By interleaving and spacing throughout the semester, students learn and remember what we teach them in the *middle* of the school year in November or February, not just information taught in September or May. Retrieving after forgetting and thinking while discriminating are desirable difficulties that dramatically boost learning. As you'll read about in Chapter 6 on combining Power Tools, we might already use some of these Power Tools, we can combine them and use them even more effectively in our classrooms.

Emerging Research on Interleaving and Discrimination

Looking forward as scientists conduct more research on interleaving, here are three caveats about this Power Tool to keep in mind:

- Mixing everything up doesn't mean it's always beneficial for learning.
- Taking one concept and presenting it in different ways is not interleaving.

- Some students may need scaffolding when using Power Tools.

First, mixing everything up doesn't mean it's always beneficial for learning. One study indicated that mixing up different course subjects – for example, chemistry and history – does not increase learning.[18] Why? Simply because this doesn't involve discrimination; the content areas are too different. It's important to interleave *similar* concepts so students really have to think about the subtle differences.

> *It's important to interleave similar concepts so students really have to think about the subtle differences.*

Second, an interleaved set of problems is *not* one in which students solve equations for slope and also solve word problems for slope. In this instance, students could use the exact same strategy for both types of problems, potentially even solving a word problem without reading the words! Practice sets that require students to *choose* a strategy is what improves learning, not practice sets on the same content in different formats.

Third, research suggests that a "hybrid approach" may be more effective for student learning, where some blocked practice initially is followed by interleaved practice.[19] This scaffolding may provide students with a foundation of knowledge initially, which they can then apply effectively with interleaved concepts.

Power Up

Which type of spaced retrieval practice is most beneficial (provides the biggest "bang for your buck") for long-term learning?[20]

    A. Retrieval before a lesson
    B. Retrieval during a lesson
    C. Retrieval immediately after a lesson
    D. Retrieval a few days after a lesson

Spot the Difference Between Spacing and Interleaving!

At some point in your life, you have probably played "spot the difference," where you compare and try to figure out what has been changed between two pictures: the types of trees, the number of cars, and so on. It's a fun challenge, and even more fun because once you spot the difference, it's hard to "un-notice" it.

But can you spot the difference between spacing and interleaving? This is a tough question, and rightfully so! Spacing is how we spread out content over time, whereas interleaving is how we mix things up. The critical difference is that interleaving refers to what happens *in between* spacing. When you're spacing content, you could fill the gap with unrelated content (this would be spacing) or highly related content (this would be interleaving).

Spacing is how we spread out content over time and interleaving is how we mix things up. The critical difference is that interleaving refers to what happens in between spacing.

Let's revisit the example practice problems from earlier, and also add a third problem set:

Problem Set 1: AAAA BBBB CCCC DDDD

Problem Set 2: ABBB ACCC ADDD ABCD

Problem Set 3: ACBD DABC BCCA DBAD

Set 1 is blocked; all the A problems are followed by B problems and so on. Set 2 is spaced; the A problems are spread across all the items. Note, however, that the As are followed by blocks of B, C, and D questions – no interleaving involved. Set 3 involves both spacing and interleaving; the A problems are spread over time *and* they are mixed up with other problems.

A related reason why spotting this difference is tough is because interleaving requires spacing by default, whereas spacing does not require interleaving. This is akin to "a square is a rectangle, but a rectangle is not always a square." In this case, Set 3 shows that "interleaving is spacing" whereas Set 2 shows that "spacing is not always interleaving."

When it comes to classroom practice, spotting the difference between spacing and interleaving can be fun (maybe even hard to "un-notice" once you've got the hang of it), but be sure to *focus on the big picture*: desirable difficulties improve learning and decrease forgetting. As a spaced reminder of our recommendation from earlier: when it comes to retrieval, spacing, and interleaving, more is better and any is better than none! So focus on the Power Tools that work best for you and your content, whether it's spacing, interleaving, or both.

POWERFUL CLASSROOM STRATEGIES FOR INTERLEAVING

Spacing and interleaving can be planned in advance – but they don't have to be! Here are small adjustments that require minimal planning, create a low-stakes atmosphere, and put students in charge of mixing it up.

- Instead of asking, "What did you learn today?," ask students, "What did you learn *yesterday*?" By being purposeful with this question, suddenly learning has gone from asking about today (and moving on) to asking about yesterday (and bringing information back to mind using spacing).

- Foster and support positive classroom culture around spacing and interleaving by using phrases such as Blasts from the Past, "space, don't race!," Throwback Thursdays, and Flashback Fridays.

- An increasing number of online tools provide the ability to quickly create and customize retrieval practice. Explore a simple "shuffle" feature for Mini-Quizzes and flashcards, which would take advantage of both spacing and interleaving.

Also, take a look at your teaching materials. An analysis of six popular middle school math textbooks found that more than 80% of the practice problems were blocked.[21] How can you interleave or mix up similar concepts so that students must discriminate and choose which strategies and approaches are appropriate for retrieval practice? As we demonstrated with the word problems earlier, try to avoid situations where students can simply plug and chug. If you assign students practice problems from a textbook (which are likely presented in blocks!), assign problems from previous chapters, the current chapter, and similar topics. *No need to change the problems* – simply mix up what you assign.

Instead of asking, "What did you learn today?" ask students, "What did you learn yesterday?"

Here are three strategies we use in our own classrooms to combine spacing and interleaving: the Dice Game, the Fishbowl, and the Lightning Round. Importantly, these three strategies *don't* require a massive amount of coordination, but they do require a little bit of advance planning; they start with a list of past, present, and related topics. This combines spacing over time, as well as interleaving and discrimination of similar topics.

The Dice Game Strategy: Put Students in Charge of Interleaving

1. Students pair up or join small groups.
2. Students get a numbered list of similar vocabulary words, math problems, or related concepts.

3. One student rolls a die (or dice for more than six items).

4. The student who rolls then retrieves the number they roll. (They can be asked to define a word, apply a concept, solve a problem, etc.).

5. The other student provides feedback.

6. Switch turns.

Voilà! *Because the list already contains similar concepts*, students are taking charge of retrieving, spacing, interleaving, and feedback, all by the roll of a die.

The Fishbowl Strategy: Switch It Up for Different Classes

1. Write past and current topics on slips of paper and put them in a fishbowl, a hat, or even a backpack, or use an electronic list where topics are numbered.

2. Have a student draw a slip or choose a number randomly, followed by Think-Pair-Share before drawing the next one.

The Fishbowl strategy is very similar to Patrice's Mini-Quizzes mentioned in Chapter 3. After each class, you can put the slips of paper back into the fishbowl and draw a new interleaved set of questions for the following class. To maximize the benefits from the Fishbowl strategy, try to ensure that *all* students are retrieving. We recommend having individual students write down their answer before sharing in pairs, which will also facilitate discussion because students don't feel put on the spot.

The Lightning Round Strategy: Keep Interleaving Fast-Paced and Low-Stakes

1. Create a list of past and current topics (to build in spacing). Better yet, have your students create the list!

2. Have one student call out concepts from the list at random.

3. Have all students retrieve and write down their answers.

4. Give students feedback at the end of the lightning round to keep it fast-paced.

For the Lightning Round, even though it's a fast-paced activity, keep it low- or no-stakes. This should *not* be competitive. As we mention throughout the book, by using low- and no-stakes retrieval practices, you emphasize that retrieval, spacing, and interleaving are *learning* strategies, not assessment strategies.

Want to take the Dice Game, the Fishbowl, and the Lightning Round even further? Over the course of an entire semester, model Patrice's Big Basket Quiz strategy and accumulate important content you want students to remember on slips of paper or a numbered list (spreadsheets can also work well for this). To make the most of interleaving, use these three strategies throughout the semester with the ongoing list you develop. This way, students are retrieving information that's spaced from earlier, not just retrieving the unit you're currently teaching.

NOTES

1. Rohrer, D., and Taylor, K. (2006). The effects of overlearning and distributed practice on the retention of mathematics knowledge. *Applied Cognitive Psychology* 20: 1209–1224.

2. Maddox, G. B. (2016). Understanding the underlying mechanism of the spacing effect in verbal learning: A case for encoding variability and study-phase retrieval. *Journal of Cognitive Psychology* 28: 684–706.

3. Carpenter, S. K., and Agarwal, P. K. (2018). *How to Use Spaced Retrieval Practice to Boost Learning.* Iowa State University. Available at www.powerfulteaching.org.

4. In neuroscience and cognitive science, this process is called consolidation. Consolidation also occurs when we sleep, changing

learning from short-term memory into long-term memory. Dudai, Y., Karni, A., and Born, J. (2015). The consolidation and transformation of memory. *Neuron* 88: 20–32.

5. Cepeda, N. J., Vul, E., Rohrer, D., et al. (2008). Spacing effects in learning: A temporal ridgeline of optimal retention. *Psychological Science* 19: 1095–1102.

6. McDaniel, M. A., Agarwal, P. K., Huelser, B. J., et al. (2011). Test-enhanced learning in a middle school science classroom: The effects of quiz frequency and placement. *Journal of Educational Psychology* 103: 399–414.

7. Uner, O., and Roediger, H. L. (2017). The effect of question placement on learning from textbook chapters. *Journal of Applied Research in Memory and Cognition 7*: 116–122. See also Weinstein, Y., Nunes, L. D., and Karpicke, J. D. (2016). On the placement of practice questions during study. *Journal of Experimental Psychology: Applied* 22: 72–84.

8. Murre, J. M. J., and Dros, J. (2015). Replication and analysis of Ebbinghaus' forgetting curve. *PLoS ONE* 10: 1–23.

9. Rohrer, D., Dedrick, R. F., and Agarwal, P. K. (2017). *Interleaved Mathematics Practice: Giving Students A Chance to Learn What They Need to Know.* University of South Florida. Available at www.powerfulteaching.org.

10. Rohrer, D. (2012). Interleaving helps students distinguish among similar concepts. *Educational Psychology Review* 24: 355–367.

11. Brown, P. C., Roediger, H. L., and McDaniel, M. A. (2014). *Make it Stick: The Science of Successful Learning.* Cambridge, MA: Harvard University Press.

12. The first two problems require the Pythagorean Theorem (the answers are 52 and 50, respectively), whereas the third problem requires simple subtraction (the answer is 42). For more examples, see Rohrer, D., Dedrick, R. F., and Burgess, K. (2014).

The benefit of interleaved mathematics practice is not limited to superficially similar kinds of problems. *Psychonomic Bulletin & Review* 21: 1323–1330.

13. Taylor, K., and Rohrer, D. (2010). The effects of interleaved practice. *Applied Cognitive Psychology* 24: 837–848.

14. Rohrer, D., Dedrick, R. E., and Stershic, S. (2015). Interleaved practice improves mathematics learning. *Journal of Educational Psychology* 107: 900–908.

15. Pan, S. C. (2015). The interleaving effect: Mixing it up boosts learning. *Scientific American*. Available at www. scientificamerican.com.

16. There's even research on the serial position effect with our sense of taste! Daniel, T. A., and Katz, J. S. (2018). Primacy and recency effects for taste. *Journal of Experimental Psychology: Learning, Memory, and Cognition* 44: 399–405.

17. Roediger, H. L., and DeSoto, K. A (2014). Forgetting the presidents. *Science* 346: 1106–1109.

18. Hausman, H., and Kornell, N. (2014). Mixing topics while studying does not enhance learning. *Journal of Applied Research in Memory and Cognition* 3: 153–160.

19. Yan, V. X., Soderstrom, N. C., Seneviratna, G. S., et al. (2017). How should exemplars be sequenced in inductive learning? Empirical evidence versus learners' opinions. *Journal of Experimental Psychology: Applied* 23: 403–416.

20. Answer: Research demonstrates that all retrieval practice conditions boost long-term learning more than no retrieval practice at all. Based on both laboratory and classroom studies, the optimal spacing for retrieval is a few days after the lesson (option D), which increases desirable difficulties or consolidation of knowledge.

21. Rohrer, D., Dedrick, R. F., and Stershic, S. (2015). Interleaved practice improves mathematics learning. *Journal of Educational Psychology* 107: 900–908.

Chapter 5

Engage Students with Feedback-Driven Metacognition

We've all been there. As teachers, we know what it is like when a student approaches us before a test exclaiming, "I studied last night for *two hours!*" As you go through your stack of grading, you smile when you get to this particular student, in anticipation of success. And then, the smile fades. You question, "Was it for *my* class and for *this* test that the student studied?" The student scored poorly. There is a reason, a common reason, a research-based reason why this happens: students' *metacognition.*

Power Tool #4 is *feedback-driven metacognition.* When students engage in retrieval, they are able to reflect on what they know and what they don't know – what cognitive scientists call metacognition.

POWER OF FEEDBACK-DRIVEN METACOGNITION IN PATRICE'S CLASSROOM

At the beginning of each year, I ask my students this question: "Who was Lady Murasaki Shikibu?" As clueless eyes scan the room, I explain, "You didn't have to think about it . . . right away, you either knew the answer or you didn't. There is no shame, no guessing; you simply have not yet been taught that information." I encourage the students to embrace the feeling of not knowing the answer. It is this feeling of not knowing an answer that will help students succeed.

I ask the students if they had ever studied for a good length of time for a test, took the test, and were surprised that they hadn't done well. Usually, about 95% of my students' hands go up. Next, I explain the role of metacognition. It is quite common for students to study what they already know; it is powerful and builds confidence. In my class, however, it is my duty to teach students *how to learn*. I teach them how to differentiate between what they know and what they don't know. I urge them to remember the feeling of "not knowing" with my Lady Murasaki Shikibu example. There was no shame; instead, I emphasize the attitude of "I don't know that *yet*." (I have used this phrase for over 15 years; it continues to be relevant year after year!)

A slogan I began using many years ago was *active engagement with feedback*. This phrase relates well to how I teach metacognition. Students remain actively engaged in my classroom by writing on whiteboards, using clickers, Think-Pair-Share, work within study buddy groups, and so on. The strategies can be individualized and endless. In fact, a great many teachers already use these techniques. The critical component, however, is *feedback*. Without feedback, how else do students understand if they know, or don't know, the material?

Teachers know that students learn at different speeds. I have found that these different speeds can often be traced to metacognition.

When I picture all my students and the impact of feedback, I think about three groups:

- Group 1 tends to be students who easily learn and retain information through the use of feedback.

- Group 2, the most common, includes the students who learn best when a topic is introduced, followed by review and reinforcement through feedback, and then additional review and reinforcement through feedback.

- Group 3 includes the students who, despite the introduction, reinforcements, and feedback, still struggle with information. Their frustration often impacts their motivation.

Students in Group 1 do well in my class; they do well in all their classes. Students in Group 2 also do well in my class. It is the students in Group 3 that benefit most from feedback-driven metacognition.

Every year after receiving first-quarter report cards, I often have students tell me, "I can't believe I am getting a B (or even an A) in your class!" This is almost always followed by, "I always fail this subject" or "I never get good grades," or the one I always dread the most, "I'm not smart." By middle school, students have often internalized failure. How can we change this? As I've stated earlier, my mission is to teach students *how* to learn. How can we teach students to differentiate what they already know from what they still need to learn? We can use feedback-driven metacognition. It is what separates those who do well from those who don't.

THE SCIENCE BEHIND POWER TOOL #4: FEEDBACK-DRIVEN METACOGNITION

When students are aware of *what they know and don't know,* learning is more successful in the classroom and studying is more successful outside the classroom. Of course, the opposite is also true. When students are *not* aware of what they know and don't know, learning and studying are *less* successful. If Patrice's story seems all too familiar, where students invest a lot of time studying only to fail a test, we have some good news and bad news.

First, the bad news: Research confirms that students frequently *think* they know something, when actually, they don't. Also, students are typically *overconfident* when they predict or assess their own learning.

Here's the good news: Cognitive scientists have developed evidence-based recommendations for improving students' metacognition by incorporating frequent feedback. In order to examine metacognition scientifically, researchers ask students to make two types of ratings:

1. *Judgments of learning,* or a student's prediction of *future* learning or memory

2. *Confidence judgments,* or a student's confidence in *recent* or *past* learning

Before you move on, answer these two questions (and write down your ratings!):

Power Up

1. On a scale from 0% to 100%, what percentage of Chapter 4 on spacing and interleaving will you *remember* in one week?
2. Who invented the polio vaccine? On a scale from 1 (guessing) to 5 (definitely sure), how *confident* are you in your answer?

The first question is a judgment of learning (JOL, predicting your future learning), while the second question is a confidence judgment (rating your previous learning).[1]

It's this relationship between the students' understanding of their own learning, compared to their actual learning, that has significant implications for long-term learning, study habits, and motivation – inside and outside the classroom. In your classroom, begin to ask these questions: Were students' predictions consistent with their final test performance? Was a student overconfident, thinking he did better on an exam than he really did?

Illusion #1: When Students Think They Got Something Correct, They Probably Did

In one laboratory study, Pooja and her colleagues examined ideal retrieval practice conditions for both learning and metacognition.[2] College students were asked to read six science passages about a variety of topics (e.g., fossils, wolves, and twisters). After students were done re-reading or retrieving, they were asked, "How well do you think you will remember this passage in one week?" Students made their JOLs on a scale from 0% (I won't remember anything) to 100% (I'll remember the passage perfectly).

Before we tell you how students rated their metacognition, answer this (spaced) question:

> ### Power Up
>
> Do you think college students predicted they will remember more after re-reading passages or after retrieval practice?

As you know by now, college students were extremely *overconfident* in their predictions after re-reading. On average, they estimated they'd remember 64% of the reading passages, but one week later, they only remembered 48% of the passages. This is an example of the first illusion of metacognition: *Students think they know something when they actually don't.*

Why are students' predictions so far off from what they actually remember? As we know from our classroom experience, when learning activities are easy, students tend to think they "just know it." In one specific condition, we asked students to re-read a science passage three times, after which they made their JOL. Imagine you've just read something three or four times, over and over. You'd probably feel pretty confident that you now know the passage like the back of your hand. Sure enough, students felt the same way – they had much higher predictions of their future test performance after re-reading a passage three times (71% prediction) compared to their actual test performance one week later (54% performance).

As educators, we hope that students *know what they know* accurately. But how can metacognition, even for advanced college students, be so poor? Part of why this occurs is what's referred to as the *illusion of fluency*. Typically, when current learning feels *fluent* or effortless, students think that learning and retention will be effortless and easy in the future.[3] In this example, it is precisely the repeated re-reading of material (an easy learning activity) that gives students an illusion of fluency, resulting in much higher JOLs for final test performance.

In contrast, when learning activities are challenging, students' predictions of their own learning are more realistic and accurate. As you may have guessed, retrieval practice dramatically increases student learning *and* improves their metacognition. As part of the same laboratory study, researchers asked college students to read a brief passage once, take a quiz, and then predict their future test performance. In this condition, students predicted that they would remember 66% of the passage in one week. On the final test one week later, students' metacognition was accurate – their test performance was literally 66%!

This illusion of fluency is consistent across a wide range of research studies. When learning is easy (e.g., re-reading, listening to lectures, etc.), students struggle to accurately predict their own learning. On the other hand, when learning is challenging (e.g., brief quizzes, interleaved lessons, etc.), students make more accurate predictions because they become familiar with their learning along the way – almost like formative assessment, *but for the student*.

But keep in mind that it's not just our students who can have an illusion of fluency! As professor and host of the Teaching in Higher Ed podcast, Bonni Stachowiak, observed:

> We all have a tendency to miss some of these counterintuitive aspects to teaching and learning. It's really complex, and rather than see such a great distance between our learners and ourselves, we should see that we all have the potential to predict wrongly about the effects of our actions.

Illusion #2: Students' Confidence is Always in Sync with Their Learning

Turning to our second illusion of metacognition, students can fall prey to the *illusion of confidence*. As we know from our own classroom experience, just because a student is confident does *not* mean they've learned something. Researchers have been studying this fascinating confidence-accuracy tradeoff for a long time, both because of the theoretical and real-world consequences.[4] Take, for instance, the number of false convictions based on eyewitness testimony. Juries have a tendency to believe highly confident witnesses, even though their memories frequently turn out to be inaccurate.

In the classroom, it's important for us to keep this illusion of confidence in mind when students are evaluating their own progress. Just because a student is confident doesn't mean that they've learned as much as they (and we) think they have. The next time a student does poorly on an exam and exclaims, "I studied last night for *two hours!*" point out the difference between confidence and accuracy. One does not always match the other!

The next time a student does poorly on an exam and exclaims, "But I studied last night for two hours!" point out the difference between confidence and accuracy. One does not always match the other!

The illusion of fluency and illusion of confidence are intertwined, and both illusions can be detrimental to student learning. If learning feels fluent, students may be overconfident in their own learning. And if a student is overconfident, they may only study what they already know, giving them the illusion that they "know it" when they actually don't.

> ## Power Up
>
> In thinking about metacognition in your classroom, ask yourself:
>
> - Do students *really* know it, or do they simply think they do?
> - Have students assessed their own learning through retrieval, or are they relying on their intuition that they learned something because it felt easy?
> - Are students confident in their knowledge, and if so, what might be contributing to their confidence?

So far, we've discussed cognitive scientists' approaches to examining students' metacognition:

- Scientists use two main measurement techniques: JOLs and confidence ratings.
- There are two common metacognitive illusions: the illusion of fluency and the illusion of confidence.
- Students' confidence-accuracy mismatches (incorrect answers with high confidence and correct answers with low confidence) can be remedied with feedback.

Whew! Next, we present specific recommendations for fostering metacognition based on a wealth of scientific research and years of classroom practice.

In Chapter 2, we presented a study by Roediger and Karpicke where students' predictions about how much they would remember after one week mismatched their actual performance after one week. Retrieve and write down Two Things about that study!

RESEARCH-BASED RECOMMENDATIONS FOR FEEDBACK-DRIVEN METACOGNITION

As we discuss in earlier chapters, when it comes to evidence-based Power Tools, remember: The more the better, and some is better than none. With this in mind, here are four recommendations for boosting students' metacognition.

Boost Learning with Feedback for Incorrect *and Correct* Answers

When we challenge student learning – using retrieval practice, for example – students are better able to understand what they still need to learn or what they still need to study. Although retrieval indicates whether we know or remember something, we also need feedback in order to tell us whether we are correct or incorrect. Otherwise, students may retrieve information, think they are correct, and then move on. Without feedback, students' metacognition can remain overconfident and out of sync with their actual learning.

Without feedback, students' metacognition can remain overconfident and out of sync with their actual learning.

In laboratory research, studies consistently demonstrate that feedback is magical. What do we mean by magical? Think of feedback like a fairy godmother's wand – you wave it and all evil things disappear. We're being dramatic, but feedback does have dramatic benefits when it comes to correcting mistakes, improving metacognition, and doubling long-term retention of information. There is also evidence from Pooja's research that feedback is particularly beneficial for students on the lower end of the learning spectrum – proof that feedback is an essential part of learning.[5]

To extend laboratory findings into the classroom, Pooja and her colleagues examined feedback in seventh-grade science classrooms.[6] Using the teacher's lessons on bacteria and plants, they compared students' learning after these three conditions:

- Clicker quizzes *with* feedback
- Clicker quizzes *without* feedback
- Regular lessons without any quizzes

Learning was measured using the teacher's unit test about three weeks later. They found that students' test performance dramatically increased when students received clicker quizzes with feedback (94%) compared to when they received clicker quizzes without feedback (83%) or didn't receive any clicker quizzes at all (80%).

In other words, when students received something as simple as a green check mark after clicking in responses for a multiple-choice question, their learning increased *by an entire letter grade*. Even though students didn't receive individual feedback or an explanation as to why something was correct or incorrect, the teacher still saw large benefits for learning using very little class time.

Before we tell you about the next part of the study, humor us and answer these two questions:

- What is the capital of Australia?
- What is the capital of Kentucky?

For the first question, you may have guessed that Sydney or Melbourne is the capital of Australia. You may have also been highly confident in your answer. Actually, the capital of Australia isn't either of these cities.[7] (Surprise!) In this first example, you were highly confident *but* incorrect. In this situation, feedback gives students the opportunity to reflect and think, "Wow, I really thought that that was the answer, but I got it wrong!" In this way, feedback creates what Janet Metcalfe, a scientist from Columbia University, calls a *hypercorrection effect*.[8] When students are absolutely positive they know something and it turns out to be incorrect, they're much more likely to retrieve the correct answer in the future. Chances are you'll never forget the capital of Australia ever again!

For the second question, you might have guessed that Frankfort is the capital of Kentucky. If so, you were guessing *and* correct. In situations like question 2, students may think, "Wow, I was just guessing and I'm glad I got it correct!" In other words, *students don't have to know the correct answer to get the answer correct.* This is precisely where feedback is so valuable: it solidifies correct answers. In other words, feedback is important for *correct* answers, not just incorrect answers.

In one of the studies in Patrice's classroom, when students received feedback during clicker quizzes, their long-term learning for incorrect *and* correct answers increased, as well as their match between confidence and accuracy.[9]

Feedback is such an important part of learning – yet we and our students tend to gloss over it! Be sure to boost learning with feedback for incorrect *and* correct answers. When you hand back a graded paper or quiz, encourage students to look at what they got correct and incorrect. This will increase students' metacognition and confidence in their own learning, too. Here's how Lisa Pulley, a high school social studies teacher from Missouri, put it: "A more confident learner is willing to take a risk, and taking a risk leads to more learning."

Prioritize Elaborative Feedback to Boost Students' Transfer of Knowledge

You may be wondering, what *type* of feedback is most effective for improving learning and metacognition? Overall, students benefit from two types of feedback: *elaborative feedback* and *correct answer feedback*. Elaborative feedback is where we provide students with explanations about why an answer is correct, whereas correct answer feedback provides students with a simple indication of whether an answer is correct or incorrect.

As we discussed in Chapter 2, elaborative feedback (especially with examples) is particularly beneficial for students' transfer of knowledge to new contexts. Students don't just learn whether they retrieved the answer correctly; they learn about the correct answer and *why* it's correct.[10]

I (Patrice) have found using elaborative feedback during my Pre-Tests to be especially effective. It allows me to explain *why* an answer is correct *and* tie it back to previously learned content. For example, I might give the students a multiple-choice question on the board, such as:

What is a revolution?
A. A war between groups within one country
B. A sudden or great change
C. A war between countries
D. The raising of crops and animals for human use

After students see the question and I read it aloud, they select the answer they think is correct (using clickers, a homemade whiteboard, colored index cards, etc.). When I reveal the correct answer (a revolution is a sudden or great change), often quizzical looks emerge because the definition did not include fighting. Elaborative feedback follows, with class discussions regarding the American Revolution, French Revolution, and Russian Revolution.

Rather than thinking about fighting, the questions turn to, "What sudden or great changes resulted? What was happening in society when the Revolution occurred?" This elaborative feedback promotes metacognition, retrieval, spacing, interleaving, and deep learning. Think how different the outcome would be if I simply gave the correct answer!

Of course, elaborative feedback can take more classroom time. But as we've mentioned before, when it comes to Power Tools, any is better than none! Laboratory research suggests that elaborative feedback is more potent than correct answer feedback,[11] and our research in K–12 classrooms demonstrates similar benefits from both types of feedback after weeks and months.[12] Provide as much feedback as you can and include elaborative feedback when possible.

Give Students Feedback Immediately *or* After a Delay

Another question we frequently encounter is *when* to give feedback: during or after a lesson versus delayed by a day or two. Some laboratory research suggests a greater benefit for delayed feedback,[13] whereas classroom research demonstrates similar benefits for both types of feedback.[14] Provide feedback when it works best for you – any is better than none! Also, the more the better; give feedback immediately *and* after a delay to combine feedback and spacing.

One of the ways Patrice uses both immediate and delayed feedback is with Mini-Quizzes. As soon as the Mini-Quizzes have been collected, she gives immediate feedback by stating the question and the correct answer. Patrice also conducts a 15-minute analysis of the Mini-Quizzes after school providing corrective feedback. Because Power Tools foster learning, the majority of Mini-Quizzes are accurate; providing corrective feedback requires little time. Delayed feedback occurs the following day when the

Mini-Quizzes are returned to students and the questions and correct answers are stated again. At the college level, feedback in Pooja's classroom is identical: After completing weekly retrieval practices, she facilitates an immediate class discussion about the answers. She then returns students' retrieval practices a week later with written feedback for individual students.

Of course, we only have so much time in our classrooms and feedback is so powerful for learning. Whether feedback is immediate or delayed, do what's practical in your classroom – just make sure to give feedback!

Encourage Students to Make Mistakes

You've probably heard the phrase, "We learn most from our mistakes." At the same time, when it comes to retrieval practice, we might be worried that students will make *too many* mistakes. What if students don't get anything correct? Won't they keep retrieving and remembering incorrect information? Great questions, and this is exactly why feedback is so important!

Sometimes we have an knee-jerk reaction to prevent our students from making errors. Scientists refer to this idea as *errorless learning*, which became a popular educational approach in the 1950s. Somewhat akin to steadying a baby when it's first walking, we want to help. It can make us cringe to see someone struggling when we can simply help them out and provide the answer. How often do we give our students the opportunity to make mistakes, and importantly, how often do we *encourage* them to make mistakes?

With retrieval practice, mistakes are a *good* thing for learning.[15] Even if students can't retrieve information they've learned, or they retrieve information but it's incorrect, there's a wealth of research demonstrating that retrieval – even with errors – improves learning.[16] Feedback after that incorrect information or lack of information is especially critical for metacognition, filling in the knowledge gaps, and swapping misinformation for deeper learning and understanding. Plus, when students make errors in low-stakes environments – not just high-stakes environments – they continue to build confidence in their metacognition and learning.

 Give feedback for incorrect and correct answers

 Give elaborative feedback to boost transfer

 Give feedback immediately or after a delay

 Give feedback while encouraging mistakes

FEEDBACK-DRIVEN METACOGNITION STRATEGIES IN PATRICE'S CLASSROOM

Where do I (Patrice) begin to teach metacognition? How do I take my students from blank slates in terms of the Eastern Hemisphere to knowledgeable inquirers? Let me introduce you to my classroom where Power Tools prevail. My classroom is a safe, comforting, respectful, energizing, and welcoming place.

On day 1, I teach my philosophy to the students along with a guided tour of the room. In particular, I explain my four key wall signs:

- We all need time to think and learn.

- It's okay to make mistakes. That's the way we learn.

- We can do more and learn more when we are willing to take a risk.

- It's okay to ask for help. No one need do it all alone.

I discuss these signs in more detail in Chapter 8: Foster a Supportive Environment, but for now, it's important to know that my signs are vital in setting the stage for boosting students' metacognition and awareness of their own learning.

On day 2, students learn about Lady Murasaki Shikibu and the metacognitive process begins.[17] After explaining what metacognition is, I have students repeat the word *metacognition* after me and then to each other using Think-Pair-Share or Turn and Talk. I use repetition, and by mimicking me, students become familiar and comfortable with the word. Each day thereafter, I begin class with choral work and Think-Pair-Share with vocabulary and definitions of metacognition. When I am confident that students understand this concept, we continue to discuss it on a daily basis. (I've even had students change the name to *Metacogtricktion*! You'll read about it in Chapter 9 on sparking conversations with students.)

I teach my units using the same approach I use for teaching the word *metacognition*. For each term, person, and place, choral work, Think-Pair-Share, and repetition are used. I state a definition and students, in unison, give the answer. This is where feedback is vital. Even if a student is unsure of an answer, the correct answer is heard and reinforced immediately. At first, feedback is instructor-led. Eventually, I turn the process over to students for self-feedback. Through the use of Retrieval Cards, the Four Steps of Metacognition, and Metacognition Sheets, students give themselves feedback. Independently, students determine what they know and what requires further study – this is metacognition!

Retrieval Cards and Four Steps of Metacognition

At the end of each lesson, students complete what I (Patrice) call *Retrieval Cards*. The Retrieval Cards are one sheet of paper divided into 8–10 boxes (see Figure 5.1 using four boxes). In each box, I include a definition and a blank for students to write in the appropriate key concept or term.

Figure 5.1 Retrieval Cards differ from flashcards because students make judgments of learning and complete the Four Steps of Metacognition. Answers for the Retrieval Cards, clockwise from the top left: industrial revolution, factories, middle class, textiles.

Retrieval Cards

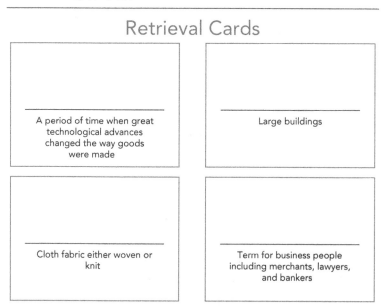

Importantly, students complete Retrieval Cards using the *Four Steps of Metacognition* (see Figure 5.2 for an example; the four steps can also be downloaded at www.powerfulteaching.org.):

Step 1. Students examine their own knowledge, even before they write it down. If they know an answer, they put a star in the box containing the definition (a happy face works well for younger grades). If they don't know or are unsure of the answer, students put a question mark in the box. Again, students complete Step 1 *without* writing down the answer. In Step 1, students simply make a judgment of their own learning – do I know it or not? After going through Step 1 for *all* the Retrieval Cards, only then do students move on to Step 2.

Figure 5.2 With the Four Steps of Metacognition, students make judgments of learning, retrieve information, and receive feedback.

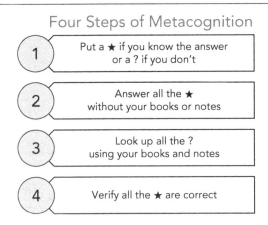

Four Steps of Metacognition

1. Put a ★ if you know the answer or a ? if you don't
2. Answer all the ★ without your books or notes
3. Look up all the ? using your books and notes
4. Verify all the ★ are correct

Step 2. Students retrieve the answers for all of their stars (terms they feel they already know), but *without* books or notes. By challenging students to retrieve what they know without access to books or notes, students are better able to judge whether they truly know something or not.

Step 3. Students turn their attention to their question marks, or terms they don't know. To answer these items, students use their books and notes.

Step 4. Students return to their stars and verify that what they retrieved during Step 2 is correct, again using books and notes.

Retrieval Cards are similar to flashcards, with *one key difference*: With traditional flashcards, there's no retrieval involved while creating them; students simply look up concepts and answers while writing them down. With Retrieval Cards, students have the opportunity to retrieve and go through the Four Steps of Metacognition from the beginning, boosting further learning.

Do students ever go back to old habits and not do well? Of course they do. The step students are most tempted to skip is Step 4: Verify that the answer is correct. While students are completing the Retrieval Cards or Metacognition Sheet, I walk around and look at their answers. If there is an error, they did not do Step 4. I let students know there is an error on their sheet (correct answer feedback), but I don't let them know which item has an error! Students must then verify each answer they wrote down to check which are correct and which are incorrect.

For several reasons, I prefer to use one piece of paper for Retrieval Cards, rather than index cards. Here's why:

- Students have just one piece of paper for studying.
- Students can quiz themselves by folding the paper.
- If students are retrieving in class, you can monitor progress.
- Grading is a breeze.
- You won't find nameless index cards in the hallway!

Importantly, a student *cannot fail* using this exercise! Soon, even the most reluctant student can complete all Four Steps independently. One year, I taught sixth-grade World History and two sections of eighth-grade US History. Because I teach in a small district, most of the eighth-graders were in my classroom for sixth-grade, as well. To my delight, students continued to use the Four Steps of Metacognition – even two years later. When I unexpectedly run into former students, I'm often greeted with, "Mrs. Metacognition!"

With Retrieval Cards, students make JOLs, engage in retrieval practice, and receive feedback. Afterwards, students have a study tool, too. *Voila!*

Metacognition Sheets: Students Reflect on Their Knowledge During Learning

Research in laboratories and classrooms indicate that metacognition can also be improved using *Metacognition Sheets*. With Metacognition Sheets, students make JOLs and/or confidence ratings *during* learning.

Evidence from Research on Metacognition Sheets

In one classroom study by John Nietfeld and colleagues, college students listened to lectures, while other students listened to lectures and also received Metacognition Sheets.[18] Using Metacognition Sheets during each class, students rated their understanding of the day's lecture, wrote down any difficult concepts, and reflected on how they could improve their understanding.

For example,

- On a scale from 1 (very unclear) to 4 (very clear), how would you rate your overall understanding of today's class?

- What are Two Things you learned in today's class?

- On a scale from 1 (not confident) to 4 (very confident), how confident are you that the Two Things you just wrote down are correct?

- What concepts from today's class did you find difficult to understand?

- Specifically, what will you do to improve your understanding of the concepts that were difficult?

In this scientific study – conducted in an authentic classroom – students in the Metacognition Sheet group consistently scored significantly higher than students in the lecture-only group (Figure 5.3).

Figure 5.3 When college students completed Metacognition Sheets and reflection questions at the end of lectures, their exam performance was nearly a letter grade higher than lectures alone.

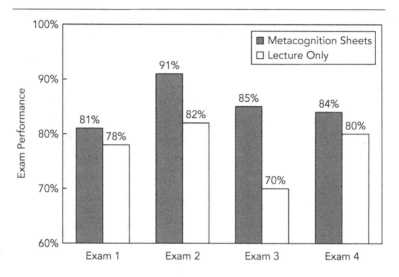

Figure 5.4 Metacognition Sheets allow students to make judgments of learning, combine all four Power Tools, and serve as an additional study tool.

Metacognition Sheet

★	?	Items to Know	Answer
		Maximilien Robespierre	
		Definition of "revolution"	
		How did each revolution change the lives of working people?	
		How did the social pyramids change as a result of the revolutions?	

Metacognition Sheets in Patrice's Classroom

Before each chapter exam in my (Patrice's) class, students complete a Metacognition Sheet (see Figure 5.4 for an example).

Each Metacognition Sheet contains four columns:

- Columns 1 and 2 are narrow and include a star or question mark at the top, which students use to complete the Four Steps of Metacognition.

- Column 3 lists *Items to Know*, which often include essential questions and essays. In this way, Items to Know can be tailored to the level of your students and the content covered. Importantly, just because something is on a Metacognition Sheet does not mean it has to be on the exam; it may simply be a concept to discuss later in the semester (spacing!).

- Column 4 provides space for students to write in their answers. (A template for Metacognition Sheets can be downloaded at www.powerfulteaching.org.)

There are two key differences between Retrieval Cards and Metacognition Sheets:

- Retrieval Cards contain content from a week-long lesson, whereas Metacognition Sheets include content from an entire chapter (i.e., 4–6 lessons); depending on the length of the unit, the Metacognition Sheet could be one-sided or longer.

- Retrieval Cards ask students to retrieve key terms and definitions, whereas Metacognition Sheets ask students to answer not only key terms and definitions but also essential questions and complex ideas.

Similar to Retrieval Cards, by completing the Metacognition Sheet, my students not only retrieve and receive feedback; they create their own study tool, too. And, to my delight, students no longer study for two hours and do poorly on a test. In fact, study time is *reduced* because students know which areas need focus. In my students, I see confidence. I see good grades. I hear the synthesis of information and deep conversations. Best of all, I no longer hear, "But I studied last night for two hours!"

Power Up

Challenge yourself with the Four Steps of Metacognition! Who Was Lady Murasaki Shikibu?

1. Do you *know* the answer (a star) or are you *unsure* (a question mark)?
2. If you know the answer, retrieve it and write it down. On a scale from 1 (guessing) to 5 (definitely sure), how *confident* are you in your answer?
3. If you're unsure, look up the answer (we mentioned her earlier).
4. Give yourself feedback and verify that your answer is correct.

FEEDBACK-DRIVEN METACOGNITION STRATEGIES IN POOJA'S CLASSROOM

As mentioned in Chapter 3 on retrieval strategies, I (Pooja) give my college students weekly retrieval practices. Each retrieval practice includes four to five short-answer questions about material from previous classes *and* material from the reading for the day's lesson (i.e., incorporating spacing and interleaving!). In terms of feedback and metacognition, here are two of my teaching strategies: Breath and Retrieve, and Metacognition Line-Up.

Breathe and Retrieve: Encourage Students to Reflect During Retrieval Practice

While students complete weekly retrieval practices, students *Breathe and Retrieve*. Next to quiz questions, students circle one of two phrases: *Nailed It!* or *Not Sure!* In this way, students have to take *a deep breath* and really think about how well they understand material based on their *retrieval*. In order to decide whether they nailed it or are not sure, I encourage students to engage in *self-explanation*, by asking themselves, "How does this relate to what I've already learned?" or, "How does this question spark new ideas?" In addition to JOLs and confidence ratings, self-explanation has been shown to also boost students' metacognition and understanding of their own learning.[19]

Once students complete their retrieval practice, we have a class discussion for about 20 minutes, which provides students with immediate elaborative feedback. For delayed feedback, I grade retrieval practices and hand them back the following week. Students are then able to view their grade *and* their self-rated confidence. In other words, with Breathe and Retrieve, students receive immediate and delayed feedback, correct answer and elaborative feedback, and opportunities to reflect on their metacognition.

There are two important things to keep in mind when it comes to Breathe and Retrieve:

- Don't include these confidence ratings for open-ended opinion questions, such as, "Do you think we should conduct research on animals?" Students will feel pressured that there is a correct answer for the question, detracting from retrieval being a learning opportunity.

- Avoid asking students to rate their confidence on a numerical scale (e.g., "I'm not at all confident" to "I definitely know it" on a five-point scale). In fact, before I used the Nailed It! and Not Sure! approach, I had students rate their confidence on a numerical scale. Even though I emphasized that the confidence ratings wouldn't affect their grade, they were hesitant to use the quick strategy as a metacognition tool.

If you are going to use a numerical or Likert scale, keep in mind that it's beneficial to provide an even number of options (e.g., four options, such as: disagree, slightly disagree, agree, definitely agree) rather than an odd number (e.g., five options: disagree, slightly disagree, neutral, agree, definitely agree). People often pick the middle number, which doesn't provide you or your students with much information at all. Nailed It! and Not Sure! provide just two options for a confidence rating, without a third option where students can hedge their bets.

Most importantly, emphasize that *feedback does not equal grades*. Because retrieval practices are for learning, not assessment, they provide feedback about progress and achievement, not end-all-be-all grades.

Metacognition Line-Up

With *Metacognition Line-Up*, students reflect on their metacognition as a *class*, not just individually. This strategy (which can also be called a Metacognition Rainbow for younger grades) was developed by Megan Nellis, a teacher and program director of a non-profit education program in South Africa. This tool has five steps:

1. Students gather on one side of the room. The teacher announces a word, key term, or concept, and students silently try to bring that information to mind.

2. Students move along a spectrum (the span of the room) based on their metacognition. One side of the room is designated as space if students feel they "Confidently Retrieved It;" the middle of the room is "Kind of Retrieved It;" and the opposite wall is "Not Sure" (or, what her students like to call "Darn you, Forgetting Curve").

3. Students match up with the person *closest* to them and spend one to two minutes talking through what they know or don't know with their partner.

4. Next, students match up with a person as *far away* from them as possible to discuss, share, and teach (another one to two minutes).

5. Students who originally couldn't retrieve share what they *learned* with the class. Ask students if they noticed any common misunderstandings.

As we'll discuss in upcoming chapters, it's important to establish a supportive environment and normalize the process of forgetting before starting a Metacognition Line-Up. In this way, students won't feel vulnerable when choosing "Not Sure" in front of the class. Over time, with trust and practice, students become comfortable recognizing if they don't understand a concept *and* students become excited to teach each other, too.

It might seem like a lot of steps, but Metacognition Line-Up moves quickly and can be completed in less than five minutes per round. Regardless of grade level or content area, this quick, flexible strategy infuses retrieval, feedback, and metacognition into the classroom – and gets students up and moving, too. It's a powerful strategy to provide a positive classroom culture, support feedback-driven metacognition, and boost student learning.

ENGAGE STUDENTS IN FEEDBACK WITH THREE QUICK STRATEGIES

Recently, a high school computer science teacher asked us, "How do I maintain students' attention when they *think* they already know something (but they don't)?"

Great question! We know that students don't always pay attention, especially when it comes to feedback. Often, students look at their grade with delight, satisfaction, or concern; or they look through what they got incorrect, but not what they got correct. In other words, when students are "looking over" feedback, they're usually just "overlooking" it.

The best way to maintain their attention is to *involve students in the process of feedback.* Four Steps of Metacognition, Metacognition Sheets, Breathe and Retrieve, and Metacognition Line-Up get students actively involved in thinking about their own learning, rather than simply glossing over feedback.

In other words, when students are "looking over" feedback, they're usually just "overlooking" it.

Here are some additional strategies for providing feedback that are engaging, quick, and don't require any additional grading:

- *Combine Brain Dumps* with Turn and Talk: Students discuss similarities and differences in their writing for just one to two minutes. This way, students receive elaborative feedback from a peer, without grades or judgment.

- Make it *Three* Things: Students write down Two Things about a previous or current topic. Next, students swap papers with a peer, add one more thing, and pass the paper back.

- Use Think-Pair-*Square*: In a spin on Think-Pair-Share, two pairs of students get together in a *square* for a quick, small-group discussion.

- Ask follow-up questions: To help students *look* at feedback and not *overlook* it, ask them to *do* something with it: What surprised you about the feedback? Why do you think you got something correct or incorrect? What is your next step? Beware, however, of giving opportunities to immediately retake a quiz or redo an assignment. That would be cramming! It would also emphasize grades, not learning. Be sure students are re-engaging and re-retrieving, not just looking to improve their grade.

By teaching our students to identify what they know and what they don't know, feedback-driven metacognition becomes a valuable Power Tool. Based on both research and classroom experience, metacognition and learning go hand in hand: When we boost one, we boost the other. As a next step, ponder this question:

Power Up

When you provide students with feedback, are you also giving them opportunities to examine their metacognition? Or are they simply looking at a grade and moving on?

NOTES

1. We hope you'll check your memory for Chapter 4 next week, perhaps with a Brain Dump! The polio vaccine was invented by Jonas Salk.

2. Agarwal, P. K., Karpicke, J. D., Kang, S. H. K., et al. (2008). Examining the testing effect with open- and closed-book tests. *Applied Cognitive Psychology* 22: 861–876.

3. Brown, P. C., Roediger, H. L., and McDaniel, M. A. (2014). *Make it Stick: The Science of Successful Learning*. Cambridge, MA: Harvard University Press.

4. Roediger, H. L., and DeSoto, K. A. (2014). Confidence and memory: Assessing positive and negative correlations. *Memory* 22: 76–91.

5. Agarwal, P. K., Finley, J. R., Rose, N. S., et al. (2017). Benefits from retrieval practice are greater for students with lower working memory capacity. *Memory* 25: 764–771.

6. Agarwal, P. K., Roediger, H. L., McDaniel, M. A., et al. (in preparation). *Feedback increases middle school students' resolution and retention of correct responses.*

7. Canberra is the capital of Australia. Frankfort is the capital of Kentucky.

8. Metcalfe, J., and Finn, B. (2012). Hypercorrection of high confidence in children. *Learning and Instruction* 22: 253–261.

9. Agarwal, P. K., Bain, P. M., and Chamberlain, R. W. (2012). The value of applied research: Retrieval practice improves classroom learning and recommendations from a teacher, a principal, and a scientist. *Educational Psychology Review* 24: 437–448.

10. Finn, B., Thomas, R., and Rawson, K. A. (2018). Learning more from feedback: Elaborating feedback with examples enhances concept learning. *Learning and Instruction* 54: 104–113.

11. Butler, A. C., Godbole, N., and Marsh, E. J. (2013). Explanation feedback is better than correct answer feedback for promoting transfer of learning. *Journal of Educational Psychology* 105: 290–298.

12. Agarwal, P. K., Huelser, B. J., McDaniel, M. A., et al. (in preparation). *Optimal feedback conditions for student learning: Immediate, delayed, or elaborative?*

13. Sinha, N., and Glass, A. L. (2015). Delayed, but not immediate, feedback after multiple-choice questions increases performance on a subsequent short-answer, but not multiple-choice, exam: Evidence for the dual-process theory of memory. *Journal of General Psychology* 142: 118–34.

14. Agarwal, P. K., et al. (in preparation). *Optimal feedback conditions for student learning: Immediate, delayed, or elaborative?*

15. Metcalfe, J. (2017). Learning from errors. *Annual Review of Psychology* 68: 465–489.

16. Hays, M. J., Kornell, N., and Bjork, R. A. (2013). When and why a failed test potentiates the effectiveness of subsequent study. *Journal of Experimental Psychology: Learning, Memory, and Cognition* 39: 290–296.

17. For curious readers, Lady Murasaki Shikibu lived from the late 900s to the early 1000s. This Japanese woman is often credited for having written one of the world's first novels, *The Tale of Genji*.

18. Nietfeld, J. L., Cao, L., and Osborne, J. W. (2006). The effect of distributed monitoring exercises and feedback on performance, monitoring accuracy, and self-efficacy. *Metacognition and Learning* 1: 159–179.

19. Wiley, J., Griffin, T. D., Jaeger, A. J., et al. (2016). Improving metacomprehension accuracy in an undergraduate course context. *Journal of Experimental Psychology: Applied* 22: 393–405.

Chapter **6**

Combine Power Tools and Harness Your Toolbox

By this point in our book, you've probably been thinking, "I already use Power Tools in my classroom."

Yes, you probably do! And for many content areas – like math and foreign languages – Power Tools like retrieval practice and spacing are a core component of instruction. Students have to practice what they know; they have to *use it or lose it.*

We feel that all good teachers already use Power Tools in their classroom. So now what? What can you do to take the next step? Whether you're already using Power Tools or just starting out, in this chapter you'll find out how to create an effective combination of Power Tools – your very own *Toolbox*!

In fact, take a moment and ponder this Power Up:

> **Power Up**
>
> For each of the four Power Tools, write down how you are
> *already* applying it in your instruction or curriculum.
>
> - Retrieval Practice
>
> - Spacing
>
> - Interleaving
>
> - Feedback-Driven Metacognition

The challenge is spotting where you think you're combining Power Tools vs. where you're using them, but in isolation.

As you may remember (and we hope you do!), we introduced the formula in Figure 6.1 in Chapter 4 on spacing and interleaving. Combining Power Tools may seem intuitive and straightforward, just like this formula. But the challenge is spotting where you *think* you're combining them vs. where you're using them, but in isolation.

Consider these questions:

- Do you already give low-stakes quizzes? If so, how can you follow up with *elaborative feedback*, rather than providing points or grades that students glance over?

- Do you space your content throughout the semester? Is there a way you can *interleave* content so students have to discriminate between similarities and differences?

- Do your students already reflect on their own learning? How can you provide just *a few more opportunities* for students to examine their metacognition?

Figure 6.1 Combining the Power Tools of retrieval, spacing, and interleaving leads to powerful learning. This figure is available online at www.powerfulteaching.org.

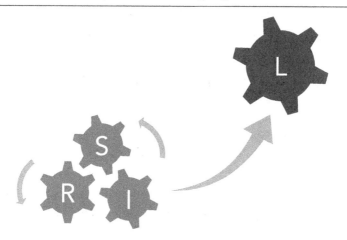

After taking the four Power Tools and effectively combining them in his classroom and instruction, Justin, a high school history teacher we mentioned in Chapter 4 on spacing and interleaving, reflected:

> So many of us are discipline experts, but small changes in how we deliver content and measure learning in our classrooms can be unlocked by strategies based on the science of learning. These strategies are obvious tools to have in a toolbox. In some ways, these strategies should be *THE* Toolbox.

THERE'S MORE THAN MEETS THE EYE WHEN HARNESSING YOUR TOOLBOX

Here are just a few examples where we *assume* Power Tools are combined by default, but when you take a closer look, that's not always the case.

Learning to Play the Guitar

Let's say you're learning to play the guitar. You could:

- Practice your instrument over and over.

- Concentrate your practice a few days before a performance.

- Receive feedback from a friend who says, "That's correct!" or "That's wrong!," without giving you more information.

In this way, you would be combining retrieval practice, spacing, and feedback – congratulations! Except the small amount of spacing and correct answer feedback might only help you on a performance in the short term, but not learning in the long term. Besides, *how* are you going to improve if you don't know *what* to improve upon?

Learning During Firefighting Training

What about skills-based learning, such as learning how to perform surgeries? Doesn't that require retrieval practice, at least? Consider this example from Dan Johnson, a firefighter and Training Division battalion chief in Bothell, Washington:

> Fire instructors in the greater Puget Sound area must complete a 14-week pre-service academy. Our industry standard is called Fire Instructor 1. The classroom is predominantly lecture-based and students are encouraged to ask questions as they need.
>
> A classroom topic is covered once, usually Monday or Tuesday. Practical topics are covered a few times in a half-day session; for example, raising ladders in the morning and extending fire hoses in the afternoon. On Fridays, students take tests over the textbook chapter from the week. Importantly, these tests must be passed to remain in the academy.

Our feedback is typically corrective, on-the-spot coaching after students perform. In recent years we have started interrupting students if they are performing incorrectly. We correct the technique and have them start over. Our corrective feedback is very specific, while our reinforcing feedback is often quite vague: "Good job!" or "You got it right that time, way to go!"

Sounds like a mix of retrieval practice (e.g., raising ladders), spacing (covering topics across a week), and feedback, right? Dan observed that firefighters were passing their tests in the short term, but they weren't remembering these skills in the long term. Even if you're combining Power Tools, they could be boosting short-term *performance*, but not long-term *learning*.

Learning Statistics with Practice Problems

In graduate school, I (Pooja) took a statistics course.[1] I bought the textbook, I pored over the syllabus, and I was ready to dive in. After 15 weeks of rigorous lectures, practice problems, and exams, I felt prepared to tackle any statistical nightmare that came my way. But now, in retrospect, here's how I'd sum up my experience: *I learned a lot, but I don't remember much.* There was very little retrieval, spacing, or interleaving – even in a math class.

How could a math class lack retrieval? The homework practice problems were challenging, but they were all open-book. I could easily look up the answers along the way. I made homework easy on myself so I could complete the assignments quickly, get good grades, and avoid the uncomfortable feeling of being wrong. (Sound familiar?) During class, we also completed practice problems with peers, but I could lean on them rather than retrieve the answers myself.

How could a math class lack spacing and interleaving? One week we'd learn about various types of probability distributions and the next week we'd move on to chi-square distributions – without ever returning to earlier concepts or discriminating between the two. Once a chapter unit was "learned," we moved on – never to see it again.

Even classes like algebra, foreign language learning, and lab sciences might seem like they use and combine Power Tools by default. And what about homework and worksheets? Aren't they retrieval practice? Well, it depends. Are your students actually retrieving? If students aren't learning much from homework or worksheets, it's probably because *they're not retrieving*; they're re-reading, reviewing, or looking up the answers.

Swap Reviewing for Retrieving

For each of the previous examples, retrieval practice is already built in! Students retrieve when they complete practice problems, respond to writing prompts, and practice an instrument. Even so, constantly ask yourself this: *Are we reviewing or retrieving?*

Recently, a college professor was describing his typical lesson plans. He reflected and shared that he always starts class by saying, "Alright, here's what we did in class yesterday." Take a moment. Based on what you've learned in this book, what could he do differently?

He could simply *ask the students*! When setting the stage for class, asking, "What did we do yesterday?" takes just as long as, "Here's what we did yesterday." The simple swap from you reviewing to students retrieving makes a big difference. So, pay attention to whether you are *reviewing* information with students ("Here's how the writer crafted the introduction") or whether students are *retrieving* ("How did the writer craft the introduction?"). Take advantage of retrieval that's

> *Regardless of your content area, ask yourself, "Are we reviewing or retrieving?"*

already built into your subject area, but also make sure you're not defaulting to reviewing!

When combining Power Tools, take a careful look at what you're already doing – and see if you can make it even more powerful. We'll provide research and strategies soon, but first, let's address another classroom strategy: *cumulative exams.*

> ### Power Up
>
> What's the difference between spacing and interleaving?
> This Power Up is tough! Do your best to retrieve first, and then get feedback from Chapter 4 only *after* you retrieve. Remember, this is no-stakes, so take a guess!

CUMULATIVE EXAMS ARE NOT THE SAME THING AS SPACING AND INTERLEAVING

Do your students take an end-of-the semester cumulative exam over all your course content? If so, you may be thinking, "That's spacing and interleaving!" Maybe, *but maybe not.* Here are two reasons why:

- Students can still cram for cumulative exams.

- Content from the entire semester may be related, but not necessarily similar.

First, *students can (and will) cram for cumulative exams.* They're typically high-stakes, and the amount of knowledge students are being tested on can be daunting. Students re-study material introduced months prior to the exam – a definite form of spacing – but they likely cram in all that information during a panic-filled all-nighter. Is this type of "spacing" the night before an exam going to boost long-term learning? Probably not. As we know from the study by Roddy Roediger and Jeff Karpicke in Chapter 2 on cramming, students will do well on an exam in the short term, but they won't remember much in the long term.

Second, just because content on a cumulative exam is related, *it doesn't mean it's interleaved.* For example, let's say that students in a semester-long course on earth science learn about plate tectonics and the formation of rocks. Do questions about the two related topics require careful discrimination? Probably not. Similarly, a cumulative exam in math could include algebra problems related to linear equations, polynomials, and irrational numbers, but that doesn't mean students are engaging in interleaving. As we mentioned in Chapter 4, the key to interleaving is mixing up *similar* concepts, not just related concepts.

Even if an exam is cumulative, students can (and will) cram!

When it comes to cumulative exams, here are three recommendations:

- Cumulative exams are good, but *frequent lower-stakes cumulative quizzes are better.* By making all course content "fair game" on quizzes (not just from the most recent chapter or unit), students have more frequent retrieval opportunities; they'll space their studying outside of class, and they'll be relieved they don't have to cram. Take the cumulative *exams* you already use and simply split them up into smaller cumulative *quizzes.*

- Ensure that cumulative quizzes, activities, and exams include *similar* concepts that require careful discrimination, not simply related concepts.

- Use spacing and interleaving as *learning* strategies *throughout* the semester, not just strategies that pop up on a high-stakes cumulative exam.

YOUR COURSE DESIGN DRIVES *STUDENTS'* TOOLBOXES

In my (Pooja's) graduate-level statistics class mentioned earlier, there were four chapter tests, followed by a cumulative final exam. How did I study? *I didn't.* I crammed for about 30 minutes right before each test and exam, and guess what – I got perfect grades!

The irony was that I was taking graduate courses on cognitive science the very same semester. Based on what I already knew about how learning and memory work, here's what I should have done as a student:

- I should have answered all the practice problems using a *closed-book* approach and checked my answers afterward. But I had no reason to do so! Had the teacher offered closed-book assignments during class each week, even for five minutes, I wouldn't have been able to "cheat myself" with an open-book approach at home.

- I should have *spaced* my studying throughout the semester. But again, I had no reason to do so. Had the teacher returned to course content throughout the semester and mixed up similar topics, not just on a cumulative exam at the end, I wouldn't have been able to get by with cramming before tests.

In typical high school, college, and even graduate-level course design, students don't have to retrieve, space, interleave, or pay attention to feedback.[2] Unless we take a close look at our course design – even if it includes frequent practice – students will continue to get by with no Toolbox at all. Are we promoting short-term understanding or long-term learning?

> ### Power Up
>
> What is one change you would make to Pooja's statistics course design in order to effectively combine Power Tools?

THE SCIENCE BEHIND COMBINING THE FOUR POWER TOOLS

First, why should you combine Power Tools? Can't they be used separately, depending on the content, lesson, students, and settings? Yes, each Power Tool dramatically improves learning on its own. But when it comes to combining them, long-term learning becomes even more robust, flexible, and memorable.

Scientists have demonstrated that combining Power Tools significantly boosts learning beyond using them in isolation. For example, Katherine Rawson and colleagues conducted a study with college students in an introduction to psychology course. Students participated in the following conditions:

- Spacing *with* retrieval practice. Students used a computerized flashcard program throughout the 14-week semester (e.g., three days after material was presented, after five days, after eight days, etc.).

- Spacing *without* retrieval practice. Students used the computerized program throughout the semester, but they were shown the answers along with the flashcard question (a re-study condition).

- No spacing/no retrieval. Students didn't use the computerized program during the semester (a *business as usual* condition).

The results from this study confirmed exactly what you'd expect: On course exams, student performance was highest in the spacing with retrieval practice (84%), followed by the spacing without retrieval practice (78%), and lowest in the no spacing/no retrieval condition (74%). In other words, combining Power Tools boosted students' learning by an entire letter grade compared to lessons alone![3]

After our discussions about combining Power Tools with Dan, the firefighter and battalion chief, here's how he explained his new approach to academy instructors:

> We will now be combining retrieval practice, spaced practice, and interleaved practice to fasttrack your mastery. *Because your life depends on it.*

Powerful indeed!

Retrieval Practice

Retrieval practice boosts learning by pulling information out of students' heads, rather than cramming information into students heads.

Spacing

Spaced practice boosts learning by spreading lessons and retrieval opportunities out over time so learning is not crammed all at once.

Interleaving

Interleaving boosts learning by mixing up closely related topics, encouraging discrimination between similarities and differences.

Feedback-Driven Metacognition

Feedback-driven metacognition boosts learning by providing the opportunity for students to know what they know and know what they don't know.

PATRICE'S TOOLBOX FOR POWERFUL TEACHING

First, before beginning a chapter or unit in your classroom, I (Patrice) encourage you to ask yourself these *power questions*:

- What is the *essential question* for this chapter?
- What information do my students *have to know* in order to answer it?
- How will I support students in *retrieving* this information?
- At what intervals will I *space* retrieval practice?
- Am I able to *interleave* content and mix it up?
- What types of *feedback* can I use to support my students' *metacognition*?

Perhaps overwhelming at first, these six questions have become my basis for lesson planning. For a chapter on Ancient Greece, here's how I plan my lessons using my six power questions and my Toolbox:

- My essential question and most important takeaway is this: How did the government of Ancient Greece differ from that of Ancient Rome?
- The key facts/terminology/people that are pertinent to my essential question include oligarchy, monarchy, democracy, assembly, republic, representative, Senate, dictator, Caesar, and Pax Romana.
- Students will retrieve key facts through Mini-Quizzes, Retrieval Guides, Retrieval Cards, and Brain Drains. My end-of-unit celebration of everything students have learned will be an essay answering the essential question.
- Retrieval will be spaced through end-of-week Big Basket Quizzes (BBQs), Four Steps to Metacognition, and Power Tickets. In addition, I plan spaced retrieval by jotting down questions into my calendar. As I do lesson planning, I have previous learning ready to go at just the right time. (And I don't forget to include it!)
- I incorporate Blasts from the Past linking and interleaving new knowledge to previously learned knowledge. This, too, I add into my calendar.

- To ensure students are able to identify metacognition, I incorporate daily choral work and Think-Pair-Share. I also provide feedback on Mini-Quizzes, BBQs, and Retrieval Cards.

My sample lesson plan in Figure 6.2 includes essential questions, retrieval activities throughout the chapter, and low-stakes assessments. Please note that when information is read and discussed, I am not imitating a class scene from *Ferris Bueller's Day Off!* My classes are lively, filled with stories, video clips, reenactments, ponderings, interaction, songs, and humor.

Figure 6.2 A sample lesson plan Patrice uses to incorporate and combine Power Tools throughout the week.

Monday	Tuesday
Introduction to the Essential Question	Mini-Quiz over Monday's material
Ponder and link to previous learning	Turn in Mini-Quizzes and discuss
Introduction to the new chapter	Choral work with Monday's Retrieval Guide
Choral work with pertinent terms	Read, discuss, and complete new Retrieval Guide
Read, discuss, and complete Retrieval Guide	Turn and Talk/Exit Ticket
Turn and Talk/Exit Ticket	

Wednesday	Thursday
Hand back and discuss Tuesday's Mini-Quiz	Hand back and discuss Wednesday's Mini-Quiz
Mini-Quiz over Tuesday's material	Mini-Quiz over Wednesday's material
Turn in Mini-Quizzes and discuss	Turn in Mini-Quizzes and discuss
Choral work with Tuesday's Retrieval Guide	Think-Pair-Share from Wednesday's activity
Activity (e.g., Reader's Theater)	Ponder and link to the Essential Question
Turn and Talk/Exit Ticket	Read, discuss, and complete new Retrieval Guide
	Turn and Talk/Exit Ticket

Friday	
Big Basket Quiz (BBQ), turn in and discuss	
Choral work on all key terms	
Think-Pair-Share with Essential Question	
New activity	
Turn and Talk/Exit Ticket	

Incorporate Power Tickets into Your Toolbox

Power Tickets are a tool I developed as a way to incorporate retrieval, spacing, interleaving, and feedback. Note this tool can be used at various grade levels and most disciplines. Ideally, they should be given every three weeks. This guarantees that students have an opportunity to retrieve over multiple lessons, chapters, and units. (*Hint:* A good rule of thumb is to schedule it on your calendar; as you write up your weekly lesson plan you will remember to include it.)

Power Tickets are *not* used as assessments; rather, they are an opportunity for students to examine their metacognition through the use of Power Tools and create a study tool for exams. Make sure you choose topics based on essential questions. Here is how a Power Ticket works:

1. Give a blank copy of the Power Ticket to each student.

2. Teacher announces topics based on essential questions and important information. You can be general (Today we talked about the Cold War, last month we talked about World War II, etc.) Or, you can start out more specific (Today we talked about Josef Stalin, last month we talked about President Roosevelt, etc.). You can make the topics general or specific – it depends on what you want your students to retrieve.

3. Individually, students write down three facts about each topic. Students choose where to begin and how to complete the Power Ticket. This should take about five minutes or less.

4. For another few minutes, students compare their answers with two other students, adding to their Power Tickets.

5. Students come together to share in a whole class discussion, adding to their Power Tickets with additional facts (Figure 6.3).

A popular spin on Power Tickets are *Retrieval Grids*. Kate Jones, a teacher in the United Arab Emirates and author of

Figure 6.3 Example of a Power Ticket: Retrieval, spacing, interleaving, and metacognition at your fingertips!

Power Ticket
What did we talk about...

	Today?	Yesterday?	Last week?	Last month?	Last quarter?	Last semester?
	The Cuban Missile Crisis	Cold War Alliances	China's Cultural Revolution	World War II	The French Revolution	Ancient Rome
Write one fact						
Write a second fact						
Write a third fact						

Love to Teach: Research and Resources for Every Classroom, first created Retrieval Grids after learning about Power Tools and desirable difficulties. In Retrieval Grids, each box contains a specific prompt for retrieval practice (e.g., who was Josef Stalin?). Questions about spaced material are in color-coded boxes (e.g., blue for info from the previous week, yellow for the previous month, etc.), but mixed up all over the grid. Again, like Power Tickets or even a bingo card, students jump around and answer Retrieval Grid questions at their own pace. As Kate put it, Retrieval Grids encourage students to "recap, recall, revise!"

Of course, Power Tickets and Retrieval Grids combine Power Tools perfectly:

- Spacing: Students are challenged to retrieve a concept or answer to a question from previous lessons.

- Interleaving: Power Tickets and Retrieval Grids can include similar concepts (e.g., names for different historical figures) that require students to discriminate.

- Feedback: After completing this activity, students can check their work individually, Think-Pair-Share, and/or receive elaborative feedback from you.

As always, keep this low- or no-stakes! If you want to give students points for filling in boxes, keep the point system minimal. You could give points depending on how far back they can retrieve concepts, but there don't have to be any points at all.

Develop Mnemonics to Support *Students' Toolboxes*

How, as teachers, can we aid our students remembering information? Saying something once certainly doesn't work. Spaced practice is a known and effective strategy. In addition, research demonstrates that if students can connect a cue using mnemonics, they retain information even better.[4] When students generate their own mnemonics, this benefit increases even more.[5]

I (Patrice) figured this out when I was in high school. Throughout high school, college, and beyond, I realized that what works well for me is to make an association or mnemonic. Ever since, I actively look for ways to create connections. As a teacher, it became a research-based strategy I shared with students, too.

For example, when studying the ancient civilization of Mesopotamia, students learn that Sargon ruled Sumer for 56 years. Taking a closer look at this mnemonic, how many letters are there in Sumer? Five. How many letters are there in Sargon? Six. How many years did he rule? 56 years (Figure 6.4).

About three months after the students learned this, one day I randomly asked the students, "How long did Sargon rule Sumer?" Over half of the class took a brief moment and responded in unison, "Fifty-six years!"

Figure 6.4 Mnemonics and visual clues helped students remember that Sargon ruled Sumer for 56 years.

As another example, I taught students about Ancient Rome and the three branches of government. The most powerful branch that controlled the money was the Senate. On the board, I wrote the mnemonic $enate. After a few months, as a Blast from the Past, I asked the students, "Who controlled the money in the early Roman Republic?" Probably 99% of the class didn't even hesitate before shouting out the answer – the Senate!

I also like to share personal stories when creating mnemonics, which makes them more memorable. For example, I lived in Chicago long ago and I was an avid Cubs fan. I spent many an afternoon in the bleachers at Wrigley Field. In my classroom, when we discuss World War II, I write on the board: CUBS F. Then I would ask my students, what does my being a Cubs fan have to do with the main Allies in World War II? Years later, they have no trouble remembering that the Allies were *China*, *United States*, *Britain*, *Soviet Union*, and *France*!

Power Up

Take a look at your curriculum. Can you find mnemonics and links that may help your students make connections to aid retrieval?

By adjusting my lesson plans, using Power Tickets, and sharing mnemonics in my classroom, I went from simply using Power Tools to creating and harnessing my own powerful Toolbox. By taking a look at strategies I was *already* using and adding a few tweaks, I turned them into *powerful* strategies. By teaching students how to learn, they in turn, helped me create new ways to incorporate Power Tools.

PRACTICAL STRATEGIES FOR A POWERFUL COMBINATION IN YOUR CLASSROOM

Combining Power Tools in your classroom may sound daunting. But it isn't! As Jay Dennis, a high school economics teacher from Mississippi, said:

> This research is directly responsible for my class doubling their AP Micro scores from previous years. My class went from a 30% pass rate to a 60% pass rate when I began utilizing Power Tools. The principles from this research have given me the ability to show tangible results in the classroom and instill that confidence in my students.

For Jay, and also for you, combining Power Tools doesn't require an overhaul of what you're already doing; just a little creativity to unleash the science of learning.

> **Power Up**
>
> Think back: At what age did King Tut become a pharaoh?[6]

Combine Power Tools with Brain Dumps

Brain Dumps, described in Chapter 3 on retrieval practice strategies, are simple, quick, and demonstrated to boost learning. They're powerful as a standalone activity, but here are two ways you can incorporate spacing and feedback:

- To quickly add spacing, ask students to write down what they can remember from *yesterday* or last week.

- To quickly add feedback, have students discuss their similarities and differences with each other (Turn and Talk or Think-Pair-Share) for only a minute or two before moving on.

Combine Power Tools with Write, Leave, Retrieve

We love the Toolbox strategy *Write, Leave, Retrieve* by Maggie, an early intervention coordinator from Wisconsin:

1. Have students *write* down what they know using a Brain Dump, Two Things, entry ticket, etc.

2. *Leave* the retrieval as-is and move on to your day's lesson or another topic.

3. After a while, have students *retrieve* the same information again.

In other words, students *write* what they know, *leave it* for spacing, and *retrieve again*. You could provide feedback on the first retrieval, the second retrieval, or both. Even if you don't provide feedback, it's a simple approach to combine retrieval with spacing.

Think-Pair-Share? Think Again!

Think-Pair-Share is engaging. Whether you teach at an elementary school or a medical school, you've probably heard of the instructional strategy *Think-Pair-Share*.

Here's how it typically works:

1. Students *think* about a topic in response to a question or prompt.

2. Students *pair up* with another student and talk about their reflection.

3. Students *share* their thoughts in a larger class discussion.

Think-Pair-Share is a fantastic way to facilitate student engagement. Simple, quick, and interactive – the trifecta for a valuable instructional strategy. But wait! *How can we ensure that students are learning during Think-Pair-Share*, instead of talking about their favorite Netflix shows and brainstorming plans for the weekend?

During Think-Pair-Share, it's possible (or probable) that:

- Not all students are engaged in thinking.

- Not all students are engaged in sharing.

Here's how to put your Toolbox to use and make Think-Pair-Share even more powerful in your classroom:

- Engage *every* student in retrieval practice by having students write down their response to a prompt, *instead of simply thinking about it.*

- Engage *every* student in spacing and interleaving by asking about closely related topics from *the day before* or the week before, not material you're covering right now.

- Engage *every* student in feedback by having students switch papers and add one or Two Things to another student's paper that were *not* already included.

Think-Pair-Share can also encourage students to reflect on their metacognition during or after the exercise. Add these two questions, developed by Bonnie Nieves, a science teacher from Connecticut:

- Did you write down any misinformation?
- Why do you think you remembered what you did?

With each of these Think-Pair-Share recommendations, you can make small adjustments to combine Power Tools *and* help students drive their own retrieval, spacing, interleaving, feedback, and metacognition. Again, take what you already do and just make small adjustments for even more powerful learning!

To create your Toolbox, take what you already do and make small adjustments for even more powerful learning.

COMBINE POWER TOOLS WITH TECHNOLOGY

So far, we've emphasized the simplicity of Power Tools and how to implement evidence-based strategies using good, old-fashioned paper and pencil. Of course, technology apps, tools, websites, and programs have enormous possibilities for using Power Tools, too! They often have a variety of prompts for retrieval practice, provide immediate feedback, track student performance over time, and enable you to space out and mix content over time.

But until recently, conversations around educational technology focused on *engagement*, not learning. For example, in 2008, I (Pooja) read an article in the *New York Times* with dismay. It was about how clickers were all the rage in schools across the country. It featured colorful photos of students using clickers and quotes from teachers who were thrilled with students' newfound enthusiasm in class.[7]

The article focused on how clickers could help boost engagement and gamification in the classroom. *But it only mentioned the word "learn" twice.*

As cognitive scientists who conduct research on learning, my colleagues and I were baffled. By the time the *New York Times* article was published, research on retrieval practice had clearly demonstrated huge benefits for learning. So why wasn't learning featured more prominently in an article about clickers in schools? (My colleagues and I wrote a letter to the editor of the *New York Times*; it didn't get published.)

As you now know, based on the simple research-based principles behind Power Tools, technology can increase long-term learning, higher-order thinking, and transfer of knowledge, not just engagement and motivation. But *which* tech tools are best for boosting achievement, based on the science of learning? We're asked this question often, and because tech tools change year to year (even day to day!), we want to empower *you* to answer this question, since you know your content and classroom best. Here are some questions to think about when exploring tech tools and harnessing the science of learning:

- Big picture: Which tech tools incorporate research-based features and strategies derived from Power Tools? Does the technology company discuss or cite any research from the science of learning?

- Does the tech tool truly require students to actually retrieve what they know, or can students get by with simplistic matching games and flashcards they can flip over too easily? Research has shown that when students quiz themselves at home via websites, student exam performance can increase by an entire letter grade.[8]

- Does it provide flexibility in terms of retrieval format, including free-recall (Brain Dumps), multiple-choice questions, or short-answer questions? What about control over how many times a student has to get a question correct before moving on? Is retrieval practice timed, or can it be self-based to decrease student anxiety?

- Does it provide no-stakes or low-stakes grading? Does it emphasize formative and/or summative assessment?

- Does it let you control the amount of spacing between content? Is content ever repeated back-to-back? Is there a shuffle feature to incorporate interleaving?

- Does it let you control the type of feedback (e.g., right/wrong, elaborative feedback, etc.)? Is feedback immediate or delayed?

- Does it allow students to track their own data over time so they can reflect on their metacognition? Can students provide judgments of learning, predictions of future learning, or confidence ratings?

- Of course, time and money are additional constraints. Does the tech tool provide content or provide a crowdsourced resource of retrieval practice questions? Do you have to manually write in feedback, especially if it's elaborative?

In asking these questions, we want you to think critically. Cognitive scientist Stephen Chew described this interaction between technology and the science of learning well:

> You don't need technology to harness the power of the science of learning, and just because you use technology doesn't mean you're truly harnessing the power of cognitive science, either.

You're probably using edtech tools in your instruction and you're probably using Power Tools already, too. With these questions, ask yourself, "How can I shift conversations about strategies that focus solely on engagement, to conversations about engagement *and* learning?"

CLASSROOM STRATEGIES FOR YOUR POWERFUL TOOLBOX

It's time for a Brain Dump! (We warned you, we practice what we preach.) For each strategy in the first column, describe it in your own words in the second column. Don't cheat!

Strategy	Write your own description!
Brain Dumps	
Two Things	
Retrieve-Taking	
Retrieval Guides	
Mini-Quizzes	
Weekly Quizzes	
Pre-Tests	
The Dice Game	
The Fishbowl	
The Lightning Round	
Retrieval Cards	
Four Steps to Metacognition	
Metacognition Sheets	
Breathe and Retrieve	
Metacognition Line-Up	

NOTES

1. These course details have been changed. Pooja remembers a lot from her graduate-level statistics courses!

2. For tips on combining Power Tools in online environments and blended courses, we recommend the book *The Productive Online Professor* by Bonni Stachowiak, as well as her website, www.teachinginhighered.com.

3. Rawson, K. A., Dunlosky, J., and Sciartelli, S. M. (2013). The power of successive relearning: Improving performance on course exams and long-term retention. *Educational Psychology Review* 25: 523–548.

4. Putnam, A. L. (2015). Mnemonics in education: Current research and applications. *Translational Issues in Psychological Science* 1: 130–139.

5. Tullis, J. G., and Finley, J. R. (2018). Self-generated memory cues: Effective tools for learning, training, and remembering. *Policy Insights from the Behavioral and Brain Sciences* 5: 179–186.

6. Check Chapter 2 for the answer. This is a perfect example of combining retrieval practice, spacing, and feedback!

7. Hu, W. (2008, January 28). Students click, and a quiz becomes a game. *The New York Times*.

8. Roediger, H. L., Agarwal, P. K., McDaniel, M. A., et al. (2011). Test-enhanced learning in the classroom: Long-term improvements from quizzing. *Journal of Experimental Psychology: Applied* 17: 382–395.

Chapter 7

Keeping It Real: Use Power Tools to Tackle Challenges, *Not* Add to Them

We're educators. And we know what it's like to throw the baby out with the bathwater or revamp your teaching. That's why, in this chapter, *we're keeping it real.*

As educators, there are a number of mountains to climb before we can make changes to our instruction: time, resources, and support – to name just a few. In this chapter, we address nine challenges when implementing Power Tools, even if you're just making small tweaks like using Brain Dumps and Two Things. We're not asking you to completely upend what you've been doing. But we hope that by keeping it real, we can make powerful teaching even easier for you.

NINE HESITATIONS, CHALLENGES, AND MOUNTAINS BETWEEN YOU AND POWERFUL TEACHING

1. Do I have to spend more time preparing for class if I use Power Tools?

2. Do I have to spend more time grading if I use Power Tools?

3. When I spend time using Power Tools, how can I cover the same amount of material?

4. Will my students get lower grades if I use Power Tools?

5. How can I adapt Power Tools for diverse students from a range of backgrounds and abilities?

6. Do I have to spend money on Power Tools?

7. There are so many Power Tools and strategies. Where do I start?

8. There's a lot of stuff out there about "brain-based learning." Is that the same thing as Power Tools?

9. When I use Power Tools, how can I find support beyond my school?

First, we break down three of the most common challenges: limited time before class, during class, and after class. Whether we're trying to cover everything we've planned or tackle a mountain of grading, there's always more to be done than hours in the day. It's no surprise, then, that the most frequent concerns about Power Tools have to do with time – whether you'll need to prepare far in advance, if they increase grading, and how long they'll take to use in class.

DO I HAVE TO SPEND MORE TIME PREPARING FOR CLASS IF I USE POWER TOOLS?

Nope, no extra prep time. The key to minimizing prep time using Power Tools is to identify what you're *already* doing and tweak it, even just a little bit. Here are four quick tweaks that require no prep time whatsoever:

- Instead of reviewing, "Here's what we did yesterday," *ask your students*, "What did we do yesterday?"

- When a student asks a question, have the class retrieve and provide the answer (instead of you retrieving it). Again, no additional planning, just flip the source of retrieval from you to your students.

- Ask students to retrieve and write down Two Things they remember about a lesson last week, Two Things about a fictional character, Two Things about the brain . . . anything! There's absolutely no planning needed for Two Things – you can come up with the question on the fly.

- You can even encourage students to come up with retrieval questions in advance, so you can use them during a following class – literally no prep whatsoever!

DO I HAVE TO SPEND MORE TIME GRADING IF I USE POWER TOOLS?

No extra grading! In fact, keeping Power Tools *as grade-free as possible* improves learning, decreases student anxiety, and emphasizes that they're learning strategies, not assessment strategies. Here's another way to think about it: Do we really have to give students a grade *every time* they retrieve something?

Why do we get so stuck on grading anything and everything students retrieve? When you're implementing Power Tools, *remove grades altogether*. There's no need to collect papers, assign points, or enter anything into the gradebook. Power Tools *free* us from grading; they don't increase grading. We're not saying grades aren't important; we're simply saying that, by focusing on Power Tools as *learning* strategies, there's nothing additional to grade. Power Tools *maximize learning* and *minimize grading*, not the other way around.

In Chapter 8, we focus specifically on building a supportive environment by reducing the stakes for students and deemphasizing grades (decreasing grading, too!). In the meantime, here are two quick tips to give students *grade-less feedback*. For example:

Power Tools free you from grading! Harness them to maximize learning and minimize grading, not the other way around.

- Facilitate a brief discussion after Two Things, rather than collecting papers and spending hours grading.

- After a Brain Dump, have students keep their papers as notes – no need to collect or grade them, either.

WHEN I SPEND TIME USING POWER TOOLS, HOW CAN I COVER THE SAME AMOUNT OF MATERIAL?

There's so much we need and want to cover, but we also want students to remember all that content, too. How can we implement Power Tools in our classrooms, but cover all our course content at the same time?

Take a look at Figure 7.1 and consider this example:

If you teach 100 facts and students remember 60% without retrieval practice, that's 60 facts.

If you teach 90 things and students remember 80% *with* retrieval practice, that's 72 facts.

In this example, you're teaching slightly less, *but students are remembering more*. This tradeoff is small, but it can yield a large impact for student learning. Because students learn more from retrieval practice, we *save* time – we don't have to re-teach what students already forgot.

Figure 7.1 When it comes to Power Tools, teach a little less content and get a huge bang for your buck. Swap students' forgetting of lots of content for students' robust learning of a little less content.

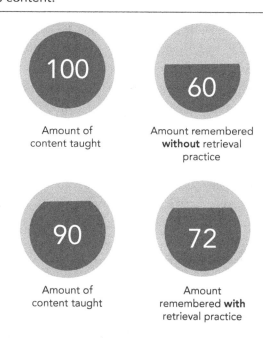

Amount of content taught: 100

Amount remembered **without** retrieval practice: 60

Amount of content taught: 90

Amount remembered **with** retrieval practice: 72

As another example, K–12 educator and author Matt Miller describes a time tradeoff he makes in his classroom: He gives students a few minutes to run around and use up energy at the start of class, so they come to class more ready to learn. Does he trade-off a little teaching time for physical activity? Yes. But it's the benefit he sees *after* that tradeoff – just a small adjustment of teaching time – that counts most.

We always have time tradeoffs to make – in teaching and in life. And we have a single priority in our classroom: learning. Start small by swapping students' forgetting of lots of content for students' robust learning of a little less content. *We need to make sure that our time spent teaching is time spent learning* – not time spent reviewing past content or zooming through new content. In thinking about tradeoffs, ask yourself this question from cognitive scientist Joseph Kim: "Am I giving lessons to be remembered or lessons to be forgotten?"

You may not be able to cover the exact same amount of content, but with Power Tools, students *remember more and forget less*. Why cover more content that will be forgotten, rather than less content that will be remembered? After spending more time on retrieval and less time on content, Heather, a microbiology instructor, realized the following:

> I think my students have a better grasp of material this semester. They seem to be able to use previously covered information in a more nuanced way, making relationships to new content easier. In fact, I'm wondering if my class could be a bit more "rigorous" as a result of the students being able to apply material more effectively this year.

When I (Patrice) first started teaching, my content was world history and the textbook covered *everything*; it was an unrealistic curriculum that led to shallow, forgetful learning. I worked together with my principal, Dr. Roger Chamberlain, to define a curriculum that would increase breadth and depth for our students. We limited the content to three continents. We looked at how my content scaffolded into the overall district map. Together we made a realistic plan. Soon, I found Power Tools to be the missing link that added the breadth and depth.

This topic is an important conversation I frequently have with teachers and administrators. Questions I ask:

- What is the most important information for your students to learn?
- How is it defined?

- What's in the curriculum map?
- How does it align with the district map?
- What is on the standardized tests?

These are valid questions, often determining purposes of particular classes. I encourage teachers and administrators to take a hard look and separate the "stuff from the fluff." What truly is the important "stuff" that students need to know versus the "fluff" that aids discussions but doesn't require retrieval? Use Power Tools only on the "stuff." You will find that you are not only able to cover the important information, you will spend much *less* time on reviews for tests, semester exams, and tying in previously learned information from previous years.

> *With Power Tools, students remember more and forget less.*

WILL MY STUDENTS GET LOWER GRADES IF I USE POWER TOOLS?

Students will struggle with Power Tools initially, but you and your students will see a boost in learning over time. When it comes to desirable difficulties, Power Tools challenge learning. But that initial struggle is a *good* thing for long-term learning. When it comes to learning, *easier doesn't mean better.*

Because Power Tools might lead to students performing more poorly, it may give students, teachers, and parents the impression that these strategies don't work. Students might give up too soon, and we might be tempted to give up too soon, as well. Try to avoid this common misconception that poor initial performance means poor long-term learning. Based on a century of research, how learning works is often *opposite* from our intuition. Here are three things to keep in mind:

- How you do now is *not* how you'll do in a few days.

- Don't stop just because it's hard.

- Don't stop just because it seems like it's not working.

Easier said than done, right? We don't want to abandon Power Tools, but if our students struggle, we might feel that it's time to try something else. In upcoming chapters, we present how to approach conversations with students and parents about desirable difficulties, and what that means for learning in both the short term and the long term.

Just like a New Year's resolution to go to the gym, you may be excited to exercise for a few days or weeks. But soon, you don't notice any improvement, old habits set in, and you stop exercising. The same thing can happen with Power Tools! The trick is making it through the initial struggle, sticking with it, and looking forward to the benefits over the horizon.

We also want to point out that sometimes, desirable difficulties can be *too* difficult. It's tough to pinpoint exactly when that happens. Simply being mindful and gauging your students' discomfort level is important. Are they struggling a bit outside their comfort zone, or are they having a *really* hard time keeping up?

Again, start small. Simply include a few quiz questions from earlier in the semester; do a quick Brain Dump in class; or simply give students a retrieval prompt as they enter the classroom. We know that Power Tools aren't challenging to implement, but they will be challenging for learning. We hope this quote from Claudia, a math coach in New York, puts this challenge into perspective:

> Teachers need to trust that if they let go of the trapeze bar they are on, the trapeze bar they see ahead will actually be in their grasp.

HOW CAN I ADAPT POWER TOOLS FOR DIVERSE STUDENTS FROM A RANGE OF BACKGROUNDS AND ABILITIES?

When it comes to diverse learners, research demonstrates that Power Tools boost learning for students with cognitive disabilities,[1] lower-ability students,[2] students with attention deficit/ hyperactivity disorder (ADHD),[3] and second language learners.[4] Power Tools also improve learning beyond traditional classroom settings, and diversity comes in many forms. There's also research demonstrating that retrieval practice improves learning for people with traumatic brain injury,[5] multiple sclerosis,[6] and HIV.[7]

How can we effectively adapt Power Tools in our classrooms with diverse learners? When we consider our own students in middle school and college, they represent quite a diverse range of abilities, backgrounds, and experiences! We know that Power Tools aren't "one size fits all." But they're powerful because they're *flexible*. Here are techniques we use to adapt Power Tools and accommodate all learners, abilities, and disabilities.

Keeping It Real with Power Tools in Patrice's Classroom

I have all types of students. Every public education classroom has diversity in some form, some having more diversity than others. I would like to share how Power Tools have been successful for my students.

Special Education

I usually have between 10 and 16 students with individualized education plans (IEPs) each year; they are interspersed across my classes. As the use of Power Tools became more prevalent in my teaching repertoire, questions emerged for me to explore:

- How best can I assist the special education teacher with the introduction of new material?

- How can we strengthen our collaboration with students?
- Are Power Tools effective for IEP students?
- How likely are students able to retain introductory information from my class and carry it over for small group instruction with the special education teacher?

In all classes, Pre-Tests, post-tests, and reviews are implemented using clickers. Questions are on the SmartBoard; I read all questions and answer options out loud. By sharing this clicker information with my fellow teacher, we were consistent in terminology. I also shared my mnemonics (as did the students!). This consistency gave the IEP students increased opportunities for retrieval and spacing.

I saw phenomenal change between the Pre-Tests, post-tests, and reviews. I made no modifications for IEP students; *the same questions were used for all students.* Upon my own analysis, I discovered that most of my IEP students *doubled* their own scores from Pre-Test to review. Chapter after chapter. Year after year.

I used the same Retrieval Routines for all students as well: Mini-Quizzes, Retrieval Cards, Retrieval Guides, Metacognition Sheets, Brain Drains, and more. I worked closely with the special education teacher to identify if any modifications were needed on an individual basis; however, the great majority of students did not need any of the strategies to be revised.

I specifically remember a student; I shall call her Bailey. By the sixth-grade, Bailey had always been in self-contained special education classrooms. It was thought by her teachers that she would benefit from the socialization she would acquire in my class. However, not only was she getting the socialization; she was also learning the material! She was doing very well in my class. In fact, one day, I had asked her special education and speech therapy teachers to observe. When asked the following question, "When did World War I end?" she was able to answer: "The eleventh hour of the eleventh day of the eleventh month, 1918." Needless to say, jaws dropped.

My takeaways from Power Tools with special education:

- The Retrieval Routines of Power Tools and strategies work for all students.
- Coordination of Power Tools and strategies with the special education teacher provided increased opportunities for retrieval practice, spacing, and feedback-driven metacognition.
- Retrieval Routines strengthen modifications and provide added support for students.

Social-Emotional Learning

A topic receiving increased press recently is *social-emotional learning,* and one particular aspect I have witnessed in my own classroom deals with trauma. I've seen students whose families have gone through bitter divorces. Some parents have cancer, other parents have died. Some students live with grandparents or other relatives. In some homes, drugs are prevalent. Some parents are in prison. One student may live in a mansion while someone else in the same class lives in a trailer with so many cracks the winter winds swirl inside. There are those who have been mercilessly bullied and those who have internalized failure. My students are 11 years old.

Every single student found success in my safe classroom using Power Tools. How can we, as teachers, allow students to fail or feel defeat when it seems, for some, life hasn't given them a single break? I want to shout from the mountaintops how vital it is to teach students about learning and provide them with an avenue for accomplishment! I have been so lucky to have former students contact me as successful adults, telling me how experiences in sixth-grade helped them get through some really tough times.

What if Power Tools began in elementary school and continued through high school and beyond? Could this have an impact on future dropout rates? Maybe poverty levels? Or social-emotional learning? Power Tools make a difference for all students – even beyond learning.

Keeping It Real with Power Tools in Pooja's Classroom

Recently, I had a college student from Madagascar whose father passed away during the middle of the semester. Another student was a first-generation college student who struggled to navigate the financial aid system, and many of my students pay their way through school by juggling multiple jobs. Also, more than 30% of my students are English language learners who have difficulty reading, writing, or speaking in English.

Even with these challenges, all of my students are in school to learn. They have a range of abilities, backgrounds, and responsibilities, but to me, learning is universal. Here are my approaches to diversity and accommodations in my classroom and how I adapt Power Tools to transform learning for *all* learners.

Diverse Learners

I aim to treat *all* of my students equally, regardless of race, ethnicity, origin, disability, ability, gender, sexuality, or socioeconomic status. As a cognitive scientist, I know that this may not always be the case (we all have internal biases that are difficult to change), but it's a core principle in my teaching. Just because a student has a disability, for instance, does *not* mean that they can't learn and contribute as much as – or more than – other students. Diversity comes in many forms, as does learning, but my expectations for all students are the same. This does not mean I expect all students to get the same grades; it means that my application of basic research-based principles (like Power Tools) applies for *all students*, not just some students.

In order to apply Power Tools for all students, it's so important to me to build a supportive environment from Day 1. In Chapter 8, we present a number of strategies for creating a welcoming space for students, but in the meantime, I find that empathizing with students goes a long way in helping them feel comfortable – across the diversity spectrum. For instance, when my student's father passed away, my response was, "Wow, that's tough. How are you feeling?" rather than, "I'm sorry for your loss." Simply asking how students are doing, especially during the first minute of class as students walk in, makes them feel welcome. The same goes for learning with Power Tools: I check in with students frequently, acknowledge the initial challenge of the desirable difficulty, and point out the small "wins" when students remember something from the previous week or month.

Diverse college students have diverse responsibilities in life, too. How can I even begin to encourage them to show up to class and be open to Power Tools? *By making Power Tools low-stakes.* In my class, students are present to learn and retrieve, not just to take a midterm or a final. My attendance and grading policies are firm, but accommodating. When it comes to my weekly retrieval practices, for example, I drop the lowest four grades and each one is worth only 2% of students' total grade. This lowers the stakes and students become *more* mindful of missing class versus picking up an extra shift for their job, going to a doctor's appointment, or catching up on sleep. (Note that if they blow off *all* of my retrieval practices, their grade will be lowered by 25%.) I once had a student say, "This is the best attendance policy ever!" It gives students wiggle room when they need it – whether for religious holidays, sleep, work, or otherwise – but it also sets a clear expectation that all students are held to the same standard.

If a student requests a particular accommodation, I try my best to provide it while still using Power Tools. For example, I created a notebook system with one of my students who had ADHD and frequently spoke out of turn; I developed methods to support another student who is blind who couldn't check her email regularly; and I worked hard to avoid using idioms (e.g., "choking under pressure") during class to avoid confusing any students who were not familiar with these phrases. With low-stakes Power Tools, I've been able to incorporate these accommodations, in large part, because my students feel *more* comfortable asking for help when they need it – they feel comfortable retrieving and writing down what they can in my supportive classroom environment.

Adult Learners

What about adult learners? Here is an email I received from Dan Johnson, the firefighter and battalion chief mentioned in Chapter 6:

> Many firefighting classes we teach during recruit academies and in-service training have no classroom setting. The common perception of adult learning in the field includes treating students nicely, never saying anything negative, aiming to be their best friend, etc. Are there best practices or recommendations for field classes with adult learners?

I also teach adult learners in my graduate-level courses (about science and education, not firefighting!). Adults, including us as educators, are always learning new knowledge and seeking ways to improve their skills. Which brings me to this question: How do we apply Power Tools outside the classroom, especially with adult learners?

Based on my experience, I recommend starting a conversation with adult learners using everyday life examples beyond the classroom: What did you do last weekend? What is the name of your first childhood friend? Where did you park your car? These types of questions get us all engaged in thinking about learning and memory in ways we don't on an everyday basis.

We provide more examples of everyday learning questions (we call them Retrieval Warm-Ups) in Chapter 8, but this entry into how learning works applies for all learners – regardless of age or setting.

Next, extend the conversation to a context more appropriate for adults. For example, ask adult learners, "If you just met someone new at a work event, how can you remember their name better?" or "If you're training a new employee, which Power Tools can you use to help *them* remember?" Engage adult learners in the conversation not just about their own learning, but about learning around them too.

Also, when it comes to learning outside the classroom, we provide a number of recommendations in Chapter 6 to build on what you're already doing. Many adults use at least one Power Tool, perhaps without realizing it. With adult learners, a greater depth of conversation can be explored, and basic Power Tools work just the same for all learners.

All of this might sound like I don't make any accommodations at all. To the contrary, I do. By emphasizing learning strategies, spacing out content, interleaving and mixing it up, and providing elaborative feedback, (1) flexibility is built in, (2) students learn more and feel more confident, and (3) everything is low-stakes, so they feel more comfortable holding themselves to the same expectations as other students in class. Power Tools aren't confining for diverse learners – they're empowering.

Power Tools aren't confining for diverse learners – they're empowering.

DO I HAVE TO SPEND MONEY ON POWER TOOLS?

No! This is one of the reasons we love Power Tools. You can implement retrieval, spacing, interleaving, and feedback simply on paper and pencil. Of course, there are many popular tech tools that incorporate Power Tools, but even strategies like Brain Dumps and the Four Steps to Metacognition are powerful, simple, and free.

THERE ARE SO MANY POWER TOOLS. WHERE DO I START?

Start small. Pick one just strategy or one Power Tool that seems doable to you, with your students, and your content. Ask yourself this question: How can I implement a strategy or Power Tool *tomorrow*?

To get your feet wet, think about implementing retrieval, spacing, interleaving, or feedback-driven metacognition in your own life. How could you use Power Tools to help you remember where you parked your car or what you did last weekend?

Also, check the Retrieval Guide at the end of this book to get an idea of which Power Tools are clearest to you and which strategies resonate most. There's no need to dive straight in! As a high school teacher realized, "It's so important to move in gradually with a small behavior change, instead of trying to go from 0 to 100 mph instantly."

THERE'S A LOT OF STUFF OUT THERE ABOUT "BRAIN-BASED LEARNING." IS THAT THE SAME THING AS POWER TOOLS?

Let's talk about "brain-based learning." First, take a look at Figure 7.2.

Next, here's a quick Power Up:

Power Up

What are the first five words that pop into your head when you look at Figure 7.2 or think about the word *brain*?

Figure 7.2 It's just a brain!

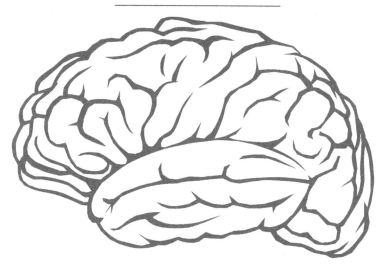

It's no surprise that brains are fascinating. People love to talk about brains, look at pictures of brains, and read about brains. But let's be honest: "brain-based learning" doesn't really mean anything. Everything we do as human beings is brain-based! When we walk, talk, cook, think about summer vacation, and brush our teeth, we're using our brain.

That's why you can swap "brain-based learning" with neuro-learning, hemispheric-integration, brain-based teaching, or any other words that look neuroscience-y. These phrases don't mean anything specific, and they're what scientists literally call *neuro-babble*. More and more frequently, you can find brain pictures on educational products, books, t-shirts, and websites. (We've collected a few of those brain-shaped squeezable stress toys they hand out at conferences, too.)

What does this mean when it comes to the science of learning, Power Tools, and your classroom? As a powerful teacher, you need to be aware of how brains are being used to *impress* you, not to *inform* you. We want to empower you to know the difference and make informed decisions about research you can trust versus neurobabble.

First, *buyer beware*. Brain pictures are everywhere, and it's because brains are mysterious and intriguing. In a clever research study by scientists Dave McCabe and Alan Castel, college students were asked to read fictional news articles related to neuroscience (e.g., "Playing video games benefits attention").[8] Half of the articles contained pictures of brains and half of the articles did not. When students were asked to rate how much the article made sense, they consistently gave higher ratings for the articles with brain pictures than those without brains. In other words, even college students (who were taking psychology courses!) placed more trust in something when they saw a picture of a brain. Be aware of this "brain bias" the next time you're confronted with a brain.

Also, be judicious when it comes to brains in professional development programs and resources. Why? Because of what are called *neuromyths*. We're all fascinated with brains, but that also means there are many misconceptions about brains – and people who take advantage of our misconceptions.

For example, which of these statements do you think are true and which ones are false?

	True or False?	
We only use 10% of our brain.	T	F
Children are less attentive after consuming sugary drinks and/or snacks.	T	F
Short bursts of motor coordination exercises can improve integration of left and right hemisphere brain function.	T	F
Students learn better when they receive information in their preferred learning style (e.g., auditory, visual, kinesthetic).	T	F
The production of new connections in the brain can continue into old age.	T	F
A common sign of dyslexia is seeing letters backward.	T	F

	True or False?	
Some of us are "left-brained" and some are "right-brained," and this helps explains differences in how we learn.	T	F
Listening to classical music increases children's reasoning ability.	T	F
Academic achievement can be negatively impacted by skipping breakfast.	T	F
Brain-training games and crossword puzzles increase cognitive function and reasoning skills.	T	F

Before we reveal the answers, how do you think other people did on this "quiz"? In a large survey, researchers asked the general public, educators, and people who took neuroscience courses in college to identify whether these statements (and additional statements) were true or false.[9] They found that people in the general public endorsed more neuromyths than the other two groups. In other words, the general public said "true" when the statement was false more often than educators and people with neuroscience course experience. On average, 68% of the general public incorrectly endorsed the most common neuromyths, compared to 56% of educators and 46% of people with exposure to neuroscience. (Now that you know the results of the study, check the answers in the Retrieval Guide in Chapter 12.)

Which myth in the table was the most commonly endorsed (incorrectly)? The one on learning styles (fourth down on the list). A whopping 93% of the general public thought that the statement about learning styles was true; 76% of educators said it was true; and 78% of people with exposure to neuroscience thought it was true. Wait, what?

While we can't go into an explanation for each neuromyth (that'd be a book all on its own!), we'd like to address learning styles in particular. Led by Hal Pashler from the University of California, San Diego, prominent cognitive scientists conducted a large review of research on learning styles and found *no evidence* that students taught in alignment with their "learning style" achieve more than students taught without designated learning styles.[10] In fact, researchers have continued to demonstrate that teaching students using a *variety* of methods is most effective for improving learning.[11] In other words, rather than concentrating on what doesn't work, focus on what *does* work: varying up teaching and learning using retrieval practice, spacing, interleaving, and feedback. In addition, as cognitive scientist Daniel Willingham put it, "Children are more alike than different in terms of how they think and learn."[12]

Why is the learning styles myth so compelling, convincing, and controversial? As Michael Norton, manager of digital learning at KIPP Texas Public Schools, explained:

> Teachers want to teach students with learning styles, perhaps because they also feel they have a learning style. Teachers need to reflect on their own learning and realize they learn lots of things in lots of different styles, not just one or two ways.

This is just one example of how debunking myths about learning and the brain is tough. If you'd like to learn more, see the notes for a 2017 neuromyths article by Kelly Macdonald and colleagues for detailed explanations, and a 2018 article in American Educator by Daniel Willingham, where he brings readers up to speed on research and misconceptions about learning styles.

Again, everyone has a brain! We use more than 10% of it (as we hope you just learned) because we use it for *everything* we do – every second, every minute, and every day. Have you ever encountered brain-based shoe buying, floor mopping-plasticity, or neuro-movie watching? Probably not. So, just because something is called "brain-based learning" doesn't mean it's based on neuroscience at all. We provide a wealth of research and articles by respected cognitive scientists and neuroscientists on our website, www.powerfulteaching.org. Scientists steer clear of neuromyths and neurobabble, *and you should, too.*

What are phrases and images you should use instead of "brain-based learning?" For phrases, we recommend cognitive science, the science of learning, and names for specific evidence-based strategies (retrieval practice, spacing, interleaving, feedback metacognition). For images, we recommend students in action! It can be hard to show a photo or illustration of retrieval, but try to find images that show students thinking, pondering, and contemplating. We also suggest images of students writing. We associate images of writing with exams and note-taking, but you can help dispel this myth by using images of students writing as an example of a no-stakes retrieval activity, rather than a high-stakes exam activity. Brain images are okay, but we encourage you to *focus on what students are doing, not what simply looks impressive.*

Also, make this image-hunting part of a conversation with students! Our students have come up with great photos, illustrations, and analogies of Power Tools during conversations about learning (see Chapter 9 with specific strategies for facilitating conversations with students). For example, what about a golden retriever who's fetching (and retrieving) a stick? Or a fruit salad that's all mixed up as an analogy for interleaving? Pictures of brains are okay, but pictures of students in action are even more powerful.

Regardless of brain games, names, myths, and pictures, focus on taking what you already do in the classroom and build on it with consistent, reliable, evidence-based Power Tools. *Let science do the talking*, not neurobabble. Because when you unleash the science of learning, you can be confident that students will achieve and succeed – no brain pictures needed.

WHEN I USE POWER TOOLS, HOW CAN I FIND SUPPORT BEYOND MY SCHOOL?

Consider this email we received from Torré Mills, a high school math teacher in Georgia:

> I started last school year with low-stakes weekly retrieval practice. However, I didn't follow through the rest of the year in using the principles that I believed in my heart would serve my kids. I had not sold my kids on the changes and they fought me all the way.
>
> What I am looking for is accountability. I would like to connect somehow with people that are using these principles in the classroom, so I can see how to best implement these principles and have someone hold me accountable to follow through for the entire year.
>
> What I underestimated was the fact that, although I believe in these principles, I myself did not learn this way. And because of that, my default setting in teaching is an old, more familiar – but less effective – way.

Wow. This email really resonated with us because it's such an important question: How can we find support and accountability using Power Tools, beyond educators in our school? Here are a few ideas, based on our own experience applying Power Tools in our instruction:

- *Visit www.powerfulteaching.org for downloads, templates, strategies, and more.* You may find inspiration from our practice guides, brief articles, research papers, and additional books that will spark ideas and energy for continuing with Power Tools.

- *Join a book club or start your own!* With book clubs, imagine the power of having colleagues right down the hall for sharing questions and exploring ideas. Talk to your local library if your school doesn't have a book club on *Powerful Teaching*. You can also join or form a book club online. It's quick and easy to join virtual book clubs – check www .powerfulteaching.org for more information. We find that in-person book clubs have more accountability than online book clubs (it's a little harder to bail on friends!), but with a few guidelines at the outset, online book clubs can be just as valuable. The *Retrieval Guide* in Chapter 12 includes book club discussion questions, so you can hit the ground running!

- *Set up a group text or weekly video call*, and join teachers anywhere in the world. Pooja started a virtual book club and teachers from Greece, South Africa, and the United States joined in! We can learn so much from each other, especially from other schools, cultures, and education systems.

- *When in doubt, look around you.* Mentally travel from classroom to classroom in your school, picturing each teacher in your building. Which teachers already use Power Tools (whether they know it or not)? Which ones might be a potential *Power Partner* as you both try out Power Tools? Which teachers might be interested and just need a little nudge? Don't be surprised to find a colleague who would love to join forces and spark powerful teaching!

- *Talk to a local college or university*, especially education and/ or psychology departments. Many colleges and universities are always looking to partner with local educators, and keep in mind that professors are teachers, too! As we've mentioned throughout this book, Power Tools aren't for K–12 *or* higher education – they're powerful for *both*!

What is it like having research conducted in your school? Dr. Roger Chamberlain, former principal of the school where our research began, wrote:

> From the beginning of the project, my concern was that the research procedures might distract from classroom instruction and learning. Instead, I found that the time away from instruction for implementing quizzes and retrieval practice was well worth the investment; indeed, all students demonstrated improved performance by nearly a letter grade, including our students with individual educational plans. The impact our middle school's participation had on student learning was an immediate return on the investment of our time and effort throughout the project.

Power Up

What is one more way to find support and accountability *beyond* your school or university as you apply Power Tools in your classroom?

WHAT IS ONE ADDITIONAL HESITATION OR CHALLENGE YOU HAVE?

We know that there are many challenges to implementing new strategies and again, we want to keep it real. Now that we've provided a few ideas for conquering uphill battles, ponder these questions:

Power Up

What is one additional hesitation or challenge we haven't addressed that applies to you? What is the first small step you can take to tackle your challenge?

NOTES

1. Powell, S. R., Fuchs, L. S., Fuchs, D., et al. (2009). Effects of fact retrieval tutoring on third-grade students with math difficulties with and without reading difficulties. *Learning Disabilities Research & Practice* 24: 1–11.

2. Agarwal, P. K., Finley, J. R., Rose, N. S., et al. (2017). Benefits from retrieval practice are greater for students with lower working memory capacity. *Memory* 25: 764–771.

3. Knouse, L. E., Rawson, K. A., Vaughn, K. E., et al. (2016). Does testing improve learning for college students with ADHD? *Clinical Psychological Science* 4: 136–143.

4. Kang, S. H. K., Gollan, T. H., and Pashler, H. (2013). Don't just repeat after me: Retrieval practice is better than imitation for foreign vocabulary learning. *Psychonomic Bulletin & Review* 20: 1259–1265.

5. Sumowski, J. F., Wood, H. G., Chiaravalloti, N. D., et al. (2010). Retrieval practice: A simple strategy for improving memory after traumatic brain injury. *Journal of the International Neuropsychological Society* 16: 1147–1150.

6. Sumowski, J. F., Leavitt, V. M., Cohen, A., et al. (2013). Retrieval practice is a robust memory aid for memory-impaired patients with MS. *Multiple Sclerosis Journal* 19: 1943–1946.

7. Avci, G., Woods, S. P., Verduzco, M., et al. (2017). Effect of retrieval practice on short-term and long-term retention in HIV+ individuals. *Journal of the International Neuropsychological Society* 23: 214–222.

8. McCabe, D. P., and Castel, A. D. (2008). Seeing is believing: The effect of brain images on judgments of scientific reasoning. *Cognition* 107: 343–352.

9. Macdonald, K., Germine, L., Anderson, A., et al. (2017). Dispelling the myth: Training in education or neuroscience decreases

but does not eliminate belief in neuromyths. *Frontiers in Psychology* 8: 1–6.

10. Pashler, H., McDaniel, M.A., Rohrer, D., et al. (2008). Learning styles: Concepts and evidence. *Psychological Science in the Public Interest* 9: 105–119.

11. Willingham, D. T. (2018, Summer). Does tailoring instruction to "learning styles" help students learn? *American Educator.*

12. Willingham, D. T. (2009). *Why Don't Students Like School: A Cognitive Scientist Answers Questions About How the Mind Works and What it Means for the Classroom.* San Francisco, CA: Jossey-Bass.

Chapter **8**

Foster a Supportive Environment: Use Power Tools to Reduce Anxiety and Strengthen Community

We'd like to start this chapter with a few trivia questions. Write down your answers and try your best, but don't cheat!

- How many bones are there in the adult human body?
- In which US city is the Baseball Hall of Fame located?
- What was the name of the ship on which Charles Darwin made his scientific voyage?

These trivia questions are pretty fun to ponder, right? You probably know someone (perhaps even you) who enjoys pub trivia or Jeopardy, where it's fun to guess, retrieve, and see if you got an answer correct.[1]

Now, ponder this question: Why is retrieval practice fun *outside* the classroom, but nerve-wracking *inside* the classroom?

It's because of the stakes. We don't put stakes on retrieval outside the classroom, but inside the classroom, retrieval and assessment are joined at the hip.

Power Up

What's the difference between retrieval practice, formative assessment, and summative assessment?[2]

How can we implement retrieval practice, spacing, interleaving, and feedback, and make these Power Tools no big deal for students *inside* the classroom? How we can reduce student anxiety and build a supportive environment so students *want* to retrieve? In this chapter, we'll share research and tips on how to *flip retrieval practice from a negative to a positive*. Unleashing the science of learning isn't about raising the stakes – it's about *eliminating* them.

WHERE DOES STUDENT ANXIETY COME FROM?

When students perceive challenges like retrieval and spacing as stressful approaches to learning, it's important to think about *why*. Where does this anxiety come from? For students from middle school to medical school, why are they reluctant to retrieve and evaluate what they know and don't know?

It's for three reasons. Anxiety *increases* when:

- Retrieval occurs infrequently (e.g., only during exams)
- Retrieval is associated with high-stakes assessments
- Retrieval is either correct or incorrect

As we'll read next, there are many quick and simple strategies to reverse this trend. In particular, anxiety *decreases* when:

- Retrieval is a standard part of every lesson and unit
- Retrieval is low-stakes or no-stakes
- Retrieval may have no correct answers at all

Because desirable difficulties are unfamiliar and uncomfortable for students, we might expect that Power Tools would increase student anxiety. On the contrary, we know from research that *Power Tools decrease anxiety.* You can use Power Tools not only to improve learning, but also to build a supportive environment.

Use Power Tools to increase learning and decrease anxiety in your classroom.

HOW PATRICE BUILDS A SUPPORTIVE ENVIRONMENT WITH POWER TOOLS

For many teachers, their classroom is their sanctuary. It is the place I (Patrice) can do what drives me most: teach. I am away from meetings, unfulfilling professional development, wasted time – the activities that drain me. I come alive when I close the door and look at my room full of students. My students and I eagerly anticipate where the next 44 minutes will take us. This positive energy comes from the culture I establish in my classroom.

Each year I am greeted with the new sets of eyes of 150+ middle schoolers (my largest was 187 students *every* day!) and I have a mini-panic attack wondering how I will possibly remember all of their names. They are curious, sometimes judgmental, eyeing me from head to toe and sizing me up. I have students who did not want summer to end and students who couldn't wait for school to begin. I have students who are considered "smart" and others who feel that adjective will never apply to them. I have students with an ideal home-life and others that come out of horror stories, and most are in-between. How do I turn a room filled with unique individuals into a classroom of positive culture?

Create Support Inside the Classroom

A crucial aspect of creating a supportive environment is introducing students to my teaching philosophy. I was very fortunate to have Dr. Merrill Harmin as my professor and mentor, a humanist who inspired my teaching. It was from Merrill that I learned the phrases, philosophies, and wall signs to which I added and molded to become my own. In fact, I still have the very same wall signs he gave me many years ago. They have always been front and center in my classroom, and students learn them on the first day. My signs are not Power Tools, but they are the basis of my teaching philosophy and lay the groundwork for building my supportive environment. The following are my signs and how I explain them to my students (see Figures 8.1–8.4; the signs in this chapter are available for download at www.powerfulteaching.org.).

My first sign: *We all need time to think and learn.* I explain that some students understand material sooner, and for some students, learning takes longer. The phrase "I don't know that *yet*" is not a flippant remark; rather, it's a sincere response after pondering.

My second sign: *It's okay to make mistakes. That's the way we learn.* I don't think I had ever heard nor seen this phrase until I was in Professor Merrill Harmin's graduate class. Prior to this,

Figure 8.1 Share with students the importance of reflection and patience with this sign: We all need time to think and learn.

We all need time
to think and learn.

my ingrained attitude was that mistakes were grave errors and needed to be avoided at all costs. My mistakes meant losing sleep, rehashing different scenarios. I was brutal on myself! It took deep pondering for me to realize that this sign was true. Making mistakes *is* the way we learn what works and what doesn't. Wouldn't it be amazing if, rather than internalizing failure, students could grasp that it is okay to make mistakes; that's the way we learn?

Figure 8.2 Acknowledge everyday life with this sign: It's okay to make mistakes. That's the way we learn.

It's okay to
make mistakes.

That's the way
we learn.

My third sign: *We can learn more and do more when we are willing to risk*. Here are some examples of risk taking I share with my students:

- Have you ever seen a toddler attempting to walk?
- Did you make a home run the first time you played tee-ball?
- Were you able to read a chapter book when you first started to recognize letters?

The examples are endless. But, I don't stop there; I follow up with these questions:

- What if the toddler fell down at the first attempt of walking and decided to totally give up and crawl for the rest of his or her life?
- Or the child who kept missing the ball the first time at bat never tried again?
- Or the kindergartner gave up reading because putting letters together didn't make sense?

The students, of course, think I am being rather silly until I point out the *thousands* of risks they have already taken. Because

Figure 8.3 Share stories and examples of learning with this sign: We can learn more and do more when we are willing to risk.

of that, they are accomplished in many ways. In my classroom, we dramatize readers' theater, deliver presentations, read aloud, complete individual and group projects; we are serious, we are funny . . . and we *can* do more and learn more because, individually and together, we are willing to take risks.

My fourth sign: *It's okay to ask for help. No one need do it all alone.* As I tell my students, no one has all of the answers, especially not me. I retell stories of my own middle school years when a teacher would ask a question, "Blah, blah, blah, blah . . . .Patrice?" (Of course, all I really did hear was the Patrice – because I clearly was not paying attention.) I remember being mortified; I wanted the floor to open up so I could fall through and escape. I don't ever want one of my students to feel humiliated or embarrassed. In my classroom, if a student does not know an answer (yet) or had taken a mental trip, they always have the option to say, "Somebody help me!" Students who know the answer raise their hands and the original student calls on one of them. This process takes a matter of seconds and we are right back on track. There is no shame, no humiliation, no guilt . . . and there is an answer. Plus, isn't it wonderful to learn at 11 years old that it *is* okay to ask for help, that no one need go through strife alone?

Figure 8.4 Build students' confidence with this sign: It's okay to ask for help. No one need do it all alone.

Build Trust Inside the Classroom

I don't spend the first day going over rules. Rather, students are invited into a classroom of respect, rapport, and adventure. I model what I preach, including making mistakes. Students quickly learn that I am kind, genuine, tough, fair, and have extremely high expectations. I am consistent. My classroom is a safe place. I teach from "bell to bell" and behavior problems (yes, even at the middle school level) are simply not an issue. *From the start, my students and I begin building trust.*

Part of this trust is empowering the students. Part of empowering students is teaching them how to learn and taking ownership of their learning. This is the process, the journey. Students learn that retrieval practice really works. They begin to understand metacognition and why it is important to study what you *don't* know and how to tell the difference from what you already know. They begin to understand that the struggles of spaced practice can be difficult and how that difficulty helps them remember more. In fact, I urge students to embrace desirable difficulties; it is a part of the learning process. And, it is the deep questioning and higher-order thinking that becomes a daily occurrence.

Often, students who had previously been labeled as "smart" begin redefining their good grades as having mastered learning strategies early on. And, to my delight, students who previously had internalized failure begin to realize that they simply hadn't *yet* internalized *how to learn*. Once realized, grades go up. Our positive culture becomes one of a team working together. Quizzes become part of the metacognitive process rather than a judgment. Tests become celebrations of what was learned versus an anxiety-producing experience. Confidence rises in all students – not only because of higher grades, but because they are able to delve into deep thinking and converse with peers (and me!) about why events happened in history.

As my confidence with content increased, I was able to focus on the individuals in my classroom. The art of pondering and questioning entered my reality. I made it a point to laugh with my students. Not just a chuckle here or there but that laugh that begins in my toes and throws back my head and spews forth sheer glee. My historical research turned into story-telling, which continued to keep my students on the edge of their chairs. I liked bringing history alive for my students. I saw students eager to walk into my class and I also began seeing a trend; students did really well in my class. I thought that, perhaps, I as a person, may have had something to do with it; yet I knew my own role was quite minimal. So, *why* were students successful? I began taking a closer look. I used choral work, study buddies, Think-Pair-Share, student engagement, feedback – the more I looked, the more I realized that student success really had nothing to do with me as a person but everything to do with the teaching strategies I employed. This became my "aha" moment and my mission to spread the word of powerful teaching.

Did I learn all of this through my teacher preparation program at my university? Did I begin my teaching career with all of these strategies – the knowledge of metacognition, spacing, interleaving, and retrieval – already in my repertoire? Sadly, no. As I stated earlier, learning is a journey, a process. Just as students enter my classroom having not yet conquered learning, I entered the profession having not yet conquered teaching. In fact, it took me years to begin being a good teacher. I believed in my philosophy and my signs; they were front and center *in my classroom*, yet, to be honest, it was difficult to have them front and center *in my mind*. The first couple years were focused on the content, learning the written and unwritten rules of my school culture, what to expect in adolescent behavior, how to manage grading, lesson plans, how to unjam the copier – I clearly remember the tears shed between classes as I wondered if I would ever feel competent. And, finally, I began to emerge. I found I could look up from the teacher manual and figure out what worked and what didn't for my students. In fact, it was when I truly embraced the philosophy of my signs, when I applied them *to me*, that I began to feel my journey take off.

DECREASE ANXIETY WITH POWER TOOLS AND RETRIEVAL ROUTINES

In a large survey of nearly 1,500 middle school and high school students we conducted in Patrice's school district, 92% of students reported that spaced retrieval practice helped them learn.[3] Critically, 72% of students reported that retrieval practice (which also included immediate feedback) made them *less* nervous for tests and only 6% of students said that retrieval made them more anxious (Figure 8.5).

For both Patrice's classroom and her entire school district, by incorporating Power Tools into *every* lesson, learning increased and anxiety decreased. Sarah Burns, a curriculum developer and STEM teacher, also creates *Retrieval Routines* in her classroom.

Figure 8.5   In a survey of 1,500 K–12 students, 94% of students reported that their test anxiety decreased or didn't change after frequent retrieval practice. (Agarwal et al., 2014)

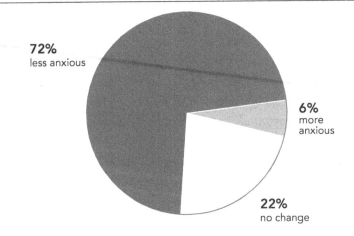

72%
less anxious

6%
more
anxious

22%
no change

As she put it, "I love making quizzes a part of daily routines so that students see quizzes as *no big deal.*"

Power Tools *decrease* students' anxiety because:

- Students become familiar with their own learning and metacognition.

- Students develop a better understanding of what they need to study and how well they'll perform on upcoming tests.

When retrieval occurs only on exams, students have not yet examined their knowledge and suddenly they are *confronted* with what they know and don't know as part of a high-stakes assessment. In other words, exams shouldn't be students' very first opportunity to retrieve! It's vital that they become comfortable with their own learning along the way.

Exams shouldn't be students' very first opportunity to retrieve!

As Patrice's first sign states, "We all need time to think and learn." Frequent opportunities for retrieval practice provide all students with time to pull information out and increase their metacognition at their own speed. All students are not only engaged in Power Tools at their own pace; they receive the *gift of time* to think and learn, too.

Power Up

Which one of these strategies could you use frequently to create Retrieval Routines?

    A. Brain Dumps
    B. Two Things
    C. Mini-Quizzes
    D. Dice Game

DECREASE ANXIETY WITH POWER TOOLS BY SPREADING THE WEALTH IN YOUR GRADEBOOK

If you've read this far, then you already know that Power Tools are learning strategies, *not* assessment strategies. At the same time, we still need to provide students with grades throughout the semester. When using Power Tools, how can we include them in our gradebook but still keep them low-stakes or no-stakes?

Spread Grades across Multiple Retrieval Opportunities

First of all, there is some scientific evidence suggesting that no-stakes retrieval practice is more beneficial for learning than low-stakes retrieval practice. In a study conducted in an introductory psychology classroom by Maya Khanna at Creighton University, college students received pop quizzes that were graded (low-stakes quizzes), pop quizzes that were ungraded (no-stakes quizzes), or no quizzes.[4] On an end-of-the-semester cumulative exam, performance was highest when students received no-stakes quizzes, compared to the other two conditions. Students who completed no-stakes pop quizzes also reported more positive feelings for quizzes than students in the other conditions. While additional findings on low-versus no-stakes are emerging, it seems that no-stakes quizzes or retrieval practice may lead to less anxiety and more learning than low-stakes quizzes.

What does this mean in your classroom? You may still want to offer students a few points for low-stakes, rather than no-stakes, retrieval, especially if that provides them with some incentive to not slack off. Finding a balance between motivating students, keeping Power Tools low-stakes, and avoiding mountains of grading can be tricky, which is why *spreading the wealth* among many retrieval opportunities works well.

In Patrice's classroom, retrieval is *not* a dreaded experience. Rather, it is a celebration of what students have learned. In her class, grades from retrieval opportunities are divided into the following:

- Mini-Quizzes

- Classwork (e.g., maps, projects, Retrieval Cards, Big Basket Quizzes [BBQs], etc.)

- Tests and exams

These three areas are not equally weighted, as Mini-Quizzes are low-stakes. The majority of points are from classwork and tests. Classwork, tests, and points vary. *All* utilize retrieval!

In Pooja's classroom, total grades are divided into quarters:

- Weekly retrieval practices (100 points)

- Individual video projects (100 points)

- Group research projects (100 points)

- In-class and out-of-class participation (100 points)

For retrieval practices, students receive a 10-point in-class quiz each week, with a total of 14 quizzes throughout the semester. To provide wiggle room for absences (and to make a nice round number of 100 points), students' four *lowest* retrieval practice grades are automatically dropped. There are no makeup retrieval practices, so if a student arrives to class after the other students have finished, they're out of luck – a good incentive to arrive on time!

When all's said and done, each retrieval practice is worth about 2% of students' final grade. Pretty low-stakes! Remarkably, this combination between no make-ups, low-stakes, and dropping the lowest grades leads to very few (if any) complaints about excused and unexcused absences. In terms of individual and group projects, students have time *in class* to work and collaborate.

Yes, this is a tradeoff in terms of time versus content we discussed in Chapter 7, but students learn so much more. The stakes are lowered and they don't have to meet outside of class.

Pooja's course structure is win-win when it comes to spaced retrieval, little grading, and big boosts in learning. Plus, students don't have any high-stakes midterms, finals, or papers! This substantially lowers students' anxiety and they no longer need to cram. From day one, the overall distribution of low-stakes assignments gets student buy-in and a sigh of relief. By the last day, Pooja's students realize that learning doesn't require high-stakes papers and exams at all:

- "I loved the class and was able to learn a lot, even with a light workload!"

- "I learned so much more than I thought I would! This class is proof that we don't need hundreds of papers/exams to learn! Thank you so much!"

Of course, many courses are high-stakes by default: Advanced Placement (AP) classes, courses for pre-medical students, and so on. While this content can be high-stakes, keep in mind that the strategies in our classrooms should *still* be low-stakes to maximize learning. When we use Power Tools, students' retention of information increases, which means they can actually study *less*. Even though we can't change the stakes of final exams, we *can* change how students prepare beforehand. Even if they cram or bury themselves in test prep, there are no-stakes strategies they can harness to decrease anxiety and increase learning.

Don't Increase the Stakes with Competitive Activities

Many educators use games like in-class Jeopardy where students are split into teams and engage in no-stakes retrieval. Be careful and mindful if you use these games in your classroom! While these games can be engaging opportunities to implement Power Tools as an ungraded activity, they can actually *increase* anxiety and *decrease* learning.

Did you ever play these types of competitive games when you were a student? We remember the feeling of getting a question correct for the team, but also the large amount of social pressure to do well and avoid mistakes at all costs. In other words, grades increase stakes, but so do situations that value accuracy and speed over reflection and retrieval. Also, there is a wealth of research demonstrating that when students retrieve in groups (called "collaborative retrieval"), it *decreases* learning and increases errors (which is pretty counterintuitive!).[5] It can be uncomfortable to get something wrong in front of peers and often, when one student speaks up with an answer, the other students fall silent and go along with the first response.

Instead of competitive games, consider having students retrieve individually on index cards, followed by collaborating as a team to select the correct answer. In Patrice's class, for example, once teams discuss the questions and answers together, one student would provide the agreed-upon final answer. This way, *all* students are participating, including special education students. Research has demonstrated that this approach removes social pressure, ensures that each student is retrieving, increases learning, and provides peer-feedback in a more relaxed environment.[6]

As Patrice's second sign states, "It's okay to make mistakes, that's the way we learn." With low- and no-stakes opportunities for retrieval, emphasis on accuracy is removed. Students are able to take a deep breath and focus on pulling information out, without worrying about points, grades, or social pressure. Especially in the context of desirable difficulties, making mistakes is a *good* thing.

DECREASE ANXIETY WITH RETRIEVAL PRACTICE THAT HAS NO RIGHT OR WRONG ANSWERS

Have you ever thought about questions where there is *no correct or incorrect answer*? In your classroom, how often does retrieval have no right or wrong answers? Of course, when students share their opinions and thoughts in response to open-ended questions, there isn't always a right or wrong answer. For example, if you had to choose one of your five senses to lose (vision, hearing, smell, touch, or taste), which one would it be, and why? Wow, that's as open-ended as it gets![8]

As another example, when we have to decide where to go for dinner, we're retrieving our previous experiences to help us decide – but no one is telling us we're objectively right or wrong (other than a stubborn dinner companion, perhaps). It's simply something we retrieve based on our own life experiences – no correct or incorrect answers at all.

When it comes to Power Tools, decrease student anxiety by emphasizing that while some retrieval practice involves right/wrong answers (followed by feedback, of course!), *retrieval practice can have no correct answers at all*. Here are two teaching strategies that ease students into Power Tools from the start – without any judgment, evaluation, or wrong answers.

Retrieval Warm-Ups

Quick: What's your *least* favorite ice cream flavor?[9] Boom – that's retrieval! Even thinking about your favorite (or least favorite) ice cream flavor is retrieving, thinking back, and pulling information out – without any anxiety about errors or failure.

More than just fun, our ice cream question in Figure 8.6 is also risk-free. As Patrice's third sign states, "We can do more and learn more when we are willing to take a risk." No-risk questions ease students into understanding that retrieval *outside* the classroom is no different from retrieval *inside* the classroom. For example, Patrice begins the school year with questions where students cannot fail: What was your favorite moment of the summer? What is your favorite food to have for lunch? If you were given $10,000, what would you do with it?

To get you started with no-risk retrieval, we've created *Retrieval Warm-Ups*. Retrieval Warm-Ups are questions with no right or wrong answer, and they're a perfect way to show students that we retrieve all the time, *without even thinking about it.*

Figure 8.6 Retrieval Warm-Ups have no right or wrong answer! They're a perfect way to show students that we retrieve all the time, without even thinking about it.

What is your *least* favorite ice cream flavor?

Retrieval Warm-Ups are flexible, too! They can be used as entry tickets, optional quiz questions, writing prompts, or icebreakers. They also work for all ages, ranging from elementary school to medical school.

Here are our Retrieval Warm-Ups. How would you answer them? Remember, there are no correct or incorrect answers!

- What is your *least* favorite ice cream flavor?
- If you could travel anywhere in the world (where you haven't been before), where would you go?
- Would you rather visit the world 100 years in the past or 100 years in the future? Why?
- If you had to wear a hat every day for the rest of your life, what type of hat would it be?
- Would you rather own a sailboat or a hot-air balloon? Why?
- What is your favorite word? Why is it your favorite?
- If you could eat only one food or dish for the rest of your life, what would it be?
- What type of animal would be a really good musician? Why?
- What is your favorite emoji? Describe it or draw it!
- If you could switch places with anyone in your family for a day, who would it be?
- What is your proudest accomplishment this semester (or year)?
- Younger students: What is your favorite thing to eat for breakfast?
- Older students: What was your favorite thing to eat for breakfast as a kid?
- Older students: Would you rather lock yourself out of your car or out of your house?
- Older students: Have you ever gone skydiving? Why or why not?

Of course, keep the warm-ups no-stakes or optional and emphasize how quick, easy, and fun retrieval practice is. After students respond, facilitate a class discussion, Think-Pair-Share, quick vote, or simply move on. Sometimes all it takes is a little warming up!

Noun-Name Tag

As powerful teachers, we know that when students feel supported, they are more engaged and better prepared to learn. As we also know, a small thing that makes a big difference for creating a welcoming environment is *remembering students' names*.

But what can you do when you have 100+ students per semester, every day? Here is a strategy Pooja developed called *Noun-Name Tag*, starting from the first day of class. Keep in mind that building a supportive classroom culture encourages students to remember each other's names, and Noun-Name Tag gets *everyone* involved in retrieving and learning, not just you. Dedicating an entire class period to remembering and practicing names is a time investment, but the benefit for building a supportive environment is huge – *from the first day of class to the last day of class*.

1. On the first day of class, ask students to write down *five words* that come to mind when they think about your subject area (e.g., psychology, algebra, world history, etc.)

2. Once students have their five words written down, instruct them to write down a *noun* that starts with the *same letter* as their first name (e.g., Pepperoni-Pooja). You may need to give students a few examples, and let them know that foods and animals work really well (e.g., Kangaroo-Kevin). Sometimes students come up with simple pairs (Kite-Kate), and other times students create really memorable pairs (Velociraptor-Vicky!).

3. Go around the room and have each student say their *name*, their *noun*, and just *one* of their words about your subject area. Everything they need to share is written down on the paper in front of them, so they don't need to worry about what to say while other students are speaking.

4. During the next class meeting (whether it's a day, two days, or a week later), play Noun-Name Tag! Start by stating your Noun-Name pair, and then say the Noun-Name for one of your students. That student then says the Noun-Name for another student, who says the Noun-Name for another student, and so on. You can announce that you'll be playing Noun-Name Tag in advance, or simply keep it a surprise.

5. Continue until all students' Noun-Names have been retrieved by all students in the class.

During the fourth step, students may freeze and be embarrassed that they can't remember anyone's name. Here's where Patrice's fourth sign comes in: "It's okay to ask for help. No one need do it all alone." Indeed, if students are stuck, they can ask for a hint of a noun first, and then the name if they're really stuck. Students are eager to jump in and help each other! But encourage students to wait and give the student who's "it" time to think and retrieve.

Importantly, Noun-Name Tag is no-stakes and non-competitive. There's a little bit of social pressure, but students ask for feedback and other students are happy to provide it. In other words, there's no embarrassment or anxiety attached to being wrong because everyone is supporting each other's retrieval process. With names, there are incorrect answers, but it's no longer a bad thing to make a mistake. Students can always ask for help.

After playing Noun-Name Tag, quiz yourself! At the end of class (or a few days later for spacing), write down all the Noun-Name pairs *you* can remember. You'll be surprised at how quickly you'll learn everyone's names. Fun perk: Students don't realize that they're actually helping *you* remember names when they're playing Noun-Name Tag!

Play Noun-Name Tag a few weeks later, a few months later, and finally on the last day of class. By the end of the semester, your students know everyone's names *and* their nouns. Throughout all of this, forgetting someone's name becomes commonplace, and even fun. Have you ever apologized for forgetting someone's name at a professional or social event? You'll find that students stop apologizing! They simply acknowledge their "error" and ask for help.

What would your own Noun-Name be? Pooja's student Jaylyn (mentioned in Chapter 4 on interleaving) remembered her noun more than a year later: Jester!

Power Up

Which Power Tools are incorporated during Noun-Name Tag?[10]

NOTES

1. The adult human body has 206 bones; the Baseball Hall of Fame is located in Cooperstown, New York; and the name of Darwin's boat was the *Beagle*.

2. After you retrieve, check Chapter 2 and give yourself feedback. How'd you do?

3. Agarwal, P. K., D'Antonio, L., Roediger, H. L., et al. (2014). Classroom-based programs of retrieval practice reduce middle school and high school students' test anxiety. *Journal of Applied Research in Memory and Cognition* 3: 131–139.

4. Khanna, M. M. (2015). Ungraded pop quizzes: Test-enhanced learning without all the anxiety. *Teaching of Psychology* 42: 174–178.

5. Rajaram, S., and Pereira-Pasarin, L. P. (2010). Collaborative memory: Cognitive research and theory. *Perspectives on Psychological Science* 5: 649–663.

6. LoGuidice, A. B., Pachai, A. A., and Kim, J. A. (2015). Testing together: When do students learn more through collaborative tests? *Scholarship of Teaching and Learning in Psychology* 1: 377–389.

7. Check your answers in Chapters 2 and 5. Spaced retrieval at its best!

8. If they *had* to choose one, Pooja would lose her sense of hearing and Patrice would lose her sense of smell.

9. Pooja's *least* favorite ice cream flavor is mint chocolate chip (scandalous!). Patrice's least favorite ice cream flavor is bubble gum (blech!).

10. All four Power Tools are used in Noun-Name Tag. But you'll have to ask for help or provide yourself feedback on what the four Power Tools are and how they're incorporated in this teaching strategy! Noun-Name Tag incorporates additional memory principles from cognitive science, including benefits from word association and visual imagery.

Chapter *9*

Spark Conversations with Students About the Science of Learning

It's powerful to use research-based principles in the classroom. *But that's not enough.* You also need *students* to recognize the value of Power Tools *inside* the classroom and adopt Power Tools *outside* the classroom.

Of course, you can't control what students do as soon as they walk out the door. How can you have conversations with students, empower them to take ownership, and get them on board with Power Tools.

We have developed *six steps* for facilitating conversations with students about how learning works, how to study effectively, and how to harness Power Tools for themselves – inside and outside the classroom.

Step 1. Empower students by sparking a *conversation*.

Step 2. Empower students by *modeling* Power Tools.

Step 3. Empower students by fostering an understanding of *why* Power Tools work.

Step 4. Empower students to harness Power Tools *inside* the classroom.

Step 5. Empower students to harness Power Tools *outside* the classroom.

Step 6. Empower students to *plan, implement, and reflect* on their Power Tools.

Incorporate Power Tools in your classroom and use these six steps to teach evidence-based strategies to students. When students experience the success of learning, students are motivated to take ownership and accountability for their own knowledge. This is why sparking conversations with students is so crucial to pass the torch.

STEP 1: EMPOWER STUDENTS BY SPARKING A CONVERSATION

If you want to transform student learning, you also need to address how students approach their *own* learning. Don't bully students into using Power Tools and *don't* dive straight into the science behind them. Instead, you can spark conversations with students about learning – *without even mentioning Power Tools*.

How Patrice Sparks Conversations with Students

I (Patrice) pass the torch of Power Tools through explaining and demonstrating, but most of all, through conversations.

On day one, I ask my students if any of them had studied at length for a test and not done well. Hands are always raised, and

I explain that this feeling is called *metacognition*. Students grasp onto this concept immediately. They know how much time they truly studied and can relate to the attitude, *Why study if I am going to fail?*

As we begin the first lesson, I ask the students the following question taught in a previous grade level: *What are cardinal directions?* Before they have the chance to answer, I ask:

- How many of you knew the answer right away?

- How many of you know you learned this at some point but can't remember the answer?

- How many of you have never heard this term in your life?

By doing this, I am asking students to make a *judgment of learning* (JOL) before answering the question. At first, I don't even ask for student responses after the JOL; I simply give the answer. My purpose is to have students begin to differentiate *what they know* versus *what they don't know*. As time goes on, I continue to have students make JOLs verbally and on paper.

By the time a quiz is given, students know what needs to be studied. I have yet to have a student not do well on the first quiz after I have set the stage for study strategies. Students understand the concept of metacognition, they find it helpful, and they continue to use the terminology throughout the year. Student confidence rises as they begin to understand the importance of metacognition and how to differentiate and prioritize what needs to be studied. And because students are experiencing success, *they are open to learning more.*

Another question I ask my students: *How many of you have been taught how to learn?* Unfortunately, very few students answer in the affirmative. I inform students that the most important part of my job is to teach and reinforce strategies that will help them learn. I then explain this quote from earlier in the book:

When we think about learning, we typically focus on getting information *into* students' heads. What if, instead, we focus on getting information *out* of students' heads?

Although this idea of getting information in versus out seems simple, it is often a new concept for students. Each year, the vast majority of my students think the entire process of learning starts and ends with the teacher. For example, they often think, "If I don't know something, the teacher didn't teach it well."

And so begins the process of teaching students how to learn. Too often, students are simply not taught this process. I explain it's my responsibility to help them encode information using methods and strategies based on research. At the same time, *all of us* (teachers *and* students) have a role in feedback and metacognition during learning. Then, it is up to *students* to retrieve information; *no one can be a substitute*. As soon as I say this, I get quizzical looks.

The conversation that follows becomes an "aha" moment for my students. With a few simple examples and exercises, students start reflecting on their responsibilities for their own metacognition and learning. My students begin to understand that learning is a *partnership*; neither teacher nor student can shirk responsibility for the roles (see Figure 9.1 as one way to illustrate this for your students). As the authors of the book *Make it Stick* put it, "The responsibility for learning rests with every individual."

How Pooja Sparks Conversations with Students

Recently, I (Pooja) had the privilege to speak with student leaders from Imagine Scholar, a rural youth development program in the Mpumalanga province in South Africa. They were energetic, curious, and full of questions for me – ranging from sleep and neuroscience, to retrieval practice and memory.

Figure 9.1 Learning is the responsibility of teachers *and* students.

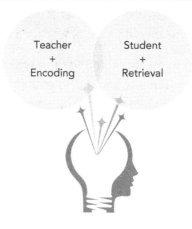

Teacher
+
Encoding

Student
+
Retrieval

Before we wrapped up, I asked the students two questions of my own:

- What is one thing that comes to mind when you think about science?
- What is one thing that comes to mind when you think about learning?

As they were sharing their thoughts to my two questions, many students started laughing. "Retrieval!" someone shouted. Students were so engaged because they were *part of a conversation on the science of learning*, not a lecture. After our conversation, the students were so invested in research-based learning strategies that they even proposed developing a workshop on the science of learning and presenting it to local teachers. Simply incredible!

Just like my virtual interaction with students in South Africa, I *don't* dive straight into talking about Power Tools in my college classroom. Instead, I ask these two questions, followed by more:

- Why is it that it's easy to learn some things and hard to learn other things?
- Why is it easy to come up with a list of our favorite movies, but difficult to come up with a list of what you did last weekend?

Without any Power Tool terminology (yet!), this exploratory discussion sparks students' awareness of and curiosity in their own learning and metacognition – something they've rarely had the opportunity to think about, *until now*.

Four Key Phrases to Empower Students

When it comes to Power Tools, it's what you say *and* how you say it.

How can we demystify the science of learning in every lesson, every day? Here are four key phrases to spark conversation and empower students that make Power Tools concrete, engaging, and familiar:

- *Let's have a pointless conversation!* With this phrase, students will be caught off guard. And that's precisely the "point!" A pointless conversation is literally no-stakes retrieval practice. You can have a pointless Brain Dump, pointless Retrieval Cards, and so on. Encourage students to retrieve and make it pointless. They'll be sure to thank you.

- *Let's learn OUTformation, not just INformation.* The contrast between getting information "in" versus "out" is a favorite phrase of ours. Now, make it even more simple with OUT-formation instead of INformation!. This simple and straightforward phrase emphasizes why retrieval practice is effective, even for younger learners.

- *What did you learn yesterday?* Here's a fun question to pose – as educators, as parents, or even as a retrieval prompt for yourself: "What did you learn today versus what did you learn *yesterday*?" Enjoy the richer conversation after thinking back to yesterday, rather than glossy-eyed looks you get when you ask students about today. This is a perfect introduction to spacing!

- *Let's flip retrieval from a negative to a positive.* We used this phrase in Chapter 8 on building a supportive environment. You can reduce student anxiety by keeping this in mind, and students can adopt this phrase, too! It's interesting to have a conversation about when and where retrieval is negative (e.g., high-stakes exams), but it's even more fun to come up with examples of when retrieval is a *positive* (e.g., playing trivia games).

STEP 2: EMPOWER STUDENTS BY MODELING POWER TOOLS

Power Tools aren't just a teaching strategy; they are a powerful study strategy, too. But in order for students to be comfortable using them, you need to model them first.

First, modeling means practicing what you preach. For instance, start by using Power Tools from day one with Brain Dumps, Retrieval Guides, and Two Things. Pretty soon, students catch on that these strategies are not only unique – they're actually helping them remember and apply information from class.

Second, model Power Tools without any grades or competitions. As we've mentioned, if students associate retrieval only with exams, they won't want to try these strategies at home – it's uncomfortable, nerve wracking, and an assessment strategy, not a study strategy.[1] Here's how we "walk the walk", demonstrating that Power Tools can work outside the classroom once students experience them inside the classroom.

How Patrice Models Power Tools in Her Classroom

I (Patrice) explain Power Tools and consistently use the terms metacognition, feedback, retrieval, spacing, and interleaving. I foster student ownership *by asking students which Power Tool I am using* during choral work and daily quizzes. Power Tools become a common language in my classroom. Throughout the year, I also often have students reflect upon a graded test or a mid-quarter grade. I usually ask two simple questions: What worked? What didn't?

By asking these simple questions, each student identifies strategies that worked best. Students truly begin to understand that these strategies do, indeed, work. I have seen the looks on the faces of even the most hardened and difficult students become relaxed and proud. Just as they had internalized failure previously, they begin to internalize success after experiencing Power Tools. All students learn that it is not a case of being smart or not smart. It is finding out the correct strategies to use. Success breeds success.

One strategy students use is note-taking. But I've never liked taking notes! I could not figure out how to listen, write, keep listening and keep writing. My frustration increased as I lacked the ability to figure out what was important versus not. Was I missing crucial information? My note-taking experiences may have allowed some information to go *into* my head – but it was jumbled and nonretrievable. How often does this happen to our students? A discussion in my classroom often shows this to be a universal concern.

Because of my own experience, I vowed when I started my teaching career that there would always be time to pause between talking and writing down notes. I have kept that vow. By simply having a discussion, followed by time to ponder, followed by time to *retrieve* notes, students are able to pull information *out* of their heads and make sense of it as we go along. Because of this opportunity for Retrieve-Taking, students listen and participate during my teaching and discussions because they are confident they will be given time for writing and retrieving later on.

Three strategies I model in my classroom quickly become strategies that students use outside my classroom: Retrieval Guides, Retrieval Cards, and Stop and Jots:

- For *Retrieval Guides*, I discuss and illustrate why particular information is important. Picking out information is a skill many of my sixth-graders have not yet mastered, so we read articles, text, etc. aloud together. It's not until after we discuss important concepts that students complete a section of the Retrieval Guide before going on. By modeling this strategy in my class, students are better able to identify important information when they study.

- For *Retrieval Cards*, students learn how to turn the traditional flashcard-making process into a powerful retrieval process. By having students retrieve an answer and write it down on one side of a card – rather than copy it out of a book – I'm modeling a study strategy before students even realize it. Because students become successful using Retrieval Cards in my class, soon, Retrieval Cards become the norm for my students when it comes to studying and learning outside of class.

- For *Stop and Jots*, I may talk for a few minutes and then give students a few minutes to write down what they thought was important or interesting. After writing and pondering, I have them share with a neighbor and then with the class

(Think-Pair-Share), and I give them another minute to jot down any other ideas they heard. Stop and Jots take a few minutes longer than simply lecturing. However, by the end of class, students' thoughts are not a jumbled mess. They have identified what is important and they will be ready for the following day's Mini-Quiz.

It is an extremely rare event for a student to fail my class. Because I use retrieval, metacognition, and spacing throughout chapters and units, I am able to monitor student progress. And yet there are occasions when a student may fail an exam. The reflection questions I ask students after the exam (*What worked? What didn't?*) are often a good place to begin to identify a problem. I follow up with a one-on-one with the student to identify strategies for the next chapter. (I know . . . there is no time, right?) However, I have found that touching base with a student, even for only a minute or two, can begin a turnaround for the next chapter.

Once students see that they *are* able to pass, I see their pride and effort increase. As a team, we look at which strategies have worked and brainstorm other strategies to try. In this way, all my students succeed; and it starts with a conversation, modeling, and strategies that work best for each learner.

How Pooja Models Power Tools in Her Classroom

In addition to directly modeling classroom strategies we've discussed earlier in the book (Two Things, weekly retrieval practices, Retrieval Warm-Ups, etc.), I (Pooja) model Power Tools in subtle ways, too. With my college students, I find it fun to step back and observe how quickly they notice their learning and retention increasing. A few weeks into the semester, I explain why Power Tools work, but until then, I don't overtly discuss them; I simply use them.

It's almost like an unspoken game for me! Here are four ways I model Power Tools, without spilling the beans:

First, I use something as simple as *remembering names* as a perfect opportunity for retrieval practice and feedback. In Noun-Name Tag from Chapter 8, for instance, students want to jump in immediately with the answer. Instead, I ask students to pause and take a guess (i.e., retrieval!). Only then are students allowed to ask for help. Students think we're playing a game, but I know that I'm modeling Power Tools for them from day one.

Second, I model Power Tools by *spacing content over time* on weekly retrieval practices throughout the semester. When my students come across a question a second time, they're a bit frustrated when they can't remember key information needed to respond. They spontaneously mention their surprise that they couldn't remember information (i.e., metacognition!). By the third time they encounter the same content, it becomes fun for them. My students are excited to find they now remember the information. Of course, I know it's because of the process of retrieval and feedback, and even though I haven't introduced the concept of metacognition, my students become aware of their own learning.

Third, I *break assignments into chunks* – not just to make them more feasible, but also to space out learning. For example, each semester, students create an individual "Science Brief" video. Their videos are geared toward a general audience (e.g., their parents and friends), must include a description about a psychology experiment of their choice, and must be three minutes or less (it has to be brief!).

Throughout the semester, students have to fill out a form for each step of the process: Choosing a topic, writing a "hook" or engaging introduction, describing the experiment, and putting it all together. Each time students fill out a form, I ask them for the same information from the previous form. This can seem redundant to students, but it's another way I use a subtle nudge to get students to retrieve: "What is my topic again? What is my 'hook' for the video going to be? What were the basics of the experiment I'm going to describe?" This is spaced retrieval practice – *without them even realizing it*. After doing this two or three times, students have the information for their video down cold. They don't have to look back at what they wrote on previous forms *and* it makes them confident in their own knowledge when they record their videos.

Lastly, if a student asks a question in class, I *encourage other students to provide a response* with elaborative feedback – beyond a simple explanation (i.e., instead of feedback from yours truly). For example, I once had a student ask, "Why is our sense of smell so intertwined with memory?" Rather than answering this question myself, students led the conversation. Once a student jumps in with an explanation, I ask a *second* student to add on to the first student's explanation. In this way, students are not only providing elaborative feedback; they're receiving it from their peers, too. At this point, students have begun to model Power Tools for themselves, without even realizing it!

STEP 3: EMPOWER STUDENTS BY FOSTERING AN UNDERSTANDING OF WHY POWER TOOLS WORK

Once you have had a broad conversation about learning and modeled Power Tools, the next step is to share the *why*, not just the *how*.

You might be thinking, "My students won't care about the research behind Power Tools." And that might be true! But through more conversations with students about how they learn, and with the success students have already experienced using these strategies in class, students will be interested in the "why" more than you might expect.

Here are three quick explanations you can share with students about why Power Tools work:

- Power Tools work because, when it comes to learning, you have to *use it or lose it.*

- Power Tools work because they provide desirable difficulties, which are *good* for learning.

- Power Tools work because they help you figure out *what you know and what you don't know.*

When it comes to conversations with students, you don't have to provide research graphs, journal articles, or long explanations. Data can come in handy and we provide *Research Snapshots* for parents in Chapter 10. But for students, whether K–12 or higher education, a few examples for each of these explanations can help. Again, when students experience Power Tools in action, they'll start the "why" conversation for you! In fact, here's a perfect analogy for why retrieval practice boosts learning from a college student:

> Definitely, the act of "retrieving" information every week makes us more able to fully dissolve the knowledge into our watery-brain! It makes us recall back the information, and by doing so, you put more room into your brain, reserved just for that info. It's like selecting homeless, wandering information and putting it into housing!

Learning is Like a Language: Use It or Lose It

I (Pooja) teach psychology, education, and neuroscience courses for undergraduate and graduate students. As soon as they walk into my classroom or join online, they look at the syllabus. "What?!" the exclaim. "We have weekly quizzes in this course?" I mention that there's research behind weekly quizzes, but I don't specify what it is, nor do I specify my area of scientific expertise (college students don't tend to ask, either).

In week two, my students encounter their first quiz-like retrieval practice. When I announce this in advance, I get blank stares. "What could Pooja possibly ask on a quiz during the second week of class?" I ask simple questions, like when and where I hold my office hours. As mentioned in Step 2 earlier, students are surprised and a bit embarrassed that they can't remember. We have a class discussion, they get feedback, and we move on.

In week three, I ask the same question about my office hours again. All of a sudden, students have an easy time remembering when and where they are! Much to their surprise (but not mine, of course), my students are so intrigued by the change in their memory from week two to week three that they initiate a conversation about *why* the retrieval practices have already helped them learn – a complete turnaround from their initial hesitations.

One reason students come up with when it comes to why Power Tools work is the phrase *use it or lose it*. Just like learning a language, my students recognize that if I hadn't asked them about office hours and they didn't use that info to visit, they would have forgotten it. By mid-semester, my students repeat my office hours in unison. I also find that this spaced retrieval literally increases students' likelihood of stopping by my office to chat.

Of course, a conversation about learning and the importance of *use it or lose it* can only get you so far. That's why it's important for you and your students to stick it out. Here's an example from Professor James Lang, author of the book *Small Teaching*:

> Tell students what the research says about the value of quizzing and retrieval practice and about your decision to use it. They still might not love taking quizzes during the long slogging weeks of October, but they will recognize their value and reap the rewards on those final assessments in December.

When students engage in frequent retrieval practice, they catch on quickly that they are *using* what they know. As students also soon realize, when they passively listen to a lecture or re-read something – *they're really not using anything at all.*

Desirable Difficulties Are a *Good* Thing for Learning

Another reason you can share with students about why Power Tools work is the framework of desirable difficulties. It's important to acknowledge that strategies like spacing and interleaving are challenging, but also that challenges are good for learning. Here's another way to put it: *Desirable difficulties don't feel good, but they're a good feeling to have.*

When it comes to conversations about desirable difficulties, Lisa Pulley, a high school teacher we mentioned in Chapter 5 on feedback-driven metacognition, gave this recommendation:

> Be very deliberate about how you approach this in the short term and long term. Explain desirable difficulties. Go into detail about the cognitive research and share the evidence with students. And prep yourself for how you're going to address moans and groans. "Do we have to?" "No, we get to!" "But this is so hard." "You're right, that's why we're practicing."

Here's a simplified explanation for desirable difficulties: Power Tools provide *a mental challenge* of having to think back and remember what we did last weekend or the name of the fourth president of the United States.[2] That sort of challenge or struggle improves learning. Students start to become *comfortable with being uncomfortable.*

Desirable difficulties don't feel good, but they're a good feeling to have.

Again, students catch onto this aspect of Power Tools quickly – and even connect it to their own study habits! One of Pooja's college students put it this way:

> The retrieval practices usually make me think a little deeper about a certain topic or subject inside of the book that I otherwise wouldn't have gone back to. The weekly memory boost is a nice way to stay present in my reading.

Metacognition Is the Cornerstone for Long-Term Learning

Another reason why Power Tools are so effective is that it shifts students' metacognition. If students are re-reading information over and over, they tend to develop the illusion of fluency and the illusion of confidence we mentioned in Chapter 5 on metacognition and feedback. Power Tools, on the other hand, challenge what students know. They realize, "Wow, I really need to study something more often," or, "I need to continue retrieving to check my understanding."

When you present research to students, light bulbs turn on. Because they are successful, they want *more* information about Power Tools and why they work. Soon enough, you're not the one explaining why they work; *your students are.* Consider this college student's sense of accomplishment and insight into their own learning when asked, "Do you think retrieval practices are helping you retain information from your book? Why or why not?"

> Yes, because it forces me to reach deep into my memory, sometimes a week in the past to grab a sliver of information. It feels good to answer questions only from memory rather than with the internet!

STEP 4: EMPOWER STUDENTS TO HARNESS POWER TOOLS *INSIDE* THE CLASSROOM

Name That Tool for Shared Vocabulary

Before students can harness Power Tools outside the classroom, it's essential to foster student ownership *inside* the classroom. One of our first strategies to help students make Power Tools their own is to have a conversation where students *Name That Tool*. In this way, you can develop a shared vocabulary you and your students use throughout the semester; a vocabulary they created, rather than one you created.

For example, a great start to building a common vocabulary would be to develop a class name for Brain Dumps or Brain Drains. You could start by having students write down everything they remember from their favorite vacation (or any other no-stakes question). Then, have a conversation with students about the process of pulling information out. Can they describe that feeling in their own words? You may want to give some examples of your own (we have a list of alternative names for Brain Dumps in Chapter 3). As we discussed in Chapter 7 on keeping it real, Name that Tool is also a great opportunity for students to brainstorm photos and illustrations that depict the process of retrieval, which can then be used on class posters, websites, and maybe even printouts for parents.

In addition to using Name That Tool with retrieval practice, spacing, interleaving, feedback, and metacognition, have students create names for desirable difficulties. Consider using Think-Pair-Share to help students describe desirable difficulties in their own words (but use our version with a spin on Think-Pair-Share from Chapter 6!). One example for an alternative name for desirable difficulties is "productive struggle," which you could share with students to start the conversation. After that, let students take the reins and drive the conversation with Name That Tool. You might be tempted to join in the conversation and provide ideas, but if students are going to make Power Tools their own, give them the space to do just that.

> ## Power Up
>
> Your turn! What is an alternative name you can think of to describe spacing to students?

Flash Forward so Students Reflect on Their Long-Term Learning

What, exactly, do we want students to remember? We often reflect on what we want students to learn and remember. But why not give the same opportunity to students? What do *they* want to remember? These are critical questions – one that you *and* your students need to ponder. So why not turn it into a classroom activity?

Toward the end of the semester, ask students to *Flash Forward*:

> *Now that you've taken this class, what is one thing you want to remember 10 years from now (and why)?*

Of course, you can change "one thing" to many things (we suggest five, max) or change "10 years" to any amount of time you want (20 years from now?).

Here are just a few benefits from Flash Forward:

- They're *retrieving*. By retrieving one thing in particular, they'll remember it even better than if you hadn't asked the question at all.

- They're *spacing*. They have to think back to course content throughout the entire semester and bring it to mind.

- They're drawing on *metacognition*. They'll reflect on what they know and also reflect on what they've already forgotten.

Flash Forward benefits for you:

- You build a supportive class culture around the process of learning.
- You get feedback on topics that were the most meaningful for students.
- You also have the opportunity for self-reflection and inspiration for the following or year semester.

Try Flash Forward, even for just five minutes, at any grade level. During discussion, students will remind each other of more memorable course topics, too. Who knows: They may even ask for *your* Flash Forward!

How Patrice Energizes Student Ownership in Her Classroom

One of my (Patrice's) overall goals has been to help create lifelong learning, critical-thinking, and educated citizens. I want to enable students to discuss, evaluate, and discern . . . not to have gone through our educational system simply copying down answers and taking everything they hear as truth without investigating it.

For example, in Chapter 6, I discussed mnemonics and the importance of building connections. I enjoy hearing students' responses and watching their eyes light up as we practice mnemonics. I feel like a magician as students say, "Boo-ya!" and raise their hands and arms as if their brains were becoming hot-air balloons.

Over the years, students have called mnemonics "Mrs. Bain's Magic" or "Mrs. Bain's Tricks." At one point, I challenged my students to name this strategy of "tricks." This was a great learning experience for me! I realized many of the learning strategies I use had become such common terms for them; they used the terminology in naming the strategy. Among my favorites are *Memory Tools, Retrieving Strategies, Memorization Shortcuts, Word Applications, w2w (Ways to Remember),* and SIMAW *(Strategic Items of Memory-Aiding Wordplay).* However, my all-time favorite was: *Metacogtricktion!*

I had several takeaways from this Name That Tool experience. If I want students to take ownership, naming strategies is a great way to get them involved with the process (Figure 9.2). I encourage all teachers to involve your students with learning and engage them in finding new strategies! My final takeaway was realizing the creative potential of my students. First semester, I am the one showing students how to make connections. However, starting second semester, I encourage students to find the "metacogtricktions" that work best for them. It has worked for me most of my life; it is pleasant to pass the torch.

Figure 9.2 One of Patrice's students recognizes the benefit of "metacogtricktion," an alternative phrase students created for metacognition.

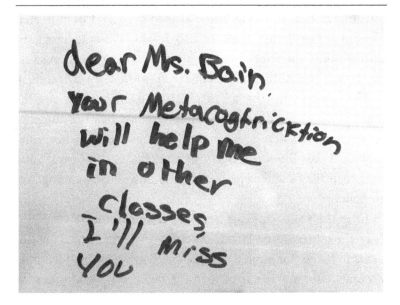

How Pooja Energizes Student Ownership in Her Classroom

Recently, I (Pooja) received an email from Luke Gangler, a middle school humanities teacher in Ecuador, with this question:

> I was thinking of having students design an experiment to test retrieval practice, in order to teach inquiry and research methods, and create buy-in for using the strategy on a regular basis. Do you have any advice for how to set it up?

I was excited to read his email, not only to learn about the strategies for his classroom but also because I do this in my psychology courses! Even at the college level, my reasons for having students design and conduct experiments are the exact same as Luke's: I spark students' interest in harnessing Power Tools for themselves. Here's what I do, which could work just as well for younger students with some scaffolding:

First, I ask my students this hypothetical question: "Which shoes make people jump higher, Nikes or Adidas?" This question is a bit silly, but I find it works really well as a starting point even for a college and graduate students. Importantly, I haven't used any scientific terminology yet (e.g., independent variables, random assignment, etc.). I have students work in small groups, and then we discuss what they came up with as a class; there are many ways to design an experiment to test this question, which adds to the fun during class discussion; there is no single correct answer.[4] I continue to use this example throughout the semester when talking about research (spacing!) and then I start asking additional questions: How would you figure out the fastest way to school? How would you figure out which type of soap you like?

Second, After some practice with these questions, I ask students how they study, why they study that way, if they were ever taught to study, and if it works for them. This makes for a very fun discussion, as students compare their personal experiences and realize most all of them have never been taught how to study effectively. Next, after a week or so (i.e., spacing again!), I ask my students: How would you figure out the best way to study? Very few of my students have thought about this before.

Third, we connect the two. How would you conduct an experiment on how to study? Students start brainstorming: studying with or without music, before or after sleeping, cramming or spacing things out, etc. After collaborating in small groups during class, students design real-life experiments to test and figure out the study strategies that work best for them.

Finally, my students conduct their experiments! They literally recruit participants, collect data, and report their results in class. By the end of the semester, students have taken true ownership of Power Tools because of their own research on how they learn. Most importantly, by conducting research on study strategies, students are learning about learning!

STEP 5: EMPOWER STUDENTS TO HARNESS POWER TOOLS *OUTSIDE* THE CLASSROOM

Now that students have experienced Power Tools through modeling, have gained an understanding of why they work, and have taken ownership inside the classroom, it's time to help them take the first steps toward using Power Tools independently *outside* the classroom.

In order for students to be successful at home, we present two additional conversations and three evidence-based study strategies that students can use to transform their studying and learning.

Give Students a Hook: Study Less and Learn More!

Students spend hours and hours re-reading and cramming, but nothing sticks. This is frustrating for us to watch, and it's frustrating for students, too! It's also tough to convince students to change old habits and place trust in Power Tools, even if you've modeled them and explained why they work.

That's where the "hook" comes into play: Power Tools *save* time. If students use Power Tools, they can study *less*. Wait, what? Yes, it's true! Think back to all the research we've presented in this book. Retrieval practice, for example, improves learning in the same amount or less time than re-reading. And, as we've mentioned, when students learn more and forget less, they don't have to keep studying over and over again. Scientists have also demonstrated that Power Tools can raise students' grades from a C to an A. This hook – spend less time studying and more time learning – can be a *huge* selling point for students!

Here's how one student, Drew, described Power Tools as time savers:

> Something that really stands out to me is that re-reading does *not* produce more learning! I used to re-read chapters in my textbook before an exam because I thought it made me more prepared. After all, it took forever, so it must be helping, right? Wrong! Learning about these strategies has saved me so much valuable time that I can now use on other things, or I can at least use that time to study in a more effective way. I spend less time studying, and I learn way more!

Talk About Ineffective Study Strategies and Why They Don't Work

Once students are intrigued by your hook, get their attention by sparking a conversation about *ineffective* study strategies that they probably use all the time. Ask these three simple questions:

- How do you study?
- Why do you study this way?
- Does it work?

Your students will be mystified! Many students have never thought about their own study habits before, and even fewer have been taught how to study effectively. After some discussion, have students write down their thoughts to this prompt: What is one *challenge* you have when it comes to learning?

When Pooja asks these questions with college students, many mention time management as their biggest challenge. Students also admit that, even though they've learned about Power Tools they don't use them. Here are a few reasons why:

- They're creatures of habit. They study how they've been studying for 12+ years.
- It takes extra time to try new strategies.
- They don't want to try Power Tools with new material (too high-stakes).
- They don't want to try these strategies with old material (they need to move on to new material).
- It's intimidating to learn new content *and* try new strategies at the same time.

Now's a great time to keep it real with students, just as we did in Chapter 7 with teachers! Have an open conversation with them. Share some of your own study experiences. Chances are, you crammed at some point in your life, too.

As teachers, we're often more aware of the *ineffectiveness* of students' study habits than they are. Here's how Alex, a teacher from Illinois, expressed his frustration with students' study habits:

> Students think they get it in class and refuse to acknowledge doing any work because they insist they get it. Which for the most part they do. But then they lose it overnight because they don't practice it. So they see math as a useless concept because they had it right up until they didn't. Then they bomb a test. Which I then have to grade. Which makes me feel miserable. Because I feel like I failed in my job to educate.

Wow. This is a powerful reflection, and there's a lot going on when it comes to students' habits outside the classroom. Let's break it down:

- Alex feels that students "think they get it," an indication of metacognition that needs improvement.
- Alex feels that students "lose it overnight," an indication that students have learned information in the short-term, but they forget it quickly over the long-term.
- Alex feels that students "don't practice it," suggesting that they aren't engaging in retrieval practice.
- Alex feels that students then "bomb a test," probably as a result of students' ineffective strategies.

Students don't like to fail, and teachers don't like to see their students fail either. Have an honest conversation about study strategies and why they don't work. This discussion can be a shock for some students, but a relief for others.

Also, let the students know that there's a lot of research about students' study habits, which typically include re-reading, taking notes, and highlighting (chances are, this is in line with how your students study).[5] And this research is clear: The most common study strategies work in the short-term, but the benefits don't last over the long-term.[6] You should also tell your students it's not just them – students from K–12 to college to medical school use the same ineffective strategies and get the same frustrating results.[7]

Many students realize they don't study effectively, but they continue to study that way anyway. Students have insight into their own habits, but they rarely discuss it. Telling students about Power Tools is a start. But give students the opportunity to share and reflect on their own study habits, too.

Power Up

Have you (yes, you!) been highlighting this book as you go along? Why?

Here are some small tweaks students can make to turn their ineffective strategies into powerful strategies.

Share How to Use Flashcards Effectively: Retrieve, Reorder, Repeat

Many students use flashcards. That's great! But here's a surprise: Flashcards don't always equal retrieval practice. Researchers at Kent State University have demonstrated that students actually "cheat" themselves by flipping cards over too early and dropping cards out of their deck too quickly.[8]

In laboratory experiments by Jeff Karpicke, when students used a flashcard program and made their own decisions (e.g., they could decide when to drop cards from the deck), there was no benefit on exam performance.[9] Similarly, in a classroom study led by Katherine Rawson, students did not remember as much when they could make their own decisions, compared to a flashcard program preset by researchers.[10]

Help students use flashcards more effectively with *Retrieve, Reorder, Repeat*:

1. *Retrieve.* Students should make sure they are retrieving the answer on the back of a flashcard *before* turning it over. One solution is for students to write down or say aloud the answer before flipping the card over. This holds them *accountable* and ensures they retrieve, rather than falling for the illusion of confidence – thinking "of course I know it" and flipping the card over prematurely.

2. *Reorder.* Students should *shuffle* their deck each time they go through it. Instead of students going through their flashcard deck in the same order again and again, they should challenge themselves with spacing and interleaving by simply shuffling the deck.

3. *Repeat.* Students should keep cards in their deck until they've retrieved it correctly *three times.* Just because a student has retrieved an item once doesn't mean they "get it." We know from research that students have a tendency to remove their cards too early, so by ensuring that students keep a card in their deck three times, students are accountable for making sure they *really* know it, rather than simply thinking they do. This also helps add space between cards in the deck (what scientists call *lag*), further increasing learning.[11]

Encourage Students to Swap Traditional Note-Taking for Retrieve-Taking

Think back to our simple strategy of swapping in-class note-taking for Retrieve-Taking from Chapter 3. (In fact, take a moment to retrieve and write down a description of Retrieve-Taking right now!)

Students can use Retrieve-Taking *outside* the classroom, too. When a student is reading a book, they can simply close the book, do a Brain Dump for one minute, and open their book again. They can do this after every page, section, or chapter. You can model this strategy in class: When students open their book, they should try to give themselves feedback and then continue reading. Research demonstrates that when students Retrieve-Take using a closed-book Brain Dump or a short-answer Retrieval Guide, compared to open-book note-taking, they remember much more in the long-term.[12] They can focus on reading or listening to a lecture, rather than juggling everything simultaneously, too.[13]

During a conversation about study strategies with a college student named James, Pooja realized he was Retrieve-Taking! Here's how he described his study strategy:

> I used to type my notes as I read, trying my best to not plagiarize, but what I found was:
>
> - I couldn't remember what I was actually learning because I was too focused on the note-taking itself.
> - I would get headaches because I was overly focused on completing the assignment thus stressing myself out because I knew that I was not really learning anything to begin with.
>
> I started taking notes by using the retrieval method a few months ago. I found that, by searching and reading for important material and remembering as much as I

could, it made the notes come out in my own words. It was also a lot quicker and easier and I was actually learning.

It was sort of like trial and error, but at the end of the day, the change happened when I decided to *try the thing I was afraid of doing* – actually reading and remembering things that weren't necessarily of interest to me. Of course, when I put this type of effort in, things that were of no interest became very intriguing. It's hard to read material that is not of direct interest, so when taking notes, kids tend to do it all simultaneously to get their assignments finished ASAP. They don't care about learning it and it's not fun, but really they have no idea until they actually tried to take notes with this retrieval method.

Additional Study Tips for Students

One question that's been popping up lately is whether students should *write notes by hand or type them on a computer.* One research study by Pam Mueller and Daniel Oppenheimer suggested that handwriting notes is more effective than taking notes via laptop.[14] Students can type as fast as a professor can speak, which means students tend to literally transcribe what's being said; there's little organization to laptop note-taking and students are simply being sprayed with a firehose. With handwritten notes, however, students have to at least think about what to write down because they can't write as quickly.

There are three things to keep in mind about this research:

1. As of 2018, there is surprisingly little research on this topic. This conclusion is mostly limited to one study, which has received a lot of press.

2. When students take notes on a computer, research demonstrates that students are more distracted during class.

3. When students take notes on a computer, they transcribe more, so they have more material to re-study, which may increase future learning compared to written notes.

Here's our opinion: Rather than worrying about typed versus handwritten notes, focus on in-class and out-of-class Power Tools like Retrieve-Taking and Two Things. Note-taking can emphasize getting information in (via firehose or otherwise). Focus on getting information *out*.

We'd like to address two additional components of students' study habits: *test prep* and *growth mindset*. Yes, students may use Power Tools (or at least practice quizzes) while preparing for high-stakes tests (e.g., Advanced Placement tests, teacher certification exams, standardized tests for graduate school, etc.). Will practice quizzes be effective? Sure, in the short-term. But encourage students to associate Power Tools with no-stakes or low-stakes activities in your classroom, *not* high-stakes exams. The more students associate Power Tools with high-stakes exams, the less likely they are to harness these powerful strategies while they study for class.

Also, you may be wondering how Power Tools are related to growth mindsets and social-emotional learning. At this point in time, there is not much research on how Power Tools affect social-emotional learning and vice versa. Based on what we know so far, research demonstrates that Power Tools increase students' confidence and engagement, as well as learning. This is another reason we love Power Tools: they foster student success in complex ways, beyond what we typically think of as academic achievement. One of the most helpful pieces of advice we've found comes from Lisa, the high school teacher we mentioned earlier: "*Having a growth mindset isn't enough. You could read* and re-read and re-read. Knowing you can change and having the right strategies go hand in hand."

From a research standpoint, we need to know more about student motivation. Why are some students inspired and driven to learn in school whereas other students are less motivated? How can we encourage students who have little interest in learning? We've all encountered a few lucky students who find an inspiring teacher who increases their drive to learn. But motivation is a complex cognitive process and the next frontier in the science of learning will require collective efforts by developmental, social, and cognitive scientists.

In the meantime, when it comes to empowering students to use Power Tools at home, it's critical to show them *how*. As Jennifer Gonzalez, educator and director of Cult of Pedagogy, put it:

> Teachers could be using these strategies with their students, but also saying to them, "You can do this at home." I feel like if teachers taught their students this stuff in September, they would see so much more success for the rest of the year. So many teachers send their students home and say, "Study for the test." Kids have no idea how to do that, and most of them will just open up their notes and look at them and open up their textbook or go online and look at the information instead of doing something with it.

Power Up

Contrary to our intuition, Power Tools – especially retrieval practice – have been proven to *decrease* student anxiety. Why?

STEP 6: EMPOWER STUDENTS TO PLAN, IMPLEMENT, AND REFLECT ON THEIR POWER TOOLS

By now, students have experienced five of the steps toward harnessing Power Tools on their own: They've participated in conversations about learning, engaged in Power Tools modeled by teachers, gained an understanding of why Power Tools work, taken ownership of Power Tools inside the classroom, and explored strategies they can use outside the classroom.

Next, encourage students to move beyond their comfort zone and try these strategies on their own, *independently*. First, students need to envision themselves using Power Tools and form a concrete plan of action. Here is a planning activity Lisa uses to support her students beyond her classroom:

During class, students are asked to write down responses to the following questions:

- What strategy are you most interested in or most likely to try on your own?

- When and where would it be possible for you to use this strategy? Choose one particular situation and write that down.

- What can you do to remember to use this strategy? Write it down and set up the reminder right now if possible (e.g., put a reminder in your phone)

- How will you keep track of whether you are using the strategy as you planned? Write down a tracking method and set it up right now.

We love this planning tool for students! It's concrete, it supports students in the classroom, and students can refer to it outside the classroom. As a follow-up activity, spark another conversation one week later: Who has already tried the one strategy you picked? If you haven't, what is stopping you from trying it? How can your peers support you with reminders and encouragement? During this conversation, have your entire class come up with a list of successes and challenges. Another follow-up (spaced!) conversation a week or two later would provide students with no-stakes support in class, again followed up by revisiting their plan outside of class.

How Students Take Ownership of Power Tools in Patrice's Classroom

We all need feedback in order to determine if we know something or if we don't. I (Patrice) give feedback purposefully and frequently. I use it after choral work, pair and share, flashcards, maps, question/answers, and Mini-Quizzes; it is second nature for me. Yet, how often are students able to analyze and reflect on this feedback over time?

To meet this challenge, I started what I call Data Analysis Day, where students review their entire semester's worth of data at the beginning of the second semester. (No, I do not spend my entire break compiling data! It is merely a click in the computer program; each student has a complete history of their classwork, Mini-Quizzes, and tests.) I use my most energetic teacher voice to announce, "It's Data Analysis Day!" I am met with incredulous looks and the pervasive feeling of "you've got to be kidding me" fills the room. My work is definitely cut out for me.

Because this is the first time my students have had this type of opportunity, I break it down step-by-step. (Depending on the ages of your students, you may want to consolidate steps.) I set the stage by having an anonymous sample of data on the SmartBoard to demonstrate how to analyze it. I compare first- and second-quarter grades; I point out how a particular student scored on Mini-Quizzes; and then I look at the chapter tests to see if they had maximized metacognition. I then ask students to look for trends – both positive and negative.

After this process, I hand each student his or her individual data sheets. Much to my delight, students become quite interested in transferring the analysis we had done together on the board to their own semester's work. After giving them a few minutes to look at their data, I ask these questions:

- How do your first quarter grades on classwork, Mini-Quizzes, and tests compare to second quarter? Were they better? Worse? Consistent? Inconsistent? And, of course, we follow up with "Why?"

- Are your grades close to 100%? Did you use the Four Steps of Metacognition to help you? Did you maximize your metacognition? Did you follow up on what you had missed on the test?

- Of all of the strategies we listed for metacognition earlier in the semester, which are the top three that work best for you?

- What are three specific ways you will maximize your metacognition second semester?

After students have responded to these questions, I take a tally. The students see that although every strategy is used, some are clear favorites. One of the most popular strategies is choral quizzing. This is when I call out a term or definition and the class answers in unison. The main reason cited for this as a favorite, especially from struggling students, was that often they weren't confident of their answers. Hearing the answers validated whether they knew it or not. Other strategies may not have had high votes, but are definitely effective for a smaller group of students. This demonstrates how important it is to provide a multitude of strategies; there is no "one size fits all."

The tally typically reveals:

- Students with top grades preferred Four Steps to Metacognition and Mini-Quizzes.

- Students who tended to struggle a bit preferred choral quizzing, Turn and Talks, and Mini-Quizzes.

I have found that my sixth-graders really ponder and analyze their data. It is easy for them to spot trends, both positive and negative. Numbers don't lie. Students feel validated when, indeed, they have maximized their efforts. My favorite lesson after Data Analysis Day is that we *all* have "off" days. For whatever reason, a student may score poorly on an assignment, a Mini-Quiz or two or three – yet can learn from it and still have a top grade at the end of the quarter.

Although the students originally did *not* want to participate in Data Analysis Day at the beginning of class, by the end, I had an energized group ready to tackle second semester with responsibility, accountability, and ownership. And, yes, I keep the analyses. I have found that when the weather begins to turn warm and spring giddiness enters my classroom, students might need a reminder of their second-semester goals. Out come the data analyses, and everyone gets back on track.

Often, when students (K–12 to college) engage in this reflection process, they wonder why they've never heard of these strategies before. Their confidence has grown and their understanding of how learning works has grown. Here is how a college student, Liz, described her realization after reflecting on learning:

> Rehearsal time does not produce learning! Sadly, neither does intent. Learning these two concepts brought forth a revelation in the way I approached studying. I would spend hours and hours with the intent of learning, going over chapters and then cram just before a test, but the results were sketchy at best. I had a difficult time understanding and I seriously considered the possibility that education was just not "my thing."

This information should be taught in grade schools to better assist students throughout their learning, because it certainly would have helped me. This has raised my self-esteem tremendously. I may still struggle learning some things, but my life has been enhanced by knowing I was studying wrong my entire life.

Power Up

How could you give a brief "elevator speech" about Power Tools to your students? Take a moment and outline it or write it out.

Bonus: Develop an activity where your *students* create a Power Tool elevator speech they can share with their parents or friends!

NOTES

1. Want to improve students' motivation to attend class, study, and learn? Model motivation, too! For research insights and practical tips on motivation, we recommend the book *Small Teaching: Everyday Lessons from the Science of Learning* by James Lang.

2. Do you remember the name of the fourth president of the US? Retrieve and write down your response before giving yourself feedback from earlier in this book!

3. Check Chapter 6 on combining Power Tools for feedback!

4. Try this out for yourself! How would *you* design an experiment to see whether Nikes or Adidas make people jump higher?

5. For more information and resources for students, we recommend the website www.learningscientists.org and the book *Understanding How We Learn* by Yana Weinstein and Megan Sumeracki.

6. Putnam, A. L., Sungkhasettee, V. W., and Roediger, H. L. (2016). Optimizing learning in college: Tips from cognitive psychology. *Perspectives on Psychological Science* 11: 652–660.

7. Agarwal, P. K., D'Antonio, L., Roediger, H. L., et al. (2014). Classroom-based programs of retrieval practice reduce middle school and high school students' test anxiety. *Journal of Applied Research in Memory and Cognition* 3: 131–139.

8. Wissman, K. T., Rawson, K. A., and Pyc, M. A. (2012). How and when do students use flashcards? *Memory* 20: 568–579.

9. Karpicke, J. D. (2009). Metacognitive control and strategy selection: Deciding to practice retrieval during learning. *Journal of Experimental Psychology: General* 138: 469–486.

10. Rawson, K. A., Dunlosky, J., and Sciartelli, S. M. (2013). The power of successive relearning: Improving performance on course exams and long-term retention. *Educational Psychology Review* 25: 523–548.

11. Pyc, M. A., Agarwal, P. K., and Roediger, H. L. (2014). Test-enhanced learning. In: *Applying Science of Learning in Education: Infusing Psychological Science into the Curriculum* (ed. V.A. Benassi, C.E. Overson, and C.M. Hakala). APA Society for the Teaching of Psychology. Available at www.teachpsych.org.

12. Agarwal, P. K., Karpicke, J. D., Kang, S. H. K., et al. (2008). Examining the testing effect with open- and closed-book tests. *Applied Cognitive Psychology* 22: 861–876.

13. For helpful tips on attention and working memory in the classroom, we recommend the books *Psychology in the Classroom* by Marc Smith and Jonathan Firth, and *Neuroteach* by Glenn Whitman and Ian Kelleher.

14. Mueller, P. A., and Oppenheimer, D. M. (2014). The pen is mightier than the keyboard: Advantages of longhand over laptop note taking. *Psychological Science* 25: 1159–1168.

Chapter **10**

Spark Conversations with Parents About the Science of Learning

Several years ago, I (Patrice) was visiting my cousin, Michelle, in Minneapolis. At the time, she had children in three different schools: one in elementary, one in middle, and one in high school. I was sharing my passion regarding student learning and she was sharing her frustration as a parent of school-aged children. Michelle and her husband are highly educated, competent, successful professionals in the business world. Their children are fun, smart, athletic, and creative. All three children are unique in personalities and views toward schools, teachers, and homework. Michelle asked me some great questions such as:

- At what point do you turn all homework responsibility onto the child?

- Should you bail out your child if they left something at home?

- I'm not sure how to best help my kids with school. What should I do?

- How much parental help is too much?

This conversation led me to deep thinking. The majority of parents have not majored in education and their basis of thought and frames of reference are often based on their own experiences. Education is quickly changing; forging ahead is met with educational jargon such as STEM and 1:1. Should it be a surprise that parents feel left out of the conversation?

As a starting point, I'd like to share with you the responses I received from parents when I conducted a nationwide survey in 2018.

Survey question	Parent response
What are the top two things that would help you with your child's learning?	(Most frequently selected) Understanding the basics of learning Understanding how to help my child study
Has your child's school, teachers, or PTA offered programs or presentations for parents on how people learn?	53%: No
There are years of research proving best methods and practices for student learning. If this information were available for parents, how likely are you to learn about it?	80%: Likely or very likely
How important is it to you that your child's teacher uses research-based learning strategies?	87%: Important or very important

Survey question	Parent response
How often have you asked your child's teacher if their teaching methods are research-based?	60%: Never
Have you asked teachers or administrators what type of professional development is available for teachers at their school?	67%: No

In this chapter, when it comes to unleashing the science of learning for *parents* (as a teacher or even for your own children), here are three important questions to ponder:

- What should you say to parents about the science of learning, given the limited time you have together?

- How can you get Power Tools into the hands of parents, so they can help their children study?

- How can you help parents understand *why* these strategies are so powerful?

MAKE THE MOST OF THE FEW, BRIEF CONVERSATIONS YOU HAVE WITH PARENTS

Teachers often spend time with the parents of struggling students. I (Patrice) have always wanted to spend time with all of the parents – to celebrate successes and share struggles. Yet, with hundreds of students, along with lesson planning, grading, copying . . . how is it possible?

One solution is parent-teacher conferences. Yes – I *enjoy* parent-teacher conferences! With my 150+ students, I am unable to meet with all parents. Our district allows 10-minute appointments, and each year I am booked solid. It has been a real boon to see how these conferences have evolved. Here is something I have noticed every year after parent conversations, which

Parents want to know how their children learn. Parents want to know how to best help their children.

was also confirmed by my parent survey: Parents *want* to know how their children learn. Parents *want* to know how to best help their children.

Ten minutes is so insufficient! To set the stage, student grade sheets are divided into three sections (these are the same papers that are shared with students on Data Analysis Day in Chapter 9): Classwork, Mini-Quizzes, and chapter tests.

A mother came to the conference perplexed; she was, one might say, a bit angry. She had noticed that her son received a couple of Fs on his Mini-Quizzes. Keep in mind that my Mini-Quizzes are low-stakes, no more than five points, so when a student only gets three points, it's technically an F. His grades in other classes averaged in the C range.

When she confronted her son, his replies were: "Oh, that's okay, Mom. They aren't really Fs. It was my metacognition showing I hadn't mastered it yet. This helps me know what to study so I can retrieve the information later." Say, what??? I was absolutely delighted! We then looked at the chapter tests; each one was 100%. I explained the process and she was surprised her son had pretty much nailed it. Our conversation changed from him being grounded to what he had simply not yet learned. A smiling mom left the conference.

I have found that centering conversations with parents around research and strategies has helped me strengthen the bond I have with them. Parents *want* tips and strategies to help their children. A brief, five-minute "mini-lesson" on Power Tools creates a bridge between school and home. Giving a synopsis of metacognition, spacing, interleaving, and retrieval, along with *why* these tools are effective, helps parents understand how their children learn. The very conversations regarding Power Tools that

I give to students are shared with parents. We become a team with shared language and shared strategies. I've always liked the acronym for TEAM: Together Everyone Achieves More. This is clearly evident as the parent, child, and myself become a triangle of learning.

I also enjoy presenting parent seminars on helping guide their children's learning outside of the classroom. (Parent seminars are also a way to fill the gap for the inability to meet with every parent during conferences.) Having the opportunity to inform parents of the research and strategies enables the use of Power Tools each year from the homefront.

I have had many conversations and emails with parents over the years expressing gratitude. It has been a game-changer. Countless parents have told me that using Power Tools has led to more efficient study time, better grades, and less struggle at home.

My takeaway is this: If a child is struggling, it is important for a parent to feel *empowered* rather than defeated.

Power Up

How do you set up your parent-teacher conferences?
Do you focus on how learning works?

PATRICE'S EVIDENCE-BASED STRATEGIES PARENTS CAN HARNESS AT HOME

In all of my years of teaching, I (Patrice) have yet to meet a teacher or parent who wanted to reinvent the wheel each and every year. These suggestions are not new; in fact, parents may have used them earlier in their own educational careers. *What makes these old strategies new is the way they are used.* Having parents – and students – aware of the research allows all to be purposeful and intentional in studying. Time is not wasted. Gone are the low grades that once appeared after hours of study. Here are two of my strategies:

Tell Me Three

- Whether in the car, over the dinner table, or anywhere, encourage parents to simply ask, "Tell me three things you learned today in (math, science, social studies, language arts, etc.)."

- Parents can also ask, "Remind me of three things you learned yesterday."

- When students bring work home, create a file (or jot down your own list), pull out a piece of paper, and have them write down three facts about a specific topic.

Tell Me Three uses retrieval practice. In addition, when using material from previous learning, this strategy uses spacing. Simply changing the question from "How was your day?" ("fine," end of dialogue) to "Tell me Three . . ." results in retrieval. I have found when parents use this tool, the students tend to listen differently in class. When students anticipate being asked "Tell me Three," they automatically use retrieval to make sure they have specific stories to retell later.

I cannot begin to estimate the number of parents who told me their carpools and meals are filled with "Mrs. Bain's Stories." If this type of daily dialogue began in the early years, think how fascinating the interaction and learning would be as the child progressed through school!

Powerful Flashcards

Parents may be very familiar with the use of flashcards, a widely used activity. In fact, parents may ask, "Using flashcards? Asking my child about his or her day? What is new or scientific about that?" My quick response would be, "Oh, I am so glad you asked! Let's talk!"

Rather than having children mindlessly go through flashcards, using metacognition purposefully increases learning. I would start at a young age and provide parental support. By middle school, I encourage studying with a buddy (within earshot of the parent). By upper middle school and high school, after seeing the benefits of flashcards, students tend to take ownership and include flashcards in their learning strategy repertoire. (See Chapter 9 on conversations with students for more flashcard tips.)

Parents can turn this age-old practice into Powerful Flashcards with these tips:

- Encourage children to retrieve by saying an answer aloud before flipping over the card; keeping a card in the deck until it's retrieved correctly three times; and shuffle the deck each time they go through it.

- Flashcards can be made on colorful index cards, with different colors to denote different categories of people, places, terms, ideas, etc.

- Have parents, siblings, or friends quiz using flashcards.

- Consider using websites, apps, and devices. There are numerous apps that can be used in place of index cards.

Point out to parents that these flashcard modifications use retrieval practice, spacing, interleaving, and feedback. In other words, all four Power Tools!

RESEARCH SNAPSHOTS TO EMPOWER PARENTS

As Patrice noted, parents often feel left out of the conversation when it comes to how their child learns. Parents also know that their access to research is limited, so it can be a challenge to fully buy into Power Tools.

Here are *Research Snapshots* you can share with parents to include them in the conversation. Research and data are very compelling, and sharing this with parents in conferences or evening seminars is so important for empowering parents, who can then empower their children.

By using these Research Snapshots, you don't need to spend hours digging into academic journals in order to share it with parents (unless you'd like to!). As Rebecca, an educator at a technical school in Missouri, told us:

> I want to make a difference in my students' lives. Often, I feel overwhelmed by the demands of my job. I try to pace myself, and finding practical strategies like yours is a balm to my tired soul. No need to research the validity of a practice; you and your colleagues have already done that!

With our Research Snapshots, parents will thank you, too. Here is an overall approach you can use with parents: *Pain, Promise, Proof.* Using this as a guide, discuss the *Pain* or problem parents are experiencing. Is it that their child studies for hours and doesn't see any results? Or perhaps that the parent doesn't even know where to begin?

Second, give parents a *Promise.* To do this, draw on Power Tools and the research you've already learned about in this book. For example, retrieval practice can boost students' grades from a C to an A; it increases learning for a variety of ages and subject areas; and it improves students' higher-order thinking and transfer of knowledge. As part of the *Promise*, you should also explain the why: *Why* do Power Tools work?

Power Up

What are two reasons why Power Tools improve learning that you can share with parents?

Third, give parents the *Proof*. Present these brief Research Snapshots to capture parents' attention and interest, even if you only have 10 minutes![1]

Research Snapshot: Retrieval Practice

- *Punchline.* Researchers demonstrated that when students quiz themselves at home via a website, exam performance increased by an entire letter grade.[2]

- *Procedure.* Sixth-grade students from Patrice's social studies classroom participated in this study. Using a website after school, students were encouraged (but not required) to self-quiz. Students' exam performance was compared between material that was self-quizzed vs. material that was not available on the website (but covered in class).

- *Results.* On the chapter test, students' performance increased by nearly a letter grade (90% vs. 82%). Even at the end of the semester, there was still a benefit for self-quizzing vs. no-quizzing by a letter grade (74% vs. 65%).

- *Takeaway.* At-home quizzing is beneficial, but students don't always follow research-based tips when left to their own devices.[3] Parents should discuss effective (and ineffective) ways of using flashcards and self-quizzing.

Research Snapshot: Spacing

- *Punchline.* Researchers demonstrated that spacing improves learning, but when students quiz themselves, use Retrieve-Taking, or engage in retrieval practice while reading a textbook, any spaced retrieval pratice while reading boosted learning by nearly two letter grades.[4]

- *Procedure.* College students read long biology textbook chapters and they completed quiz questions within the chapter, after reading the chapter, both locations, or they re-read information but didn't engage in retrieval practice.

- *Results.* After two days, the retrieval practice conditions led to greater final test performance than the re-read condition (62% vs. 45%), regardless of whether retrieval questions were within or after the textbook chapter. Answering repeated questions both during and after reading produced an additional benefit (65%).

- *Takeaway.* Practice questions improve learning, whether students retrieve while they read a textbook chapter or after they read the chapter. Parents should encourage students to self-quiz and use Retrieve-Taking at any point, even if students are unable to space textbook content over time.

Research Snapshot: Interleaving

- *Punchline.* Researchers demonstrated that when students mix up practice problems using interleaving, exam performance increased by nearly two letter grades.[5]

- *Procedure.* Seventh-grade students completed math problems (e.g., graph and slope problems) that were interleaved (ACB-CAB) or blocked (AABBCC).

- *Results.* After one day, interleaving improved exam performance by more than a letter grade compared to blocking (80% vs. 64%). One month later, interleaved performance was almost double compared to performance for the blocked group (74% vs. 42%).

- *Takeaway.* Interleaving is a simple strategy that dramatically boosts learning. Students can take the materials they're already studying and mix them up. Note that mixing up different course subjects (e.g., chemistry and history) does not increase learning.[6] Parents should encourage children to mix up *similar* concepts so they have to discriminate and think about subtle similarities and differences.

Research Snapshot: Metacognition

- *Punchline.* Researchers demonstrated that metacognition can be improved by prompting students to make judgments of learning and confidence ratings during learning, improving exam performance by nearly a letter grade.[7]

- *Procedure.* One group of college students listened to lectures, while another group of students listened to lectures and also received Metacognition Sheets during class. Students in the Metacognition Sheet group rated their understanding of the day's lecture, wrote down any difficult concepts, and reflected on how they could improve their understanding.

- *Results.* Across four exams, students in the Metacognition Sheet group scored significantly higher than students in the lecture-only group (85% vs. 78%).

- *Takeaway.* Prompting students to make judgments of learning while they study is beneficial for learning. Parents should encourage students to use metacognition prompts, even for just a few minutes, at the end of each study session.

Research Snapshot: A Powerful Combination of Power Tools

- *Punchline.* Scientists demonstrated that when college students used a quizzing program that combined retrieval practice, spacing, and feedback, exam performance increased by nearly a letter grade.[8]

- *Procedure.* College students in an engineering course used an online tutor that incorporated Power Tools for some course content and not other content.

- *Results.* On a final exam, exam performance was greater for content students learned using Power Tools compared to content without Power Tools (63% vs. 56%).

- *Takeaway.* Using Power Tools in combination, particularly via online websites and apps, can dramatically improve learning – including learning in STEM courses at the college level.

Power Up

Research studies we present often include a re-study condition compared to a retrieval practice condition.

Name one reason why re-study conditions are important in scientific research. If that was easy, challenge yourself: Name *two* reasons!

To empower parents, share our recommended resources at www.powerfulteaching.org, including videos, downloadable guides, books, and more. Parents are curious and hungry for the science of learning. Let's unleash it and *pass the torch to parents, too!*

NOTES

1. Note that these Research Snapshots are greatly simplified from the original studies. For more information, we encourage you to read the references we've cited for each snapshot.

2. Roediger, H. L., Agarwal, P. K., McDaniel, M. A., et al. (2011). Test-enhanced learning in the classroom: Long-term improvements from quizzing. *Journal of Experimental Psychology: Applied* 17: 382–395.

3. Karpicke, J. D. (2009). Metacognitive control and strategy selection: Deciding to practice retrieval during learning. *Journal of Experimental Psychology: General* 138: 469–486.

4. Uner, O., and Roediger, H. L. (2017). The effect of question placement on learning from textbook chapters. *Journal of Applied Research in Memory and Cognition* 7: 116–122. See also

Weinstein, Y., Nunes, L. D., and Karpicke, J. D. (2016). On the placement of practice questions during study. *Journal of Experimental Psychology: Applied* 22: 72–84.

5. Rohrer, D., Dedrick, R. F., and Stershic, S. (2015). Interleaved practice improves mathematics learning. *Journal of Educational Psychology* 107: 900–908.

6. Hausman, H., and Kornell, N. (2014). Mixing topics while studying does not enhance learning. *Journal of Applied Research in Memory and Cognition* 3: 153–160.

7. Nietfeld, J. L., Cao, L., and Osborne, J. W. (2006). The effect of distributed monitoring exercises and feedback on performance, monitoring accuracy, and self-efficacy. *Metacognition and Learning* 1: 159–179.

8. Butler, A. C., Marsh, E. J., Slavinsky, J. P., and Baraniuk, R. G. (2014). Integrating cognitive science and technology improves learning in a STEM classroom. *Educational Psychology Review* 26: 331–340.

Chapter 11

Powerful Professional Development for Teachers and Leaders

Take a moment and answer these two questions (and you can only pick one answer per question!):

> In the past two years, what is the main way you learn about education trends or new ideas that might be worth pursuing in your classroom?
> A. Social media
> B. Teacher-focused websites
> C. News websites
> D. Research journals
> E. Professional development and conferences
> F. Colleagues and word of mouth

Which of the following is most important when it comes to deciding whether you will try a new idea in your classroom?

A. It aligns with my instructional approach.
B. It's endorsed by my colleagues.
C. It's endorsed by my school and district leadership.
D. It's evidence-based.
E. It's aligned with standards.

These questions were part of a survey of 500+ K–12 teachers in the United States by the news source Education Week.[1] What do you predict was the most frequently selected choice for each question? Do you think your responses are the same as other teachers? Why or why not?

The results from this survey may (or may not) surprise you. For the first question, the most frequently selected method for learning about new instructional ideas was *professional development* – not social media, journals, or blogs. For the second question, the most important factor in trying out a new idea was whether it was *evidence-based*. In other words, evidence-based professional development was selected as the most common source for and reasons to adopt new ideas.

But how often is professional development actually evidence-based?

To set the stage for this chapter, here's how fifth-grade teacher Amber Haven felt about the need to unleash the science of learning:

> These strategies are such common tongue for me now . . . yet I am still so inspired to continue implementing them more and more. It baffles me that so many do not know about them. Don't you just want to scream it from the rooftops?!

IMPLICATIONS FOR POLICY MAKING, EDU-CATOR PREPARATION, AND LEADERSHIP

Travel back to the Introduction to our book. Whew! A lot has happened since then. Which is why we want to take a step back and remind you how we got here in the first place.

In the Introduction, we gave two reasons why we keep rein-venting the wheel when it comes to teaching:

1. The science of learning sits dormant in academic journals, rather than easily accessible in pre-service textbooks and professional development materials.

2. The science of learning has been featured in newspapers, blogs, and social media, but it's hard to know if these are trusted sources or simply people concocting more fads.

With *Powerful Teaching*, we have translated the science of learning and made it actionable. We have also provided trust-worthy research and strategies from experts each step of the way.

So now, we're going to stop driving in circles, right? Wrong! We all know that change takes time, energy, and patience. Power Tools and the strategies we provide have a huge impact on student learning in the classroom. But how can we impact learning and education on a larger scale? In particular, how can we transform education policy, educator preparation programs, and leadership with the science of learning?

When it comes to policy, there are no quick fixes. From 2006 to 2012, I (Pooja) served in a variety of roles in education policy at state and national levels. If you take a moment and retrieve, you may remember a handful of policy changes at that time, including Common Core, growth models for teacher evaluations, No Child Left Behind waivers, and Race to the Top, just to name a few. From my teacher preparation days before that, I can't begin to count the number of "portfolios" I had to put together to demonstrate my expertise as a teacher. And when I observed administrators at my school, I couldn't help but notice how burnt out they were from discipline issues and budget constraints.

Are Mini-Quizzes and Retrieve-Taking going to ease the burden in those situations? Obviously not. So, what can policy makers, teacher-educators, and leaders do? Demand evidence, of course! But that's not enough.

When it comes to education policy, *policy makers must seek evidence* from cognitive science based on the core principles in this book. Time is short and the challenges are many in the policy world. But understanding the fundamentals of retrieval, spacing, interleaving, and feedback would go a long way toward transforming education. Policy makers have a golden opportunity to take the science of learning and unleash it in districts, schools, and classrooms. And unless we begin to make decisions about education differently, we will continue adding money, programs, and computers, hoping for a quick fix.

When it comes to educator preparation, *every future teacher must have a deep understanding* of desirable difficulties, metacognition, and the critical importance of retrieval. In addition, by incorporating the science of learning into educator preparation programs, colleges and universities can add scientific rigor, encourage tougher standards for certification, enhance decision-making based on student data (rather than simply "the more data, the better"), and ultimately move us toward a higher-quality education system.[2]

When it comes to school and district leaders, *principals and superintendents must lead the charge to unleash – and initiate – research* on learning in their schools. To truly push the science of learning from the laboratory to the classroom, more research needs to be conducted *in partnership* with teachers and scientists. Even informal research in the classroom with support from school leaders can make a big difference in instilling an environment that welcomes best practices based on the science of learning.

What types of changes occur when leaders embrace research and evidence-based practices? Our 10+ year scientist-teacher collaboration wouldn't have been possible without Dr. Roger Chamberlain, former principal and current professor. Here's what he learned:

> It is imperative for principals to know how to analyze and understand student performance data, and change curriculum and instruction accordingly. I highly recommend that principals welcome the possibilities from applied research that promise to benefit your students, your teachers, and also your own professional development.
>
> I became more aware of the importance of knowing how our students were performing in order to drive instructional decision-making. Now, I am more aware of the positive impact of research on student learning, especially when research-based decision-making has never been more important for principals.[3]

In each of these cases – policy, educator preparation, and leadership – we ask this question: How can *you* be the leader that unleashes the science of learning?

AN INFORMED TEACHER IS A POWERFUL LEADER

There will always be a line of people out the door who claim to have a new and improved "evidence-based" professional development program, teacher prep curriculum, or assessment method. Often, these programs are based on anecdotes and fads, not science. So what's the big deal, as long as this professional development isn't harmful? Actually, these types of programs create a few challenges for you:

- You'll spend valuable prep time on instructional methods with inconsistent results because they're based on anecdotes.

- You'll spend precious classroom time on methods that don't improve learning, while there are actual research-based methods that are effective and improve learning.

- You'll spend money on ineffective teaching strategies and programs, when you can be unleashing the science of learning for free, without extra prep or grading time.

In line with the Education Week survey, how can you find genuine professional development that's evidence-based?

- Foundational principles from cognitive science are there for the taking! You don't need fancy professional development programs to understand the power of retrieval practice, spacing, interleaving, and feedback-driven metacognition.

- Create your own professional development! You can develop a workshop about Power Tools, which you can share with colleagues and unleash the science of learning – all evidence-based, all created by you.

- In order to separate the real stuff from the bunk, it's critical to become an informed consumer, especially when you're confronted with brains, neuroscience, and many "scientific" terms you've probably seen floating around.

- Once you dig into research on how learning works, not only do you become an informed *consumer* of science, but you become an informed *educator* – and a powerful teacher, facilitator, and leader! As a teacher-leader put it, "By understanding the science of learning, you not only hold the ball; you learn how to dribble it well, too."

This is why it's critical to learn more about research! We know this can seem daunting and we definitely know that time is a precious commodity. As high school psychology teacher and blogger Blake Harvard stated:

> While reading research and considering how it can be applicable in my classroom takes up a significant amount of time, in the long run it saves time in the classroom because instruction is more efficient and effective.

If you'd like to learn more about the research in this book, check the notes at the end of each chapter. All the research studies we discuss are accompanied by references because we want *you* to take this research into your own hands and delve into it more.

Here's a baby step: Simply Google the authors of any studies in this book you find interesting. Most scientists have websites that describe their research and link to their publications. You can also find interviews with scientists on YouTube, so you can learn about their research firsthand, sans jargon. We have many links to scientists' websites, publications, podcast interviews, and YouTube videos at www.powerfulteaching.org.

If you want to read a research article or primary scientific source, start by Googling the title of the article and reading the abstract. We also recommend looking on the Association for Psychological Science's website (www.psychologicalscience.org) for research summaries written for a broad audience. You can use their website to search by topic, scientist, keyword, etc.

Don't be shy about contacting a local college or university to learn more. Google the name of a scientist whose research interests you and email them. You'll most likely get a response, and if you'd like to conduct research at your school, they'll be thrilled! Share your expertise with them and they will be grateful. Besides, it's just an email and you have nothing to lose.

One note of caution: If someone says something is "research-based" or "evidence-based," ask for proof. Where did their data come from?[4] Who participated in the research studies? What exactly was compared or measured? Try to get a sense of whether someone is giving you the full research picture or simply citing journal articles because it looks impressive. And always be wary of brains!

It's *so* important to become an informed teacher. Why? Because, as Maya Angelou said, "Do the best you can until you know better. Then when you know better, *do better*." Now's the time to know better – and to do better.

BECOME A POWERFUL LEADER ON POWER TOOLS

It's time to lead your own professional development! Based on the EdWeek survey we mentioned earlier, teachers are clearly hungry for more evidence-based professional development. And who better to create powerful, research-based, teacher-led professional development for your team, school, and beyond? You! We have given you the research and strategies to unleash the science of learning and Power Tools in your classroom. Now, it's up to you to pass the torch; it's up to you to make an impact and share the science of learning.

As one example, Andria Matzenbacher, an instructional designer with the Federal Reserve Bank of St. Louis, shared the following:

> When I was a teacher, prior to my participation in research with Patrice, I thought of tests as a way to assess – not as a way to learn. Now, as an instructional designer, I ask learners to retrieve what they have learned. I strongly believe in the benefits of these strategies for students of all ages and I share them with instructors.

Shift your teaching to *powerful* teaching and share Power Tools with your team, school, and beyond. We can't do this for you, but *you* can. Creating your own professional development is an opportunity for agency, leadership, and transformation. It's also an opportunity to share and collaborate. Just think about the impact you can have on your students, classroom, and school!

We know it can be challenging to change people's knowledge, beliefs, and practices. In reading this book, we hope we've done that for you – with newfound scientific knowledge, shifting trust and confidence in evidence-based education, and teaching practices based on Power Tools. As a leader, you will be looking to change educators' knowledge, beliefs, and practices, too. This can be intimidating! Here are a few questions to think about:

- Imagine yourself as the teacher in this (slightly edited) proverb: Give an educator a fish and you feed them for a day. Teach an educator to fish and you feed them for a lifetime. Why is "teaching an educator to fish" important to you?

- Imagine what you want your classroom, school, or district to look like when it's empowered with the science of learning. How might the culture look the same or different?

And imagine what can happen if we pass these strategies to pre-service teachers! As educators and leaders, it's our responsibility to share these Power Tools and transform learning. If you work with college students, new teachers, or mentor teachers, have conversations about how they learn and remember, too. How powerful! You're not only using Power Tools to improve learning and modeling them for your students – you can impact *future* teachers, too.

Power Up

What is one way you can help a tutor or pre-service teacher become engaged in powerful teaching?

USE POWER TOOLS TO MOVE FROM *SIT-AND-GET* TO GETTING INFORMATION *OUT*

When it comes to professional development, you may have heard the phrase "sit-and-get." It means exactly what it sounds like: When it comes to learning, we're so used to "sitting" and "getting," without any interaction or practice. This is exactly like getting information "in" versus getting information "out!" Ironically, we know that sit-and-get doesn't work with students. So why do we keep subjecting ourselves to this during professional development?

When you unleash the science of learning, focus on getting information "out." In other words, use Power Tools and model them while sharing them! Whether you're changing your teaching individually or leading professional development with a team, here are quick retrieval strategies you can use to shift from sit-and-get to powerful learning:

- Start your professional development with Retrieval Warm-Ups. This will get teachers' attention right from the start – just like with your students.

- Complete the Do It Yourself (DIY) Retrieval Practice Guide in Chapter 12, whether individually or as a group. You can quiz each other or quiz yourself multiple times by writing in pencil and erasing it for spaced retrieval.

- As you complete the DIY Retrieval Guide, collaborate and develop a common language for the four Power Tools. Think about the progress that will happen when you and your team use shared language with each other and in the classroom.

- During professional development, model Power Tools. For example, ask one of the everyday examples at the beginning (e.g., how many bones are there in the human body?), and then throw in the same question later in the presentation or workshop.

Here is a quote from a K–12 teacher who participated in *powerful* professional development:

> There's nothing worse than sitting through professional development that's meaningless. It's really demoralizing. Being a part of this discussion, I'm *finally* learning what I should have learned in college, which totally changes how I will be teaching in the future.

USE POWER TOOLS TO MOVE FROM "ONE-AND-DONE" TO SPACING, INTERLEAVING, AND FEEDBACK

Another approach to teaching and learning you've likely experienced is the frustration with "one-and-done" programs. You might be super engaged and excited about a new idea, but soon, you've moved on. In other words, you've just experienced one-and-done. How can we use Power Tools to continue the conversation? Here are quick strategies using spacing, interleaving, and feedback:

- Complete the questions and exercises in the DIY Retrieval Guide chapter-by-chapter, or ideally, interleave and mix up the questions for yourself and fellow teachers. Don't forget to include elaborative feedback, too.

- Create a book club, whether in your team, school, or virtually. When you read a chapter each week, you're spacing!

- Even if your professional development is packed into a day or two (we know how hard it can be to find the time in the first place), send an email follow up to participants every week or so with even just one of the questions from the DIY Retrieval Guide in Chapter 12. You'll be surprised by how many teachers will respond and seek feedback each week.

- Space out opportunities for accountability. Start a collaborative spreadsheet to track how often Power Tools are used in your classrooms. Even a quick check-in for five minutes after school adds accountability – but make them no-stakes check-ins, of course!

CREATE POWERFUL PROFESSIONAL DEVELOPMENT

Here's our plan for powerful professional development. Each row represents an activity that can be done all at once (e.g., a one-day workshop) or, ideally, spaced out over time. The times listed are approximate and can be longer if you add time for discussion and additional retrieval practice questions from the DIY Retrieval Guide. The DIY Retrieval Guide is also a helpful spaced activity for participants to complete in between sessions.

Time (min)	Topic	Powerful Activities
15	Introduction	Start with Retrieval Warm-Ups and everyday examples. Retrieval practice: What's one thing you've learned so far today (if there are other workshops beforehand) or learned yesterday (about anything)? Retrieval practice: What's one thing you remember from our most recent professional development workshop?
30	Chapter 1: Discover the Power Behind Power Tools	Explain the three-part model of learning (encoding, storage, and retrieval) using a diagram or a real-life example. Activity: Have participants come up with their own example from everyday life of the three-part model. Activity: Complete the three-part chart from Chapter 2 (or space this for later).

Time (min)	Topic	Powerful Activities
60	Chapter 2: Build a Foundation with Retrieval Practice	Describe retrieval practice in your own words using the Retrieval Warm-Ups and everyday examples. Explain one of the Research Snapshots. Activity: Have participants describe retrieval practice in their own words. Explain the 10 benefits from retrieval practice and the concept of desirable difficulties. Retrieval practice: What is one way you already use retrieval practice in your classroom? Retrieval practice: What's the difference between retrieval practice, formative assessment, and summative assessment?
60	Chapter 3: Empower Teaching with Retrieval Practice Strategies	Provide teaching strategies for retrieval practice: Brain Dumps, Two Things, Retrieve-Taking, Mini-Quizzes, etc. Retrieval practice: Do a Brain Dump of everything you've learned so far! Retrieval practice: How can you incorporate one of these strategies and start small? Ask the same Retrieval Warm-Up you asked at the beginning as a transition to spacing.
45	Chapter 4: Energize Learning with Spacing and Interleaving	Describe spacing (use the spaced example you just gave). Explain one of the Research Snapshots. Retrieval practice: Why is spacing more effective than cramming? Retrieval practice: What is one example of spacing in everyday life? Retrieval practice: Do you already use spacing in your classroom? If so, how?

Time (min)	Topic	Powerful Activities
45	Chapter 4: Energize Learning with Spacing and Interleaving (continued)	Describe interleaving and give an example (song verses, fruit salad, math problems, etc.)
		Explain one of the Research Snapshots.
		Retrieval practice: Why does interleaving improve learning?
		Retrieval practice: What's the difference between spacing and interleaving?
60	Chapter 5: Engage Students with Feedback-Driven Metacognition	Describe metacognition, judgments of learning, and confidence ratings.
		Give an example where metacognition is changed with feedback (e.g., capitals of Australia and Kentucky).
		Explain one of the Research Snapshots.
		Retrieval practice: What are the Four Steps to Metacognition?
		Retrieval practice: Why is feedback so crucial for metacognition?
		Activity: Complete a Metacognition Sheet for concepts you've learned about so far.
		Retrieval practice: How would you explain metacognition in your own words?
30	Chapter 6: Combine Power Tools and Harness Your Toolbox	Retrieval practice: What are the four Power Tools? How would you explain them to students?
		Retrieval practice: How do you already use the four Power Tools in your classroom?
		Retrieval practice: How can you take one of the Power Tool strategies you've learned about and combine it with another Power Tool?

Time (min)	Topic	Powerful Activities
60	Chapter 7: Keeping It Real: Use Power Tools to Tackle Challenges, *Not* Add to Them	Retrieval practice: What is one hesitation or challenge when shifting from your current instruction to Power Tools? Develop a plan with participants to hold each other accountable for trying out Power Tools. Retrieval practice: What are neuromyths? Which neuromyths did you incorrectly endorse? Why do you think these neuromyths persist?
45	Chapter 8: Foster a Supportive Environment: Use Power Tools to Reduce Anxiety and Strengthen Community	Retrieval practice: What are three ways you can decrease student anxiety with Power Tools? Activity: Develop two or more Retrieval Warm-Ups you can use in your classroom to decrease anxiety. Retrieval practice: What is Noun-Name Tag? How does it incorporate all four Power Tools?
60	Chapter 9: Spark Conversations with Students about the Science of Learning	Retrieval practice: What are the six steps for having conversations with students about the science of learning? Activity: Create an elevator speech to explain why Power Tools work to students. Retrieval practice: What is one way you can help students form a concrete plan for using Power Tools at home?

Time (min)	Topic	Powerful Activities
60	Chapter 10: Spark Conversations with Parents about the Science of Learning	Retrieval practice: Why might parents be reluctant to use Power Tools inside and/or outside the classroom? Activity: Describe one of the Research Snapshots in your own words, as though you were explaining it to a parent. Activity: Create a resource for parents about the science of learning and Power Tools. Activity: Develop a seminar for parents to share the science of learning and Power Tools.
60	Chapter 11: Powerful Professional Development for Teachers and Leaders	Retrieval practice: What are Two Things you've learned about each Power Tool? Retrieval practice: What does powerful professional development look like to you? How does the science of learning fit in? Activity: Develop a professional development plan for the semester and the school year that includes one Power Tool you'll implement, how often you'll check in with a colleague, and how often you'll come together for additional discussion. Activity: Develop a workshop or course for pre-service teachers to share the science of learning and Power Tools.
60	Chapter 12: Do It Yourself Retrieval Guide	Activity: Interleave all of the questions and exercises in the DIY Retrieval Guide. Swap your interleaved guide with someone else, answer five questions from their guide, and give each other feedback. Activity: Develop five more questions that are not included on the DIY Retrieval Guide. Retrieval practice: What is one strategy or Power Tool you can use *tomorrow*? Retrieval practice: If you could remember only one thing about this book in 10 years, what would it be? Why?

Time (min)	Topic	Powerful Activities
45	Conclusion: Unleash the Science of Learning	Retrieval practice: Time yourself for 5 minutes and write a Brain Dump for everything you remember about this book.

Activity: Write a manifesto! Why is the science of learning and evidence-based education important to you? What is one thing you can do to help teachers focus on getting information out? What is one challenge teachers frequently encounter, and what is your advice to help them meet the challenge? |
| 60 | Reflection | Next, we have discussion questions to foster reflection on teaching, learning, and Power Tools. Pick one and dedicate at least 1 hour to guiding your colleagues through a reflection activity.

You can complete these reflections before professional development (right now is a perfect time, too!), during professional development, or afterward as a spaced activity. |

REFLECTIONS TO SPARK POWERFUL CONVERSATIONS

Reflect on Your Classroom

These are reflection questions you can use individually or to spark a conversation, adapted from Jennifer Gonzalez's "gut-level teacher reflection":

- Look around your classroom (or picture it in your mind). What does successful learning look like? What does unsuccessful learning look like?

- Open up your plan book (or spreadsheet, or wherever you keep your lesson plans from the year) and just start browsing. How often do you space things out? How often do you use retrieval as a learning strategy, and not just as a formative or summative strategy?

- Take a look at your student roster. Which students have high grades? Do they also have a keen sense of metacognition and awareness of their own learning? Which students struggle with retaining information?

Reflect on Your Rose, Thorn, and Bud

- *Rose*: What is one success you've had with Power Tools?

- *Thorn*: What is one challenge you've had with Power Tools?

- *Bud*: What is one new idea, strategy, etc. you've had with Power Tools?

Reflect on Your Implementation

- Of the four Power Tools, what is one strategy you can implement tomorrow?

- Of the four Power Tools, what is one strategy you can implement next semester?

- What are two challenges you may encounter in implementing Power Tools?

- What are two unanswered questions you have?

Reflect on Your Now and Next

- Where are we now?

- What are we currently doing in this area?

- What are our most pressing needs in this area?

- Which one of the Power Tools would most likely help us meet our needs?
- Where do we go from here?
- Who needs to be involved?
- What roadblocks might we encounter?
- How can we work around those roadblocks?

Challenge, Power, Action

In the first column, we've listed some of the *challenges* for implementation from Chapter 7: Keeping it Real. In the second column, we've listed *powerful* strategies based on Power Tools that tackle or reduce these challenges. In the third column, think about what *action* you will take in your own classroom, school, or district. For example, Power Tools help students remember knowledge year to year, but what is a specific strategy or curriculum change you can make to be sure you're focused on long-term learning, not just short-term learning? Actions speak louder than words. So how will you take what you've learned and put it into action?

The Challenge	Your Power with Power Tools	What Action will you take to make this happen?
Students don't remember knowledge from year to year.	Strengthen long-term learning for diverse students and subject areas with retrieval practice.	
Textbooks and assessment systems reinforce student cramming.	Strengthen effective and continuous learning with spacing and interleaving.	

The Challenge	Your Power with Power Tools	What Action will you take to make this happen?
Students are under-motivated and they don't take their own learning seriously.	Strengthen students' ownership, engagement, and metacognition with effective feedback.	
Classroom implementation of new strategies takes too much time.	Strengthen your teaching strategies without more preparation, classroom time, or grading time.	
Professional development programs promote fads and ineffective teaching strategies.	Strengthen teacher-led professional development and share the science of learning.	

Start, Stop, Keep

When it comes to the four Power Tools, what would you like yourself, your school, and your district to *start, stop, and keep?* It's as simple as it sounds. For example, perhaps you want to start using Brain Dumps more often, stop reviewing what happened in the previous class, and keep providing elaborative feedback.

Complete this chart as you reflect on immediate steps, what you might want to start/stop/keep next semester, or start/stop/keep the following school year.

	Start	Stop	Keep
Self			
School or Department			
District or University			

POWER TOOL IMPLEMENTATION CHECKLISTS

These Power Tool Implementation Checklists can be used for self-feedback, discussion during professional development, and classroom observation as simple reminders of key features for each Power Tool.

How to Harness Retrieval Practice

❏ Use retrieval practice as a learning strategy, not an assessment tool.

❏ Make retrieval practice low-stakes or no-stakes (i.e., not for a grade), to reduce anxiety and encourage desirable difficulties.

❏ Use retrieval practice with a variety of subject areas (science, history, etc.) and grade levels.

❏ Provide retrieval practice as frequently as possible. Practice makes perfect.

❏ Reassure students and parents that challenging learning is a good thing.

❏ Examine your teaching strategies – do they focus on getting information "in" or "out" of students' minds?

❏ Use a variety of question types: fact-based, conceptual, higher order, and transfer.

❏ Use a variety of question formats: Brain Dumps, multiple-choice, and short-answer.

❏ Use a variety of strategies to implement frequent retrieval practice: quizzes, index cards, bell work, quick writing prompts, etc.

❏ Expand meaningful retrieval practice by asking "why" and "how," not simply "what."

How to Harness Spacing and Interleaving

❏ Provide spaced retrieval practice after a lesson is complete, perhaps even a few days or weeks later.

❏ Break up lessons into smaller sessions. Instead of teaching one long lesson over a topic, divide up the lesson into smaller lessons and space them over multiple days.

❏ Revisit concepts that have been taught in previous class meetings, ideally using retrieval practice or Two Things.

❏ Harness technology to help students set a spaced study schedule (e.g., websites, spreadsheets, apps, etc.).

❏ Interleave concepts so students have to learn how to both choose a strategy and use a strategy.

❏ Simply take a few problems from a blocked assignment and mix them to create interleaved assignments.

How to Harness Feedback-Driven Metacognition

❏ Ask yourself: Are students being challenged, or is learning easy and "fluent?"

❏ Encourage students to use their knowledge in novel contexts and situations by acknowledging the challenge of transfer.

❏ Combine retrieval practice with elaborative feedback to maximize the "bang for your buck" when fostering transfer.

❏ Keep students actively engaged in their metacognition, by alternating between retrieval practice and feedback.

❏ Offer hints or prompts to ensure students recognize opportunities to transfer their learning.

NOTES

1. Where do teachers get their ideas? *Education Week* (2018, January 10). Retrieved from www.edweek.org.

2. We recommend an excellent report for teacher-educators on the science of learning by Deans for Impact, which is available at www.deansforimpact.org.

3. Agarwal, P. K., Bain, P. M., and Chamberlain, R. W. (2012). The value of applied research: Retrieval practice improves classroom learning and recommendations from a teacher, a principal, and a scientist. *Educational Psychology Review* 24: 437–448.

Chapter 12

Do It Yourself
Retrieval Guide

We practice what we preach. In this Do It Yourself (DIY) Retrieval Guide, we provide the Power Ups featured throughout the book, as well as *new discussion questions and exercises* for professional development. Keep in mind:

- This is *your* DIY Retrieval Guide! You can quiz yourself while you read this book, after you read it, or both. You might even want to complete these questions in pencil so you can erase your responses and quiz yourself again down the road for spaced retrieval.

- We intentionally don't provide summaries at the end of our chapters. We don't even give you the answers or page numbers in this DIY Retrieval Guide, so you'll need to retrieve and seek elaborative feedback for yourself!

In addition to unleashing the science of learning for yourself, we encourage you to use this DIY Retrieval Guide in a few different ways:

- As a resource for questions, strategies, and implementation checklists in your classroom
- As discussion questions and Power Ups for professional development and book clubs
- As activities and exercises for teachers, administrators, students, and parents
- As a method for modeling Power Tools by experiencing them yourself

Lastly, there are two additional things to note:

- In line with research, we've included a variety of multiple-choice, short-answer, conceptual, and higher-order questions to boost learning.
- Many of the Power Ups and questions included in this DIY Retrieval Guide were spaced throughout the book; here, we've grouped them by chapter for convenience, but we hope you'll space and interleave the questions for yourself!

INTRODUCTION TO POWERFUL TEACHING

What are five words that come to mind when you think about learning?

Have you heard of research from the science of learning before? If so, from where? If not, why do you think you haven't?

Have you ever gone along with a fad, anecdote, or new idea for your instruction? Why?

What does powerful teaching look like to you?

CHAPTER 1: DISCOVER THE POWER BEHIND POWER TOOLS

Describe the four Power Tools in your own words.

Describe these key terms in your own words: desirable difficulties, cognitive science, and the science of learning. How do these terms relate to education?

What's the difference between encoding and retrieval?

We talked about three stages of learning (encoding, storage, retrieval) in the context of going to a coffee shop. Describe the three stages of learning in a situation from *your* everyday life!

Take a moment and think about how you teach. What do students do in your classroom each day? Now, ask yourself: Are you supporting their short-term learning or long-term learning?

CHAPTER 2: BUILD A FOUNDATION WITH RETRIEVAL PRACTICE

Why are desirable difficulties a good thing for learning?

Why is having students retrieve information more powerful for learning than having them listen to or read something?

Where do you focus your teaching: encoding, storage, or retrieval? Do you focus on one stage more than another stage?

In the Roediger and Karpicke (2006) study we presented, did college students predict they would remember more after re-reading or after retrieval practice? Why?

Research studies we present often include a re-study condition. Why is a restudy condition important? Name at least one reason. If that was easy, challenge yourself: Name *two* reasons!

How do you define retrieval practice? How would you describe retrieval practice to *parents*?

In this chapter, we listed 10 benefits of retrieval practice. What are three of them?

What's the difference between retrieval practice, formative assessment, and summative assessment?

What is one reason why students struggle to transfer their knowledge?

What are two examples of retrieval practice in your everyday life where you purposely retrieve in order to remember something (rather than focusing on encoding it)?

Complete the following table, based on the three stages of learning: encoding, storage, and retrieval.

	Did you intentionally try to encode this information?	How long have you had this information stored?	How many times have you retrieved this information?
What you ate for breakfast			
King Tut's age			
Your favorite vacation			
One thing about this book			

Now, circle the boxes where you feel your own learning occurred. Do you see any patterns in what you circled? When it comes to the classroom, where do you focus your activities and teaching practices – encoding, storage, or retrieval? Do you focus on one stage more than another stage?

CHAPTER 3: EMPOWER TEACHING WITH RETRIEVAL PRACTICE STRATEGIES

Why should retrieval practice be used as a learning strategy and *not* an assessment strategy?

Do a Brain Dump about Brain Dumps! Write down everything you know about Brain Dumps.

How would you describe retrieval practice to *students*?

In the 2006 study by Roediger and Karpicke mentioned in Chapter 2, how did college students engage in retrieval practice?

As we discussed in the previous chapter, what does it mean to move from pyramid learning to powerful learning? Write a description or draw your own diagram!

As a powerful teacher, here are questions you might encounter from teachers, administrators, and parents. How would you respond to each one?

- Is retrieval practice effective for only basic information, like vocabulary and facts?
- Should retrieval practice questions be multiple-choice, short-answer, or free response?
- Are Pre-Tests before a lesson beneficial for learning?
- Which is more effective for long-term learning: open-book or closed-book quizzes?

- Is retrieval practice effective if students generate their own questions?
- Are active strategies, like concept mapping, as effective as retrieval practice?
- How is retrieval practice different from "cold calling?"
- Don't we have to start with encoding and get information in, before students can retrieve and pull information out?

Retrieval practice can take three minutes or less! How can you incorporate just one of these strategies and start small *tomorrow*?

Which of these Power Tool strategies could you incorporate into your teaching easily? Which one works best for you, given your content and your classroom?

A. Brain Dumps

B. Two Things

C. Mini-Quizzes

D. Dice Game

CHAPTER 4: ENERGIZE LEARNING WITH SPACING AND INTERLEAVING

Why do you think your students cram the night before an exam?

One additional benefit of spacing is savings. What is it? Give an example or describe it in your own words.

Why is spacing more effective than cramming? Why is interleaving more effective than blocking?

How do you already use spacing in your classroom? How can you incorporate even more?

How much spacing is optimal for learning?

Which type of spaced retrieval practice is most beneficial for long-term learning?

A. Retrieval before a lesson
B. Retrieval during a lesson
C. Retrieval immediately after a lesson
D. Retrieval a few days after a lesson

What's the difference between spacing and interleaving?

What is one example in your everyday life where you purposely *retrieve* information in order to remember it, rather than focusing on *encoding* to remember it?

Can't I just give cumulative exams? Isn't that the same thing as spacing and interleaving?

CHAPTER 5: ENGAGE STUDENTS WITH FEEDBACK-DRIVEN METACOGNITION

What is a judgment of learning? What is a confidence rating?

First, on a scale from 0% to 100%, what percentage of Chapter 4 on spacing and interleaving will you remember in one week? Second, who invented the polio vaccine? Rate how you feel on a scale from 1 (guessing) to 5 (definitely sure). Now, which of these questions is a judgment of learning and which is a confidence rating?

In Chapter 5, we presented a 2008 study by Agarwal and colleagues where students predicted how much they would remember after one week. Retrieve and write down Two Things you remember about that study!

Take a moment and think about metacognition in your classroom. What does it look like? Now, ask yourself:

- Do my students *really* know it or do they simply think they do?
- Have my students assessed their own learning through retrieval, or are they relying on their intuition that something was easy to learn so it'll be easy to remember?
- Do my students seem confident in their knowledge, and if so, what may be contributing to this confidence?

What are the Four Steps to Metacognition?

What's the difference between Retrieval Cards and Metacognition Sheets?

When you provide students with feedback, are you also giving them opportunities to examine their metacognition? Or are they simply looking at a grade and moving on?

Who was Lady Murasaki Shikibu? What is the capital of Australia? What is the capital of Kentucky? Do you know the answers or are you guessing? On a scale from 1 (guessing) to 5 (definitely sure), how confident are you in your answers?

In Figure 12.1, we've provided new "items to know" about Power Tools. Complete this Metacognition Sheet using the Four Steps of Metacognition. Provide this activity during professional development, too!

Figure 12.1   Use the Four Steps of Metacognition and explore what you've learned from this book!

Metacognition Sheet

★	?	Items to Know	Answer
		The difference between spacing and interleaving	
		The illusion of fluency	
		The most effective types of feedback for transfer	
		Why retrieval practice improves learning	

When it comes to providing students with feedback, which of these options is *true?*

A. It's optimal to provide students with feedback quickly, even while they are retrieving. This way, they won't make any mistakes.

B. It's optimal to provide students with feedback that includes elaborative examples and descriptions.

C. It's optimal to provide students with feedback after a delay. Immediate feedback doesn't improve learning; only delayed feedback improves learning.

CHAPTER 6: COMBINE POWER TOOLS AND HARNESS YOUR TOOLBOX

For each of the four Power Tools, write down how you are *already* applying it in your instruction or curriculum.

Write down four things:

- One thing teachers, students, or parents should know about the science of learning
- One thing teachers, students, or parents should know about retrieval practice
- One thing teachers, students, or parents should know about metacognition
- One thing teachers, students, or parents should know about a research study presented in this book

In order to harness Power Tools before beginning a chapter or unit, ask yourself:

- What is the essential question for this chapter?
- What information do my students have to know in order to answer it?
- How will I support students in retrieving this information?
- What types of feedback will assist students in improving their metacognition?
- At what intervals will I space retrieval practice?
- Am I able to interleave content and mix it up?

What is a Power Ticket? Draw an example or write down a description.

What are mnemonics? Come up with an example or a mnemonic you already use. Take a look at your curriculum. Can you find mnemonics that will help your students make connections and aid retrieval?

What are the pros and cons of using Power Tools separately vs. combined?

Which Power Tools improve higher-order thinking and transfer? Why?

CHAPTER 7: KEEPING IT REAL: USE POWER TOOLS TO TACKLE CHALLENGES, *NOT* ADD TO THEM

What is one hesitation, challenge, or mountain between your current instruction and using Power Tools?

Work individually or in a group and identify one way Power Tools can address each of these challenges:

- Do I have to spend more time preparing for class if I use Power Tools?
- Do I have to spend more time grading if I use Power Tools?
- When I spend time using Power Tools, how can I cover the same amount of material?
- Will my students get lower grades if I use Power Tools?
- How can I adapt Power Tools for diverse students from a range of backgrounds and abilities?
- Do I have to spend money on Power Tools?
- There are so many Power Tools and strategies. Where do I start?
- There's a lot of stuff out there about "brain-based learning." Is that the same thing as Power Tools?

What is one way to find support and accountability *beyond* your school or university as you apply Power Tools in your classroom?

What are the first five words that pop into your head when you think about the word *brain?*

Which of these statements do you think are true and which ones are false?

	True or False?	
We only use 10% of our brain.	T	F
Children are less attentive after consuming sugary drinks and/or snacks.	T	F
Short bursts of motor coordination exercises can improve integration of left and right hemisphere brain function.	T	F
Students learn better when they receive information in their preferred learning style (e.g., auditory, visual, kinesthetic).	T	F
The production of new connections in the brain can continue into old age.	T	F
A common sign of dyslexia is seeing letters backward.	T	F
Some of us are "left-brained" and some are "right-brained," and this helps explain differences in how we learn.	T	F
Listening to classical music increases children's reasoning ability.	T	F
Academic achievement can be negatively impacted by skipping breakfast.	T	F
Brain-training games and crossword puzzles increase cognitive function and reasoning skills.	T	F

CHAPTER 8: FOSTERING A SUPPORTIVE ENVIRONMENT: USE POWER TOOLS TO REDUCE ANXIETY AND STRENGTHEN COMMUNITY

In Chapter 8, we discussed three ways student anxiety increases in the classroom and three ways to decrease anxiety using Power Tools. What are they?

Do you remember what you ate for breakfast yesterday? Do you remember the name of the fourth president of the United States? How do these two questions make you feel? Do they feel fun or stressful? Why?

In this chapter, we presented our no-stakes Retrieval Warm-Up strategy. What are one or two more Warm-Ups you can create and share with your students?

First, what are the four Power Tools? Second, which Power Tools are incorporated during Noun-Name Tag?

Contrary to our intuition, Power Tools – especially retrieval practice – have been proven to *decrease* student anxiety. Why?

CHAPTER 9: SPARK CONVERSATIONS WITH STUDENTS ABOUT THE SCIENCE OF LEARNING

In this chapter, we gave six steps for empowering students through conversations about the science of learning.

- First, what are the six steps?
- Second, we gave three ways to explain to students *why* Power Tools work. What are they?
- Third, we gave three ways to help students harness Power Tools *outside* the classroom. What are they?

What is an alternative name you can think of to describe spacing to students?

Do you remember who ruled Sumer? How long did he rule? Did you experience a desirable difficulty answering this question? Why or why not?

Have you been highlighting this book as you go along? Do you typically highlight when you read? Why?

What is one way you can help students form a concrete plan for using Power Tools at home?

How could you give an "elevator speech" about Power Tools to your students? Take a moment and outline it or write it out. (Bonus: Develop an activity where your *students* create a Power Tool elevator speech they can share with their parents or friends!)

CHAPTER 10: SPARK CONVERSATIONS WITH PARENTS ABOUT THE SCIENCE OF LEARNING

What are three things you could say to parents about Power Tools, given the limited time you have with them?

We presented five *Research Snapshots* you can share with parents. Describe at least one of the research studies in your own words.

How did parents react to Patrice's nationwide survey? Were any specific results surprising to you?

How can you set up your parent-teacher conferences, so the conversation centers around research-based learning strategies and not grades?

What is one reason you could share with parents about why Power Tools improve learning?

Research studies we present often include a re-study condition compared to a retrieval practice condition. Name one reason why re-study conditions are important in scientific research. If that was easy, challenge yourself: Name *two* reasons!

CHAPTER 11: POWERFUL PROFESSIONAL DEVELOPMENT FOR TEACHERS AND LEADERS

Take a moment and answer these two questions (you can only pick one answer per question!):

In the past two years, what is the main way you learn about education trends or new ideas that might be worth pursuing in your classroom?

A. Social media

B. Teacher-focused websites

C. News websites

D. Research journals

E. Professional development and conferences

F. Colleagues and word of mouth

Which of the following is most important when it comes to deciding whether you will try a new idea in your classroom?

A. It aligns with my instructional approach.

B. It's endorsed by my colleagues.

C. It's endorsed by my school and district leadership.

D. It's evidence-based.

E. It's aligned with standards.

In this EdWeek survey, what do you predict was the most frequently selected choice for each question? Check Chapter 11 for the answers. Are your responses the same as your predictions for other teachers? Why or why not?

Imagine yourself as the teacher in this (slightly edited) proverb: Give an educator a fish and you feed them for a day. Teach an educator to fish and you feed them for a lifetime. Why is "teaching an educator to fish" important to you?

Imagine yourself as a leader, step by step: How will you support your colleagues as they make a small change from an old umbrella to a new umbrella? And what about a bigger change from an old house to a new house?

Imagine what you want your classroom, school, or university to look like when it's empowered with the science of learning. How might the teacher culture look the same or different?

Look around your classroom (or picture it in your mind). What does successful learning look like? What does unsuccessful learning look like?

Open up your plan book (or spreadsheet, or wherever you keep your lesson plans from the year) and just start browsing. How often do you space things out? How often do you use retrieval as a learning strategy, and not just as a formative or summative strategy?

Take a look at your student roster. Which of your students have high grades? Do they also have a keen sense of metacognition and awareness of their own learning? Which students struggle with retaining information?

Answer these questions:
- Rose: What is one success you've had with Power Tools?
- Thorn: What is one challenge you've had with Power Tools?
- Bud: What is one new idea, strategy, etc. you've had with Power Tools?

Of the four Power Tools, what is one strategy you can implement tomorrow? What is one strategy you can implement next semester?

What are two challenges you may encounter in implementing Power Tools?

What are two unanswered questions you have about Power Tools?

Which one of the Power Tools would most likely help you meet your needs? What steps can you take to implement this Power Tool? Who needs to be involved? What roadblocks might you encounter? How can you work around those roadblocks?

When it comes to the four Power Tools, what would you like yourself, your school, and your district to start, stop, and keep?

What are Two Things you've learned about each Power Tool?

What does powerful professional development look like to you? How does the science of learning fit in?

What is one additional way you can help a tutor, pre-service teacher, or fellow teacher become engaged in powerful teaching?

CONCLUSION: UNLEASH THE SCIENCE OF LEARNING

Time yourself for five minutes and Brain Dump everything you remember about this book!

Here are our learning objectives from the Introduction. Which objectives were met? Can you add one more thing you learned or achieved?

- Develop a deep understanding of powerful teaching strategies based on the science of learning, whether you are a past, present, or future educator.
- Go behind the scenes and explore key findings from cognitive science research.
- Gain insight into how scientifically based strategies are effectively implemented in a variety of academic settings without additional preparation, classroom, or grading time.
- Think critically about your current teaching practices and classroom environment from a research-based perspective.
- Develop tools to share the science of learning with students and parents, ensuring success inside and outside the classroom.
- Identify next steps to transform teaching and unleash the science of learning in your classroom.

RETRIEVAL WARM-UPS AND EVERYDAY EXAMPLES

Here are our no-stakes Retrieval Warm-Ups using everyday examples for retrieval practice. Just like for students (more details in Chapter 8 on building a supportive environment), these would be great to use at the beginning of professional development to get educators thinking about retrieval. You might have fun answering all of these right now, too!

- What did you have for breakfast yesterday?
- At what age king Tut become a pharaoh?
- What was your favorite vacation?
- How many bones are there in the adult human body?
- In which US city is the Baseball Hall of Fame located?
- What is the name of the fourth president of US?
- What is your *least* favorite ice cream flavor?
- If you could travel anywhere in the world (where you haven't been before), where would you go?
- Would you rather visit the world 100 years in the past or 100 years in the future? Why?
- If you had to wear a hat every day for the rest of your life, what type of hat would it be?
- Would you rather own a sailboat or a hot-air balloon? Why?
- What is your favorite word? Why is it your favorite?
- If you could eat only one food or dish for the rest of your life, what would it be?
- What type of animal would be a really good musician? Why?
- What is your favorite emoji? Describe it or draw it!
- If you could switch places with anyone in your family for a day, who would it be?
- What is your proudest accomplishment this semester (or year)?

- Younger students: What is your favorite thing to eat for breakfast?

- Older students: What was your favorite thing to eat for breakfast as a kid?

- Older students: Would you rather lock yourself out of your car or out of your house?

- Older students: Have you ever gone skydiving? Why or why not?

Conclusion

Unleash the Science of Learning

Education is in dire need of transformation. For years, parents, students, and educators have asked: Why is our education system ineffective? Instead, we urge you to ask a different question: Why do we *still* use a system that has been shown to be ineffective?

Educational curricula and methods are driven by personal experience and anecdotes passed on from teacher to teacher, not grounded in research and scientifically based practices. Teaching strategies and fads reinvent the wheel, while student achievement remains stagnant.

Education is in deep trouble and this problem hasn't been solved – yet. Because evidence-based education isn't what's actually going to transform learning. It's *you*.

Reading this book isn't enough. We can give science away and make it accessible – *but you have to unleash it*. You have the power to move mountains, no matter how small or big. Whether it's a specific student or a teacher-educator program, *you* have the power to transform education for generations to come.

Take a close look at the image from our book cover. The light bulb represents the "aha" moment of learning and the sparks illustrate getting information *out*. But why are there *five* sparks? Four sparks represent the four Power Tools. And the fifth spark? *It's you!* Whether you are a teacher, administrator, curriculum designer, or professor, it's *your* turn to ignite powerful teaching in your classroom, school, district, and university.

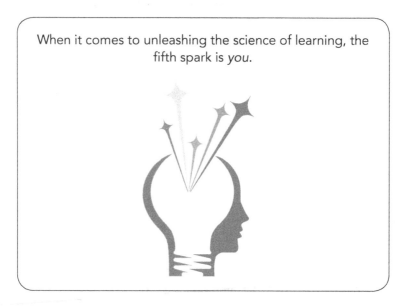

When it comes to unleashing the science of learning, the fifth spark is *you*.

We've passed the torch to you. Now, it's your turn to pass the torch to others. Will *you* unleash the science of learning? Will *you* transform teaching? Because students need your help. Parents need your help. And our entire education system needs your help.

We can't do it without you.

Education is in trouble and it can't wait any longer. The science of learning exists. *It's time to unleash it.*

Acknowledgments

We are indebted to Amy Fandrei, Pete Gaughan, and our team at Jossey-Bass, as well as Kate Gagnon, Henry L. Roediger III, and James Lang, without whom *Powerful Teaching* would have remained ideas in our heads, not pages in a book.

Roddy Roediger, Mark McDaniel, and Kathleen McDermott paved the way for classroom research on cognition and student learning, and they also paved the way for our deep collaboration and meeting of the minds. They have supported us through a research partnership, zany classroom adventures, and now, a book together. Who knew that a chance meeting on that sunny Wednesday in 2006 would lead us here?

POOJA AGARWAL

I thank those who have inspired me along the way, as far back as I can remember: Elizabeth Albro, Susan Fitzpatrick, Jennifer Gonzalez, Doug Lemov, and Daniel Willingham. Additional thanks to Matt Miller, Susan Randall, Michael Rutter, Bonni Stachowiak, the Boston Athenaeum, and the Brain Trust for the space to explore and the support to make this happen.

A huge thank you to many family and friends who have guided me throughout my uncharted blob of teaching, research, policy, book writing, and learning. I am especially grateful for my mother, Anu; my husband, Chuck; and my dear friend, Geoff. And to Liz, Jerry, Sachin, Nikhil, Sheetal, Jenn, Julia, Steve, Tim, Jason, Bec, Cindy, Wilma, and Jenny; thank you for listening to my harebrained ideas and nodding along with patience.

I sincerely thank all the scientists who have dedicated their lives to learning about learning. This book would not exist without their wealth of knowledge and expertise.

Funding for the research featured in this book was generously supported by the Institute of Education Sciences, the James S. McDonnell Foundation, the National Science Foundation, the Association for Psychological Science, the American Psychological Association, and the Harry S. Truman Scholarship Foundation.

Lastly, I am indebted to countless faculty, staff, and students from the Illinois Mathematics and Science Academy, Washington University in St. Louis, and the Berklee College of Music. Every person – from every walk of life – is a powerful teacher. Thank you for sharing your knowledge with me.

PATRICE BAIN

I am forever grateful to Steven, Jed, Amber, and Cam for their patience, for sharing with me the teaching profession, and for remaining my steadfast cheerleaders. I also wish to thank those who have supported and inspired me throughout the journey: my immediate and extended family, Roger Chamberlain, Merrill Harmin, Jack Turner, my ILSTOY and NNSTOY families, the Educational Advisory Board at the Federal Reserve Bank of St. Louis, my fellow CMS teachers, my Sioux Falls friends, and my Rowdies.

I am indebted to everyone who has made my "shouting from the mountaintop" a reality. Thank you to the Institute of Education Sciences, Annie Murphy Paul, REL Mid-Atlantic, NOVA, Digital Promise, EdSurge, and ConnectEd Learning, as well as to the readers of this book.

And to my students, who will always have a place in my heart, thank you.

Name Index

Lilienfeld, S. O., 23n.6
Lim, S. W. H., 91n.29
Little, J. L., 80, 90nn.17, 18, 19
LoGuidice, A. B., 226n.6
Lyle, K. B., 35, 51n.12
Lynn, S. J., 23n.6

M

Macdonald, K., 198, 203n.9
Maddox, G. B., 119n.2
Marsh, E. J., 23n.3, 90n.21,
   151n.11, 277n.8
Matzenbacher, A., 286
McCabe, D. P., 196, 203n.8
McDaniel, M. A., 22n.2, 34, 51n.11,
   52n.18, 88n.1, 90nn.21, 23, 107,
   120nn.6, 11, 150nn.3, 6, 177n.8,
   204n.10, 276n.2
McDermott, K. B., 34, 88n.3, 89n.13,
   91n.28, 329
Melton, A. W., 22n.1
Mestre, J., 51n.15
Metcalfe, J., 23n.4, 133, 151nn.7, 15
Miller, M., 183, 329
Mills, T., 200
Morris, C. D., 52n.21
Mueller, P. A., 255, 263n.14
Murre, J. M. J., 120n.8

N

Nadel, L., 50n.7
Nellis, M., 147
Newman-Smith, K., 50n.7
Nietfeld, J. L., 142, 152n.18, 277n.7
Nieves, B., 173
Norton, M., 198
Nunes, L. D., 120n.9, 277n.4

O

Oppenheimer, D. M., 255, 263n.14
Osborne, J. W., 152n.18, 277n.7
Overson, C. E., 263n.11

P

Pachai, A. A., 226n.6
Pan, S. C., 44–45, 52n.24, 53n.26,
   121n.15
Pashler, H., 51n.8, 197–198,
   203n.4, 204n.10
Pereira-Pasarin, L. P., 226n.5
Perkins, K., 91n.24
Powell, S. R., 203n.1
Pulley, L., 133, 241, 256–258
Putnam, A. L., 38, 51n.15,
   177n.4, 263n.6
Pyc, M. A., 263nn.8, 11

R

Rahman, S., 90n.24
Rajaram, S., 226n.5
Ratcliffe, T., 91n.27
Rawson, K. A., 23n.3, 151n.10, 162,
   177n.3, 203n.3, 253, 263nn.8, 10
Rickard, T. C., 44–45, 53n.26
Ringstead, C., 52n.20
Roediger, H. L., 22n.2, 30, 50n.5,
   51nn.11, 15, 61, 88nn.1, 4,
   89nn.8, 12, 90nn.16, 21, 91nn.26,
   28, 95, 107, 120nn.7, 11, 121n.17,
   150nn.3, 4, 6, 159, 177n.8, 225n.3,
   263nn.6, 7, 11, 276nn.2, 4, 306,
   308
Rohrer, D., 94–95, 107, 108, 119n.1,
   120nn.5, 9, 10, 12, 121nn.13, 14,
   21, 204n.10, 277n.5
Rose, N. S., 150n.5, 203n.2
Ross, B., 51n.15
Rowland, C. A., 89n.6
Ruscio, J., 23n.6

S

Sciartelli, S. M., 177n.3, 263n.10
Seneviratna, G. S., 121n.20
Shimamura, A., 23n.4
Simons, D., 23n.5

Subject Index

Page references followed by *fig* indicate an illustrated figure.

A

Achievement, 5, 15, 33–35, 40, 125, 180, 185–186, 249, 259–260, 268, 272–274. *See also* Grading

Advanced Placement (AP), 33, 218, 256

Anxiety: competitive activities, 119, 218–219, 224, 233; distribution of grades reduce, 216–218; phrases that reduce, 232–233, 257; Noun-Name Tag, 223–225; signs that reduce, 208–211*fig*; Retrieval Warm-Ups, 221*fig*–223; sources of, 206–207; survey on student anxiety, 214*fig*–215

Assessment: baking a cake analogy for, 47–49, 206; cumulative exams, 159–161, 310; difference between retrieval practice and, 47–49, 57, 78*fig*, 206–207, 216–218; file drawer analogy for, 48; formative assessment, 38, 47–49, 57, 77, 83, 128, 175, 206; influence on study strategies, 17, 84, 94, 96, 126–127, 129–130, 159–160, 215–218, 249, 256; low-stakes, 57–59, 67–68, 72*fig*, 116–118, 137*fig*, 165*fig*, 191–193, 206–207, 216–219; no-stakes, 48–49, 64, 159, 199, 216–219, 256; summative assessment, 47–49, 57, 206–207. *See also* Grading

B

Big Basket Quiz (BBQ), 98–99, 119, 164–165*fig*, 217. *See also* Retrieval practice strategies

Blasts from the Past, 97–98, 116, 164, 169*fig*. *See also* Spacing

Bloom's Taxonomy, 40–42*fig*. *See also* Higher order thinking; Transfer of knowledge

Brain Dump, 56–61*fig*, 76–77, 79–80, 86, 89n8, 149, 171, 174, 176, 179, 182, 186, 193–194, 215, 232–233, 243, 254, 291, 295, 298–299, 308–309, 323. *See also* Retrieval practice; Retrieval practice strategies

Breathe and Retrieve, 146–147, 149, 176. *See also* Retrieval practice strategies

C

Checklists for implementation, 299–300

Cognitive science. *See* Research

Confidence ratings, 129–130, 142–147, 275, 311. *See also* Judgments of learning; Metacognition

Content areas: Buddhism, 44; dressage, 44; engineering, 84, 275–276; everyday life, 12, 17, 19–20, 37–38, 49–50, 99, 113, 192–193, 307; firefighting, 156–157, 163, 192; foreign language, 32, 153, 158; history, 34*fig*, 109*fig*–110; mathematics, 108–109*fig*, 157–158; medicine, 35–36, 41; music, 156; psychology, 71–73, 162, 196, 216, 239, 247, 285; sign language, 44; sports, 107–108; statistics, 35, 157–158, 161; science, technology, engineering, math (STEM), 214*fig*–215, 266, 275–276

Cramming, 4–5, 14, 94–95*fig*, 96, 100, 105, 149, 159–161, 218, 291, 310. *See also* Spacing; Study strategies

Cumulative exams, 159–161, 310. *See also* Assessment; Interleaving; Spacing

D

Desirable difficulties: description of, 17–19, 55, 282; forgetting as a, 100, 106; interleaving as a, 113, 116, 253; retrieval practice as a, 45*fig*, 131; spacing as a, 116, 167*fig*, 253; supporting students, 62, 65–66, 88, 185–186, 191, 206–207, 212, 239, 241–243. *See also* Learning; Mistakes

Dice Game, 117–119, 176, 215, 309. *See also* Interleaving

Do It Yourself (DIY) Retrieval Guide, 22, 201, 288–289, 303–304

E

Education policy and training, 281–283

Educational technology, 15, 43, 75, 79, 173–175, 300

Encoding, 10*fig*–12, 27–29, 87, 99, 290, 305–307, 309–310. *See also* Forgetting; Learning

Errorless learning. *See* Misconceptions about learning

Exams. *See* Assessment

F

Feedback: description of, 5, 11, 14, 16, 123; elaborative feedback, 134–135, 137, 146, 154, 175, 193, 238, 300, 303; following correct answers, 131–133; following errors, 136–137, 209*fig*, 219; following multiple-choice questions, 79–82; immediate compared to delayed, 135–136, 146, 175; research in college classrooms, 142; research in the laboratory, 127–128, 132, 135; research in middle school classrooms, 132–133, 135; transfer of knowledge, 5, 38–39, 44–47, 49, 134–135, 137, 272, 300. *See also* Metacognition; Mistakes

Figures: Bang for your buck, 183*fig*; Bloom's Taxonomy, 42*fig*; Brain Drain photo, 60*fig*; Brain Drain example, 61*fig*; Combining Power Tools, 112*fig*, 155*fig*; Four Steps of Metacognition, 140*fig*, 310*fig*; Graph of interleaving compared to blocking, 109*fig*; Graph of the optimal timing of quizzes, 102*fig*; Graph of retrieval practice compared to re-reading, 30*fig*; Graph of retrieval practice compared to standard lessons, 34*fig*; Graph of research on Metacognition Sheets, 143*fig*; Graph of spacing compared to cramming, 95*fig*; Metacognition Sheet, 143*fig*; homemade white board, 78*fig*; illustration of a brain, 195*fig*; Mini-Quiz, 69*fig*; mnemonics, 169*fig*; Name That Tool, 246*fig*; Power Ticket, 167*fig*; Retrieval Cards, 139*fig*; retrieval practice from Pooja's classroom, 72*fig*; Retrieval Warm-Up, 221*fig*; Shared responsibility, 231*fig*; Sample lesson plan, 165*fig*; Sign: Time to think and learn, 209*fig*; Sign: It's okay to make mistakes, 209*fig*; Sign: Willing to risk, 210*fig*; Sign: Ask for help, 211*fig*; Stages of learning, 10*fig*; Transfer of knowledge, 45*fig*; Test anxiety survey, 214*fig*

Fishbowl strategy, 118–119, 176. *See also* Interleaving

Flash Forward, 244–245. *See also* Retrieval practice strategies; Spacing

Forgetting, 16, 32, 37, 95*fig*–96, 99–100, 105–106, 147–148, 183*fig*–185, 225. *See also* Desirable difficulties; Learning; Spacing

Four Steps of Metacognition, 138–141, 144–145, 149, 164, 176, 193–194, 260, 292, 310*fig*. *See also* Metacognition

G

Google, 43, 70, 74, 285

Grading, 13–15, 48, 58, 67–69*fig*, 75, 149, 179–182, 216–218, 284, 298. *See also* Assessment; Time management

H

Higher order thinking, 16–17, 38–43, 47, 70–71, 79–82, 259–260, 272, 299. *See also* Bloom's Taxonomy; Transfer of knowledge

I

Illusion of confidence, 129–130, 242, 253. *See also* Metacognition

Illusion of fluency, 31–32, 128–130, 242, 310*fig*. *See also* Metacognition

Interleaving: blocked practice, 107–109*fig*, 115–117, 274, 300, 310; description of, 5, 12, 14, 106–110; Dice Game, 117–119, 176, 215, 309–310, 314; difference between spacing and, 115–116, 159; example from art history, 112*fig*; example from mathematics, 107–108; example from music, 156; example from social studies, 109*fig*–110; example from sports, 107–108; Fishbowl strategy, 118–119, 176; fruit salad analogy for, 112*fig*–113; importance of discrimination for, 5, 14, 112*fig*–115, 160; Lightning Round, 118–119, 176; research snapshot about, 274; serial position effect, 113, 121n16. *See also* Spacing

J

Judgments of learning, 125–128, 130, 138–143*fig*, 175, 229, 275, 311. *See also* Confidence ratings; Metacognition

L

Learning: consolidation of, 100, 119n5, 121n20; difference between long-term and short-term, 18, 30, 82–83, 95*fig*–96, 101, 156–157, 159–161, 185–186, 241, 251–252, 297, 305; everyday life, 12, 17, 19–20, 37–38, 49–50, 99, 113, 192–193, 307; memory, 21, 26, 36–38, 41–43, 47, 226, 242; Mnemonics, 168–170, 188, 245–246*fig*, 314; social-emotional, 20, 189–190, 256–257; stages of learning, 10*fig*–12, 17, 21, 27–28, 87, 305, 307, 231*fig*. *See also* Encoding; Forgetting; Retrieval

Learning styles. *See* Misconceptions about learning

Lightning Round, 118–119, 176. *See also* Interleaving

M

Metacognition: Four Steps of Metacognition, 138–141, 144–145, 149, 164, 176, 193–194, 260, 292, 310*fig*; hypercorrection effect, 133; illusion of confidence, 129–130, 242, 253; illusion of fluency, 31–32, 128–130, 242, 310*fig*; judgments of learning, 125–128, 130, 138–143*fig*, 175, 229, 275, 311; research on Metacognition Sheets, 142–143*fig*; research snapshot

about, 275. *See also* Feedback; Study strategies

Metacognition Line-Up, 75, 147–149, 176

Metacognition Sheets, 138, 141, 142–145, 149, 176, 188, 275, 292, 310*fig*

Mini-Quizzes, 65, 67–71, 69*fig*, 76, 94, 98, 117–118, 135–136, 164–165*fig*, 176, 188, 215, 217, 236, 259–261, 268, 282, 291, 309. *See also* Retrieval practice; Retrieval practice strategies

Misconceptions about learning: brain-based learning, 180, 194–199; brain training games, 197, 199; concept mapping, 85–86; myths about learning, 16; errorless learning, 48, 136–137; learning styles, 196–198; neuro-myths, 196–199

Mistakes, 48, 57, 132, 136–137, 208–209*fig*, 212, 219, 224. *See also* Anxiety; Feedback; Learning

Mnemonics, 168–170, 188, 245–246 *fig*, 314

Multi-tasking, 23n5, 254, 263n.13

Multiple-choice questions, 22, 32, 79–82, 85, 96, 132, 134, 174, 299, 304, 308

N

Name That Tool, 243–244, 246*fig*. *See also* Anxiety

Noun-Name Tag, 223–225, 226n10, 237, 293, 317. *See also* Retrieval practice strategies

O

Open-book quizzes, 64, 75, 84, 157, 161, 254, 257, 308. *See also* Retrieval practice

P

Parent-teacher conferences, 60*fig*, 267–269, 319. *See also* Study strategies

Power Tickets, 166–168, 170, 314. *See also* Retrieval practice strategies

Power Tools: description of, 11–16, 154–155*fig*; research snapshot about combining, 275–276. *See also* Feedback; Interleaving; Metacognition; Retrieval Practice; Spacing

Powerful Flashcards, 252–253, 270–271. *See also* Study strategies

Pre-Tests, 82–83, 96–97, 101–102*fig*, 134, 188, 308

Professional development: create your own, 286–290; discussion questions, 295–298; research-based programs, 283–284; sample plan, 290–295; survey on professional development programs, 279–280. *See also* Checklists for implementation; Do It Yourself (DIY) Retrieval Guide

R

Research: bridge the gap between laboratories and classrooms, 2–6, 21, 32–33, 79, 121, 282; description of the science of learning, 3–4, 19–21, 195*fig*–199, 257, 281–282; snapshots of key findings, 271–274, 276, 319; steps to access cognitive science, 3–4, 285–286

Research on retrieval practice: free recall, 32, 56, 58–59, 79; in college classrooms, 35, 85–86; in high school classrooms, 79, 214*fig*; in the laboratory, 30*fig*–32, 46, 56, 83–85, 253; in medical school, 35–36, 41, 44; in middle school

classrooms, 33–34*fig*, 35, 41, 79, 214*fig*; testing effect, 49

Retrieval Cards, 138–141, 144–145, 164–165, 176, 188, 217, 232, 235, 310*fig*

Retrieval Guides, 65–67, 69*fig*, 76, 88, 164–165*fig*, 176, 188, 233, 235, 254

Retrieval practice: as a flexible teaching strategy, 14–16, 22, 28, 79, 187 193; as a learning strategy, 48–49, 55, 62, 78*fig*, 298–299, 308; description of, 4–6, 11, 13–14, 28, 36–38; difference between assessment and, 47–49, 57, 78*fig*, 206–207, 216–218; question difficulty, 22, 41–43; question formats, 22, 32, 79, 85, 174, 299, 304, 308; student-generated questions, 84–85, 309; ten benefits of, 38–39; research snapshot about, 273

Retrieval practice strategies: before and after lessons, 82–83; Big Basket Quiz (BBQ), 98–99, 119, 164–165*fig*, 217; Pre-Tests, 82–83, 96–97, 101–102*fig*, 134, 188, 308; swap reviewing for, 71, 94, 158–159, 184, 299. *See also* Brain Dump; Mini-Quizzes; Two Things

Retrieval Warm-Ups, 74, 193, 221*fig*–223, 236, 288, 290–291, 293, 317, 323–325

Retrieve-Taking, 63–65, 76, 176, 235, 254–256, 273–274, 282, 291

S

Spacing: Blasts from the Past, 97–98, 116, 164, 169*fig*; cramming, 4–5, 14, 94–95*fig*, 96, 100, 105, 149, 159–161, 218, 291, 310;

cumulative exams, 159–161, 310; description of, 4–6, 12, 14, 93; difference between interleaving and, 106, 115–116, 157–160, 291–292, 311–313; difference between spiraling curriculum and, 99–100; Flash Forward, 244–245; importance of forgetting during, 99–100; optimal amount of, 100–104, 310; research in the laboratory, 94–95*fig*, 101, 102*fig*–103; research in middle school classrooms, 101–102*fig*; research snapshot about, 273–274; savings of knowledge, 104–105, 309. *See also* Interleaving

Stages of learning, 10*fig*–12, 17, 21, 27–28, 87, 305, 307, 231*fig*. *See also* Encoding; Forgetting; Learning; Retrieval

Standardized testing, 185, 256. *See also* Education policy and training

Student populations: ADHD (attention deficit/hyperactivity disorder), 187, 191; benefits for all ages and grade levels, 33, 55, 148, 245; English language learners, 190; lifelong learners, 192–193; special education, 5, 60, 187–189, 219

Study Strategies: cramming, 4–5, 14, 94–95*fig*, 96, 100, 105, 149, 159–161, 218, 291, 310; flashcards, 139*fig*–140*fig*, 162, 174, 235, 270–271, 273; Powerful Flashcards, 252–253, 270–271; note-taking, 17, 63–65, 199, 234, 254–256; re-reading, 17, 28,

30*fig*–32, 64–65, 84–85, 94–95*fig*, 105, 127–128, 158, 241–242, 249, 252, 273–274, 306; Retrieve-Taking, 63–65, 76, 176, 235, 254–256, 273–274, 282, 291. *See also* Illusion of confidence; Illusion of fluency; Parent-teacher conferences; Time management

T

Tests. *See* Assessment

Think-Pair-Share, 49, 58, 66, 74, 97, 118, 138, 149, 165*fig*, 168, 172–173, 213, 223, 236, 243. *See also* Retrieval practice strategies

Two Things, 61*fig*–63, 71–73, 76–77, 131, 142, 149, 171–172, 176, 179, 181–182, 193, 215, 233, 236, 256, 291, 294, 309, 311–312*fig*, 322. *See also* Retrieval practice strategies

Time management: during lessons, 15, 57, 63, 73–75, 77, 132, 135–136, 165*fig*, 179–180, 182–185, 202, 217–218, 223, 284–285, 298, 319; for students: 65, 84–85, 96, 124–126, 145, 229, 249–250, 261, 269; grading, 13–15, 48, 58, 67–69*fig*, 75, 149, 179–182, 216–218, 284, 298; preparation time, 6–7, 82, 103, 111, 179–181, 284, 298, 323

Transfer of knowledge, 5, 38–39, 44–47, 49, 134–135, 137, 272, 300. *See also* Higher order thinking; Bloom's Taxonomy

W

Write, Leave, Retrieve, 171